PARIS
REVEALED

www.**rbooks**.co.uk

Also by Stephen Clarke

A Year in the Merde
Merde Actually
Merde Happens
Dial M for Merde

Talk to the Snail: Ten Commandments for
Understanding the French

1,000 Years of Annoying the French

For more information on Stephen Clarke and his books, see his
website at www.stephenclarkewriter.com

PARIS
REVEALED

The **SECRET LIFE** of a **CITY**

STEPHEN CLARKE

BANTAM PRESS

LONDON · TORONTO · SYDNEY · AUCKLAND · JOHANNESBURG

TRANSWORLD PUBLISHERS
61–63 Uxbridge Road, London W5 5SA
A Random House Group Company
www.rbooks.co.uk

First published in Great Britain
in 2011 by Bantam Press
an imprint of Transworld Publishers

A CIP catalogue record for this book
is available from the British Library.

ISBNs 9780593067116 (hb)
9780593067482 (tpb)

Addresses for Random House Group Ltd companies outside the UK
can be found at: www.randomhouse.co.uk
The Random House Group Ltd Reg. No. 954009

The Random House Group Ltd supports the Forest Stewardship
Council (FSC), the leading international forest-certification organization. All our
titles that are printed on Greenpeace-approved FSC-certified paper carry the FSC logo.
Our paper procurement policy can be found at
www.rbooks.co.uk/environment

Typeset in 11/14pt Minion by
Falcon Oast Graphic Art Ltd.
Printed and bound in Great Britain by
Clays Ltd, Bungay, Suffolk

2 4 6 8 10 9 7 5 3 1

Mixed Sources
Product group from well-managed
forests and other controlled sources
www.fsc.org Cert no. TT-COC-2139
© 1996 Forest Stewardship Council

FSC

Acknowledgements

Merci, first of all, to my fellow Parisians for being so very Parisian.

More specifically, *merci* to everyone who helped, knowingly and unknowingly, in the construction of the book; to all the people I interviewed (and some who interviewed me); to those who gave me access to their buildings, books, exhibitions and events; to anyone who might have been worried when I started staring at them and taking notes; and to everyone who makes life in the city possible, practical and (usually) fun.

Even more specifically, *merci beaucoup* to my editor, Selina Walker, especially for taking the trouble to nip over to Paris so often 'to see how the book's coming along'; to everyone at Susanna Lea's literary agency and especially, for this British edition, Susanna Lea and Kerry Glencorse; to all at Transworld for putting the book together (they continually prove that old-fashioned three-dimensional paper books with covers and pages are actually a nice, albeit ancient, invention); and to Marie-Christine Frison, Alain Plumey, Susan Oubari, Lyne Cohen-Solal, Brian Spence, Heather Stimmler-Hall, Sophie Boudon-Vanhille and Aline Jumeaux for their invitations and explanations.

To the Crimée Crew, and especially N, for revealing so much that is good about Paris.

To M, *bon vol*.

Paris is a bit like an ocean. It's a great place to live if you're a shark. There's loads of fresh seafood, and if anyone annoys you, you just bite them in half. You might not be loved by everyone, but you'll be left in peace to enjoy yourself.

If you're human, though, you spend your time floating on the surface, buffeted by the waves, preyed on by the sharks.

So the thing to do is evolve into a shark as quickly as you can.

(From *A Year in the Merde*)

CONTENTS

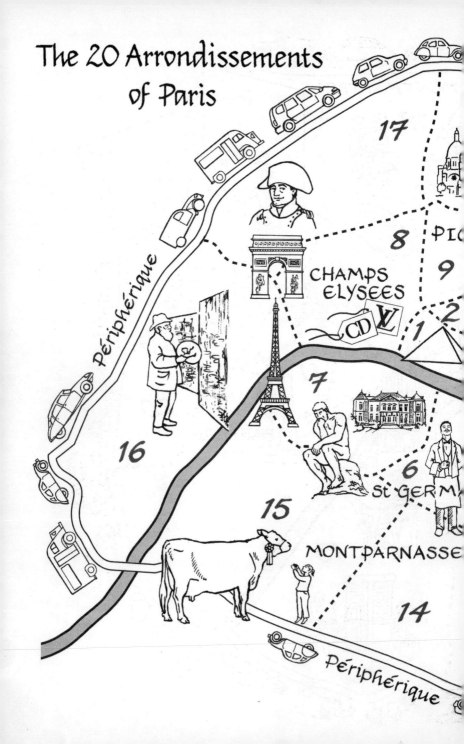

The 20 Arrondissements of Paris

Périphérique

17

8

PIC

CHAMPS ELYSEES

CD LV

9

1

2

7

16

6

St GERM

15

MONTPARNASSE

14

Périphérique

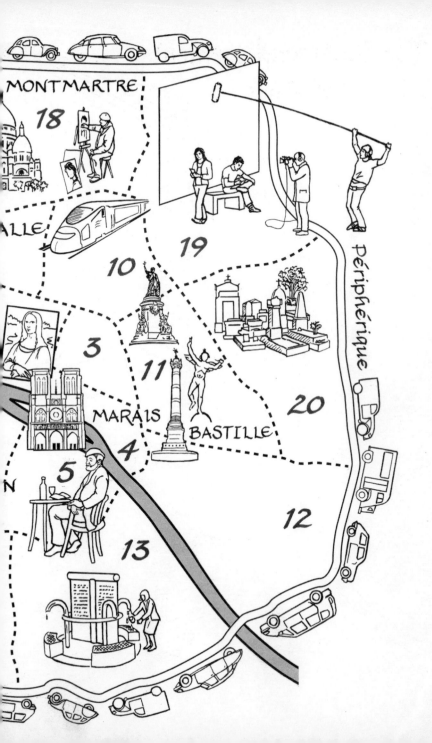

FOREWORD

PARIS IS like the world's most famous screen goddess. We've lost count of all the movies she's starred in – from romantic comedies and historical dramas to thrillers and even cartoons – and we feel as if we know everything about her thanks to all the photos, books, songs and glossy magazine covers that keep her constantly in the public eye.

But of course we don't know *everything*.

She's had many famous lovers, she's taken quite a few knocks in her long history, and like all true divas, she does her best to keep her private life very private. There are things that she needs us to know, and others she would prefer to sweep under her expensive carpet.

This book, however, is designed to reveal her secrets.

The idea is not to turn anyone off the city – on the contrary, I hope that Paris will become a real, fully rounded personality rather than the glitzy, romanticized image that is often projected at us by her fans and her backroom staff. After all, you don't truly fall in love with someone until you know what makes them tick.

And there is a lot to love. I've lived here most of my adult life and I'm still discovering seductive new eccentricities and eye-opening facts.

Make no mistake – Paris has got where she is today because she has genuine star quality. And, unlike most movie stars, this becomes more obvious when you see her close up. She even looks great first thing in the morning with no make-up and the sleep still in her eyes. Which is not bad for a 2,000-year-old.

Stephen Clarke, Paris, January 2011

'Welcome to Paris, you annoying tourist.' In fact, most Parisian waiters are very polite, much to the annoyance of visitors hoping to go home with anecdotes about grumpy service.

1

PARISIANS

Dieu a inventé le Parisien pour que les étrangers ne puissent rien comprendre aux Français.
(God invented Parisians so that foreigners wouldn't understand the French.)

ALEXANDRE DUMAS THE YOUNGER,
NINETEENTH-CENTURY WRITER

Paris is full of Parisians

PARISIANS HAVE a terrible reputation for being self-centred, rude and aggressive, and the worst thing is that they're actually proud of it. A few years ago, the daily newspaper *Le Parisien* made a series of commercials that were shown in cinemas. As the paper is the local version of the national *Aujourd'hui*, the ads were obviously aimed at Parisians themselves.

One of the films shows a pair of lost Japanese tourists begging for help from a middle-aged Parisian man. He stares blankly at them as they point at their map and valiantly try to pronounce 'Eiffel'. Then, when the penny drops, he points them back along the way they came, and they thank him as if he'd just saved their lives. He goes off in the other direction, turns the street corner, and there, looming large, is the tower. The Parisian deliberately sent the

1

tourists the wrong way. Cue the punchline, *Le Parisien, il vaut mieux l'avoir en journal* – The Parisian, it's better to have it as a newspaper.

Another ad shows a respectable-looking man peeing against the outside of a public toilet. He zips up, walks away and smiles innocently at a woman whose shopping bag is standing in the rivulet of urine he's just created.

Then there's the one in which a guy strides quickly to a super-market checkout, cutting in front of the little old lady with her meagre supply of groceries. He has been waiting in line for a few seconds when his wife turns up pushing a huge, overloaded trolley. The Parisian shrugs to the horrified old lady as if to say, well I did get here first. Cue the punchline.

And the funniest thing was that every time I saw one of these ads in a Parisian cinema, it got a huge laugh. I was astonished – it was as though the *New York Times* had put together a campaign saying that the paper was like its readers – thick and opinionated.

But Parisians don't mind the insult at all. On the contrary, they love to think of themselves as anti-social pushers-in, always trying to get one over on anyone gullible enough to fall for their tricks.

They even enjoyed the ad that went too far. In this one, a tall, chic Parisian businessman is seen leaving a café. He grudgingly accepts a business card from a small, subservient type who is leaving with him (from his grovelling demeanour, the little guy has to be a *provincial*). The Parisian goes to his flashy 4WD, reverses and hits a parked car. He's been seen by everyone sitting at the café terrace. He gets out to inspect the damage – his car is fine but he has dented the other car – and has a brainwave. He takes the little guy's business card out of his breast pocket, holds it up to show everyone what an honest fellow he is, and slips it under the windscreen wipers. The little loser is going to take the blame. One up for the totally amoral, treacherous Parisian, and the city's movie-goers cheered.

Who actually likes the *Parisiens*?

A survey in early 2010 by *Marianne*, a national news magazine, asked its readers what they thought of Parisians, and the answer was a typically French contradiction.

Overall, provincials had a *bonne opinion* of the capital-dwellers, recognizing that they were sophisticated, well-educated and trendy – while also showering them with insults.

The survey found that Parisians were seen as arrogant, aggressive, stressed, snobbish and self-obsessed, as well as being much less generous, tolerant, light-hearted and welcoming than people from the provinces.

But was the *Marianne* survey accurate, or just a reflection of the clichés bandied about in the media (including those *Le Parisien* newspaper ads)?

Parisians certainly think of themselves as a race apart, probably because the city is separated from its suburbs not only by its postcodes, which all start with '75', but also by physical barriers. The *boulevard périphérique*, the ring road that encircles Paris, is lined for much of its length with high-rise *HLMs* – *habitations à loyer modéré* (low-cost housing) – the modern version of the old city ramparts. And even though the walls have long disappeared, the twenty *arrondissements* comprising Paris itself are still referred to as *intra muros* – inside the walls. No wonder Parisians are considered snobbish – they're using a medieval term to distinguish themselves from anyone unfortunate enough to live outside the *périph'* (the abbreviation commonly used by the locals).

This sense of geographical uniqueness does seem a bit exaggerated, though. After all, a commuter who lives, say, 10 kilometres from Notre-Dame is still going to be pretty Parisian, even if he or she does live on the 'wrong' side of the *périph'*.

And commuting and working are at the root of the Parisians' famous aggression. That man pushing past you on the *métro*, or snarling at you when you ask directions in the street, probably got up at six that morning, wedged himself into a suburban train and/or a *métro* carriage, stood for forty minutes with his nose in someone else's armpit while the carriage jerked his spine out of shape, and then got told by his boss that his workload was being doubled because a colleague has been given three months' sick leave by an indulgent doctor. He's not going to smile at you if you can't find your way to the Sacré Coeur.

So, *oui*, Parisians and their suburban cousins are aggressive and stressed, but no more than the inhabitants of any big commuter city. And they seem intimidating only because they know how the city works, and therefore get impatient with people who don't – the tourists and provincials. To Parisians, cohabiting with outsiders is like going fishing with someone who has never baited a hook before. Surely *everyone* knows you're not supposed to throw the fishing rod in the water with the hook and line? No? Well, then they must be really, really stupid.

This uncomprehending impatience explains why Parisian drivers' fists seem to be permanently jammed on their hooter, and why waiters (who more often than not give perfect service, despite seeming to ignore you) can get irritable with their customers. Many diners, especially the non-French and non-Parisians, are mere part-timers in the restaurant game, and the waiters are old hands. They're simply expressing frustration at being forced to share their territory with untrained beginners.

In short, the Parisians' apparent unfriendliness is not a deliberate attempt to insult outsiders. It's just a symptom of their wish to get on with their lives.

On the other hand, the accusations of snobbishness and self-obsession are entirely justified, because right from birth, a sense of their city's greatness is hammered into Parisians' heads with a gold Chanel mallet.

Paris is undeniably the centre of the French-speaking universe.

It's only a slightly skewed interpretation on the part of some Parisians to see the city as the centre of the universe, full stop. The top dogs of pretty well every prestigious French institution – cultural, economic and political – have to be based in Paris to stay close to the centralized action, so the *crème de la crème* are always going to be here, and, being Parisian, will always think that their own particular brand of *crème* is the creamiest.

And their snobbishness is not only inflicted on outsiders – Parisians weave a tangled web of snobbery amongst themselves. For example, those in the posher *arrondissements* will look down on their less chic counterparts with a mixture of scorn and pity. Try telling someone from the ultra-snooty 7th on the Left Bank that you live on the other side of the river in, say, the 20th, and a polite grimace will come across their face as though you'd just confessed to an infestation of headlice. And it works both ways – a TV cameraman living in the northern media ghetto of the 19th will think of a blazer-wearing 16th *arrondissement* banker over in the southwest of the city as a slug-like, brainless slave of philistine capitalism. Meanwhile, someone with a loft in a pleasantly gentrified part of the 11th, but near to a poor neighbourhood, will see themselves as an urban pioneer, living much closer to the edge than a person whose apartment is 500 metres to the south.

The rules of Parisian snobbery are as complex as a 3-D chess game played on twenty boards at once, despite the fact that the city is a rough circle of only about 10 kilometres in diameter. The key thing being, of course, that if you don't live inside the circle, you're totally out of the game.

This is not to say that Parisians don't have their chinks of self-doubt. They can, for example, feel inferior to New Yorkers, San Franciscans, Londoners and the Milanese – in short, to anyone with their own superiority complex. And Parisians are scared of, and therefore a little overawed by, the poorer *banlieusards*, believing that anyone who can survive life in an ugly apartment block more than a kilometre from a cinema or decent restaurant deserves *le respect*. And the success of French rap, as well as mainstream films like *Neuilly Sa Mère* and *Tout Ce Qui Brille* (in which young Arab *banlieusards* make fun of absurdly stereotyped snobbish Parisians), have proved that Paris is losing ground in the trendiness stakes – the irony being that as soon as a *banlieusard* rapper or film star becomes famous, they move *intra muros* and turn into typical *Parisiens*.

Parisien-spotting

Paris's twenty *arrondissements* contain some 2.2 million people, who can be as different as Champagne and absinthe and yet still remain quintessentially Parisian.

There are as many types of Parisians as there are fish on a coral reef. But what makes them all Parisian, apart from simple geography, is the way they interact. Like the fish, they have to negotiate their way around the reef. The small fry have to steer clear of the sharks; the shrimps have to watch how they cross the open spaces in case a crab runs them over; and for all his or her bright colours, even the most beautiful individual will never outshine the reef itself.

Certain species of Parisian gather in certain *arrondissements*, and take on the characteristics of the neighbourhood as if trying to camouflage themselves. Of course, there are dozens of subtypes that will have to be left out to avoid turning this book into a sociological encyclopaedia, but here is a run-through of the main species of Parisian you will find in each of the *arrondissements*, and the best places to see them. And the good news is that you won't need a mask and snorkel to explore this particular coral reef.

The 1st

So much of the nucleus of Paris is taken up by the Louvre, the Palais-Royal and shops that hardly anyone lives there, except around Châtelet and Les Halles, where you can get a loft with a balcony and exposed wooden beams much more cheaply than in the nearby Marais. Though not many people want to live in an area that attracts all the suburban *racaille* (the establishment's insulting name for young wasters) who come in from the northern *banlieues* on the RER (the suburban *métro*) and hang around Les Halles, chatting each other up and getting hassled by the police. If you want to spot weekday locals, especially civil servants from the nearby Ministry of Culture and the Conseil d'État (the state's legal department), sit on the terrace of Le Nemours, the café at the entrance to the Palais-Royal gardens, near the Comédie Française theatre.

The 2nd

Until about fifteen years ago, this was an area of fascinating contrasts. The Sentier was still full of clothes workshops, while the newly pedestrianized area around the rue Montorgueil was attracting all sorts of intellectuals and their families, just metres away from the rue Saint-Denis, where prostitutes stood in every doorway. Now gentrification is almost complete – the Sentier is getting lofted up, rue Montorgueil has changed from a street market into a hipsters' food court where you can get mango sushi, and the prostitutes are being squeezed out. The only time you can see residents *en masse* is on a Sunday morning, when the buggy brigade come out to buy their baguette and grab a coffee before the sushi fans arrive. Local-watching is best outside any café on the rue Montorgueil at eleven o'clock on a Sunday morning.

The 3rd

This comprises the northern half of the Marais, gentrified long enough ago to have achieved maturity. Its remarkably quiet medieval streets house art galleries (thanks to the Picasso Museum run-off effect), tasteful estate agencies, clothes shops and ultra-trendy restaurants, peopled by exactly the kind of staff – young and slightly snooty – that you'd expect. However, the shops and cafés in the rue de Bretagne are surprisingly down-to-earth, and mainly cater to the arty young things who can afford to live nearby. Spotting spot: the Café Charlot on the corner of rue Charlot and rue de Bretagne. The interior is a bit of an 'Old Paris' theme park, but locals don't care because the terrace is so sunny. It's packed every lunchtime with *fashionistas* from the area's showrooms. The same goes for the lunchtime foodstalls in the nearby hyper-hip Enfants Rouges market.

The 4th

Forty years ago the heart of the Marais was a gloomy dump in-habited by people who had been there for ever. The *hôtels particuliers* (urban mansions) were soot-blackened and falling down. This was why the city felt free to unleash the wave of destruc-tion that gave us Les Halles (in the 1st), the Centre Pompidou (known by Parisians as Beaubourg) and the hideous modern Quartier de l'Horloge.* These days, post-gentrification, the Marais' surviving buildings are all spruced up and it's almost impossible to identify any residents, except perhaps for the second-home Americans on café terraces on a Sunday morning and the parents watching their toddlers play in the small public gardens. The area does attract some easily spotted Parisian groups, though – gays (along the rue des Archives, where I once heard a little girl ask her dad, 'Papa, why does that princess have a moustache?'), Jews

---

* For more on the demolition, see Chapter 5.

(shabat in the rue des Rosiers is a veritable falafel-fest) and shoppers. Neither the Jews nor the gays follow the old-fashioned French Tuesday-to-Saturday shopping timetable, so the area buzzes all week long. Spotting spot: the falafel bars and bakeries on the rue des Rosiers, or Les Marronniers, the gay and straight brunch place at the bottom of the rue des Archives.

The 5th

A large but subtly disguised proportion of Paris's old money is concentrated here. The Latin Quarter used to provide shelter for penniless writers like James Joyce and Samuel Beckett, but these days they couldn't afford to live there, except maybe above a *crêperie* in the rue Mouffetard. The residents of all but the tiny *chambres de bonne* (top-floor garrets) dress down so the taxman won't ask how much their apartment is worth, and these people's kids try to look sloppy so they won't get mugged by the youths who come into the area on phone-hunting trips. You see that dowdy-looking middle-aged woman with a baguette and a sprig of parsley poking out of the top of her beaten-up shopping bag? She's a property millionairess, and one day she'll leave her fortune to those schoolkids who are huddling around a café table making a coffee last for hours and smoking their cigarette as though it cost them all their pocket money (which it will do if Papa finds out they've been smoking). The locals shop for food in the rue Mouffetard, despite the heavy presence of tourists, and some of them sit in the sun at the place de la Contrescarpe, though they all retreat to their country houses in high tourist season.

The 6th

A lot like the 5th, except that the people here are more ostentatious, and the youngsters feel freer to show off their Lacoste polo shirts,

Rolexes and vintage Vespas. Look out for '80s throwbacks with knotted pullovers around their shoulders, and girls with the kind of free-flowing hair and perfect teeth you see only on billboards. This is also home to the most intellectual publishing houses, so cafés attract a concentration of loud pontificators, old guys sharing a drink with their pile of manuscript paper, and sophisticated smokers on the lookout for a woman who'll be impressed to know that she's meeting a part-time poet. Spotting spots: Les Éditeurs, the book-lined café at Odéon, where writers and publishers gather to talk loudly about book prizes. Also the café Bonaparte, on the corner of the rue Bonaparte and the place Saint-Germain des Prés. Here you can sit amongst lunching locals and watch the hyper-trendy and those with limitless expense accounts heading for La Société, the hot restaurant behind the discreet door diagonally right as you look out from the Bonaparte's façade.

The 7th

Saying that you're moving to the 7th is a bit like admitting, 'Well, I've thought it over and I now realize that I do deserve that Rolls-Royce I've always wanted.' Either that or 'I've been made director of the Musée d'Orsay.' The people there are posh and they know it. To spot the poshest of the lot, go to La Grande Épicerie, the grocer's shop next to the Bon Marché department store, and look out for the kind of person who has to tell their friends, '*Naturellement*, I always buy my Earl Grey from la Grande Épicerie.' Another excellent spot is Le Concorde, at 239 boulevard Saint-Germain, the closest café to the Assemblée Nationale, the lower house of France's Parliament. Before debates, politicians huddle here to talk amongst themselves or dictate notes to their glamorous assistants, the sexiest politics students in the country.

The 8th

The only Parisians who live here full-time are rich old ladies who wear a fur coat as soon as the temperature drops below 20 degrees centigrade, along with their ancient, ex-playboy husbands, and the newly very rich who need a large underground garage to park their 4WD BMW. Other than that, it's mostly offices, shops, theatres and fashion houses, with the Champs-Élysées running through the middle. I used to work in this part of town, and for me, the most fascinating people-watching was outside L'Avenue, the posh café on the corner of the rue François Premier and the avenue Montaigne. It is so essential to be seen there that in the middle of winter you will spot a full row of facelifts late-lunching outdoors on the terrace when everyone else is rushing back to their office to get out of the cold. If you actually want to sit in comfort and eat, wander up François Premier to L'Antenne, the café on the corner of the rue de la Trémoille. Here, office workers and media types from Europe 1 radio station gather at lunchtime for an unpretentious break from the daily grind.

The 9th

Until very recently, the area between Pigalle and the Galeries Lafayette was where people moved when they couldn't decide which *arrondissement* they liked best. Nowadays it's going the same way as the 2nd. The internet is killing both the sex shops and the guitar shops, and the neighbourhood is becoming breathlessly trendy. Drab cafés are being made over as 'traditional bistros', where *carpaccio de boeuf* has replaced *jambon-beurre* (ham baguette) on the menu, to cater for the new clientele of artfully unshaven men, and women who use Ray-Bans to hold their hair in place. You can still see a few old-style occupants of the neighbourhood – sex-shop owners and ageing prostitutes – in the small cafés just south of the place Pigalle. But beware, if an underdressed girl in a foreign accent comes up and says hello as soon as you enter a bar – you're in for a very expensive drink. To see the biggest concentration of trendy newbies, head for the Hôtel Amour's restaurant in the rue de Navarin.

The 10th

This is a bit of a no-man's-land. Around the Gare du Nord and along the boulevard de Strasbourg, it's as sordid as it ever was, though the Sri Lankan community to the north of the station is now settling in and cleaning it up, and incidentally providing some of the best and cheapest ethnic food in the city. At Château d'Eau *métro*, touts for the African hairdressers hustle women to come and get their locks braided or straightened. Fifteen years ago, the canal zone in the east of the *arrondissement* was the hippest area in Paris, and it still attracts plenty of night-time revellers, either crowding into the laid-back restaurants and bars or sitting along the waterside, watching the drunks stumble into the murky water. My favourite spotting spots are the Sri Lankan cafés near La Chapelle *métro* station, where Tamils gather for an early dinner or after-work chat, or one of the bridges over the Canal Saint-Martin when the summer-evening picnics are in full swing. And just for a taste of the really seedy side of Paris, a quick dash over the Strasbourg–Saint-Denis crossroads will take you past cheap Chinese streetwalkers and all the lowlife that these cruelly exploited new immigrants attract.

The 11th

Bastille, formerly a furniture-making area, has become a big-brand shopping ghetto, but beyond the rue de la Roquette and the rue du Faubourg Saint-Antoine, this is still a lively, varied *arrondissement*, with gentrifiers living alongside Arab corner-shop owners and ordinary Parisians who will struggle if you ask them the way to Père

Lachaise cemetery in English. The Oberkampf area is still one of the best venues for bar-crawling, and attracts slightly rough-edged crowds from the late teens to forty-somethings practically every night of the year. For cooler, terrace-based people-watching, it's best to head for the Pause Café on the corner of the rue de Charonne and the rue Keller, in the area made famous (to other Parisians, at least) by the 1996 film *Chacun Cherche son Chat* (also released under the English title *When the Cat's Away*).

The 12th

This is a far-flung *arrondissement* inhabited by a mix of middle-class people who wanted a cheaper alternative to the 11th, and poor edge-of-towners. The most interesting spots are the Coulée Verte ('green flow') gardens heading out from Bastille along the old railway track, and the hub of activity around the place d'Aligre. This is a densely packed Sunday market that makes your mouth water and your toes hurt, as you jostle to buy cheap food and get stomped on by the hurried locals. It's Paris at its democratic, people-watching best, with rich and poor vying elbow-to-elbow to get served, and stalls selling Spanish strawberries at suspiciously low prices just metres away from the old market hall where you can buy hand-picked, organic, individually boxed French varieties that cost as much per kilo as a second-hand Renault.

The 13th

This is home to Paris's biggest and most Chinese Chinatown, with some startlingly authentic restaurants and a real colonial feel near the Porte de Choisy. It's also home to the Butte aux Cailles, the hilltop village of lanes and low-rise houses that is the southern Parisians' alternative to Montmartre. I used to think that the name 'Quails' Hill' was cutely rustic until I was told that *caille* was an old word for prostitute. These days, there are no brothels, but you might see some Chinese masseuses taping their phone numbers to lampposts. In the evenings, the Butte is a young people's party zone, with student types bustling around in front of the bars and waiting patiently for a table at the incredibly popular Café Gladines, the cheap and cheerful Basque restaurant at 30 rue des Cinq Diamants.

The 14th and 15th

As far as people-watching is concerned, these are of interest only to someone doing a PhD on the Parisian middle-class family. There is absolutely nothing wrong with Parisian middle-class families, it's just that they're not the world's most colourful tribe. One of the oases of liveliness is the huge traditional brasserie La Coupole, on the boulevard du Montparnasse, where Parisians usually outnumber tourists, and gather to eat mountains of seafood. If you tell the restaurant it's your birthday, the waiters will troop towards your table chanting, 'Ça, c'est Paris', and then they will crowd around you to sing 'Joyeux Anniversaire' while you squirm with embarrassment and try to avoid getting your nose burnt by the Roman candle on top of the birthday cake – which is a dummy, by the way.

The 16th

This vast *arrondissement* is mostly a rather dull blend of *grand bourgeois* and tacky new money. In the daytime, the parks are crammed with immigrant nannies and the designer shops are full of desperate housewives. In the evening, they're all either at home or out for dinner in the 7th or the Bois de Boulogne. The deathly gentility is disturbed only on match days, when Paris Saint-Germain football fans swarm to the Parc des Princes for a session of racist chanting. Best place to spot locals in the wild is on the long walk from the *métro* station La Muette to see the Impressionist paintings at the Musée Marmottan. The 16th is also the *arrondissement* that spawned what many people see as the archetypal Parisian *homme* – floppy hair, designer jeans, effortless charm, seen-it-all (but wouldn't be seen dead in the T-shirt) attitude – though he is more usually to be found bantering his way around the bars and restaurants of the 6th.

The 17th

The 17th is so far away from everything that it's hard to imagine it's *intra muros*. Quite honestly, I have very little idea who lives here. There is an outburst of shopping activity at Ternes and a posh, 8th-style area around the Parc Monceau, with lots of lawyers' offices, but the only 17th people who have stuck in my mind are transvestites – for a short while, I lived near the Porte de Saint-Ouen, which was a cruising zone for men who like men dressed as ladies, and I once saw a kind of mini Rio carnival as three ten-foot-tall cross-dressers strutted flamboyantly towards their pick-up points.

The 18th

Montmartre is home to Paris's artists and can-can dancers, and on a good day you will see Picasso out sketching with Van Gogh, and Toulouse-Lautrec hobbling after a petticoated lady, begging to paint her portrait. Or maybe not – in reality, Montmartre today is a village populated by Parisians rich enough to have bought houses with fantastic views before the prices went crazy, slightly un-conventional middle-class professionals who enjoy walking up hills, and tourists in search of a good photo of the city's rooftops. Nearby Barbès, on the other hand, is a multi-generational logjam of people from every part of Africa that France ever managed to colonize. To observe *l'Afrique française*, just walk northwards along the boulevard Barbès on a Saturday afternoon and you'll go all the way to Senegal. Those in search of more trendy people-watching usually head up the hill to the bars and cafés on the rue Lepic to recapture the feel of the movie *Le Fabuleux Destin d'Amélie Poulain*.

The 19th

Belleville, with its cluster of big Chinese brasseries, is resisting change, but the rest is getting seriously hip, with artists' studios and film-production companies herding in. Above Belleville, the Jourdain area is a media ghetto, with about 50 per cent of the population working in TV, cinema or radio. These are the *bobos* (bourgeois Bohemians) – Parisians trying to pretend they're not. Their apparent lack of style is a style in itself and make no mistake – that rumpled shirt and ruffled hair were rumpled and ruffled by professionals. All of which means that the café terraces are crowded non-stop because these people don't work regular office hours. On sunny days, they all go to the Buttes-Chaumont park to try and picnic on the dangerously sloping lawns (downhill-rolling wine bottles and melons are a frequent hazard). Further northwest, the area around the canal basin, the Bassin de la Villette, is not yet inhabited by trendies, and is one of the last poor, mixed-race *quartiers* inside the city. Blacks, Chinese, Arabs, Orthodox and Sephardic Jews and low-income Whites co-exist in a zone that will be almost entirely lofted over in ten years' time. Spotting spots: the Buttes-Chaumont whenever it's sunny, and the Bar Ourcq on the southeastern (sunny) side of the Bassin de la Villette, where young Parisians gather for evening *pétanque* picnics.

The 20th

Until recently considered as a distant cultural and social wasteland, it's now a great place for small live-music venues. Apart from that, its location means that it is home to lots of scooter-riding *bobos* who can afford to send their kids to private schools in better areas, as well as vestiges of poor people who are hanging on in Paris but might be forced to cross over the *périph'* to the suburbs if their rents rise any further. Spot two different types of trendies on one stretch of the rue de Bagnolet – rock fans in the Flèche d'Or, an old railway station that has been turned into a cool music venue, and just opposite, much snappier dressers in the bars and restaurants of the Mama Shelter Hotel, which until recently used to be one of the city's ugliest multi-storey car parks.

How to become a Parisian

The Russian-born French actor Sacha Guitry once said, 'Être parisien, ce n'est pas être né à Paris, c'est y renaître.' In other words, to be a Parisian you don't have to be born here, it's all about being *re-born*. People re-invent themselves when they arrive, or at the very least evolve so that they will fit in.

And the good news is that it's really not too difficult to become a Parisian. There are no painful tattoos or initiation ceremonies to go through, just a change of look and attitude. And most Parisians have had to undergo this acclimatization process, because a very large proportion of them weren't born that way. They came here from all over the world, including other parts of France, and have battled their way through the city's obstacle course of manners to arrive at the finishing post as fully fledged Parisians. Even I, who was terrified of driving in Paris for the first five years, am now capable of swerving, swearing and hooting with the best of them.

Appropriately, it took a non-Parisian writer to define the process of Parisianization (Parisians don't have time to do such a thing). In 1938, the Swiss writer Charles Ferdinand Ramuz published a book called *Paris, Notes d'un Vaudois* (Vaud is a Swiss canton), in which he said that:

> Paris still enjoys the privilege of showing everyone how things should be done. And everyone living there shares this privilege. They don't need to be born in Paris. All they have to do is be in Paris and conform to Paris. The city will exclude anyone who doesn't belong there, and who does nothing to look as though they want to belong – people who refuse to adapt their appearance, their gestures and their way of speaking, and who try to impose their habits on Paris, immediately become suspect.

This need to conform is why Paris never really changes. Unlike cities such as London and New York, where newcomers bring fresh influences, everyone arriving in Paris gets pushed through the same pasta mould and ends up as a length of typically Parisian spaghetti, intertwined with all the others in the tasty but rather over-rich sauce that the city throws over everything.

And adaptation is not just about clothing and ways of speaking. What you have to do to become a Parisian is get it into your head that you are the most important being in the universe. Other people might *think* they are important, and must be humoured, but they are wrong. The only truly important thing is you and your life. Everything you want to do (or rather, *need* to do) is urgent and of vital importance, and you are therefore (regrettably) obliged to ignore the wishes of the other, lesser, beings, including your fellow Parisians. If anyone tries to stop you, you are perfectly entitled to get annoyed at them because they are just being ignorant.

And it works – as soon as you start acting like a Parisian, you will be accepted as one. Before you have completed the process, however, there is one vital skill that you have to develop as a survival tool . . .

How NOT to annoy a Parisian

A few hints on how to avoid treading on a Parisian's toes, or getting trodden on, both literally and metaphorically:

In a café or restaurant

- If you only want a drink, don't sit down at a table that has been laid for lunch or dinner. Laying these tables in preparation for mealtimes, and thereby limiting the number of drinks-only tables, is the waiters' equivalent of herding sheep. Sit in the wrong place and they will set the dogs on you (verbally, at least).

- Except in fast-food places and English- or Irish-style pubs, never order at the bar and then take your drink to a table. Usually, the bar and the tables are governed by two different cash tills and the drinks are priced differently, so by doing this, you will plunge the café into accounting hell, as well as making the waiter very indignant. Smokers wishing to drink a cheap coffee must alternate – sip of coffee at the bar indoors, puff of cigarette outside (unless they're regulars, in which case they will be allowed to take their cup – but not usually their saucer – outdoors). I have actually seen a fist fight between the owner of a café and a smoker who paid for his coffee at the bar and then came outside to *sit at a table*.

- If the waiter comes to your table while you're perusing the menu and asks whether you've chosen ('Vous avez fait votre choix?'), make damn sure before you answer 'yes' that everyone at the table really has decided what they're going to order. The slightest sign of hesitation from anyone in your party will mean that you have been lying, and the punishment for lying to a waiter is to watch him raise his eyes towards heaven and pray that God will strike you dead. And then disappear for at least ten minutes while you try in vain to attract his attention.

- Do not, under any circumstances, mention the words 'vegetarian' or 'food allergy', because doing so anywhere except in a health-food restaurant will only cause unnecessary panic, like saying 'bomb' in an American airport. Instead, you must either choose something on the menu that you're sure you can eat (and most cafés and restaurants will have something) or say, 'Je prends le/la ... sans le/la ... s'il vous plaît' ('I'll have the ... without the ... please'). The waiter will respect you for knowing what you want in life, and probably won't ask you why you want it.

- Don't just breeze into a café and ask to use the toilets. Toilets are for customers only. Simply order a coffee at the bar, wait till it's served, and then go to the toilet, which will almost always be downstairs or in a corner of the café, and is usually marked with a *Toilettes* sign. Some cafés, especially in touristy or crowded areas, will force you to ask for a token (*jeton*) at the bar, or even the key, and will only give it in return for a food or drink order.

In shops

- In *boulangeries*, people queue in an orderly fashion, mainly thanks to the *boulangères'* strict discipline. But things can go awry – when, for example, there are two women serving and one of them accidentally misses out a customer, thinking that they're already being served. If you are the missed-out one, it is perfectly OK to pipe up, politely but firmly, 'En fait, c'est à moi' ('Actually, I'm next'). If however, you are the person who has been unfairly favoured, it is best to say, 'En fait, c'est à Madame/ Monsieur' ('Actually, Monsieur/Madame is next'), because if you play dumb, and the person in front of you realizes what's going on, he or she will complain and your order will probably be put to one side, causing confusion at the till. Moral of the story: if, for once, you are in a Parisian queue that is actually working, make sure that the *status quo* is upheld. The alternative is anarchy.

- In other small shops, or at the market, there may not be an orderly queue. Under these circumstances, it is necessary to gauge how things are being managed. Even though there is what looks like an anarchic huddle in the *charcuterie/ fromagerie/boucherie/marchand de vin*, is there actually a first come first served policy? If so, you should engage in resolute eye contact with the sales assistant when it comes to your turn, and be ready with 'En fait, c'est à moi' in case someone tries to push in. If, on the other hand, it's total anarchy, just stare the assistant in the eyes until he or she looks your way for a second, then blurt out 'Bonjour' and your order before anyone else can get a word in. Bizarrely, under these circumstances, respecting the law of the jungle reassures Parisians and keeps them calm.

- There is, however, one way to annoy Parisians even while standing passively in line, with the right change, a patient smile on your face and only nine items in the 'ten and under' super-market queue. That is if it is getting near the cashier's break time and he or she tells you, 'Après vous, c'est fermé' ('After you, I'm closing my till'). This means that you have been entrusted with the moral responsibility of telling anyone who stands behind you, 'C'est fermé après moi.' Personally, I usually remember to say this once or twice and then forget, and have to annoy the three people behind me by telling them the bad news. These days, if I hear the fatal phrase 'Après vous, c'est fermé,' I either bow out and go to the back of another line, or accept my fate and stay facing backwards until I'm served – this helps me remember to tell approaching customers that there's no point joining my queue, and also makes me look so weird that few people want to risk it anyway.

In the street

- It's the most frequently repeated piece of advice, but it's valid – even if you can't speak French, don't launch straight into English or any other language when addressing a Parisian. The most gifted, multilingual Parisian will pretend not to understand you unless you start the conversation with *bonjour*, or *bonsoir* after about 5 p.m. (see 'Essential Phrases' below).

- Don't dress as though you're going to the beach (even if you are on your way to Paris Plages*. Bikini tops are not considered acceptable streetwear, except by ogling men.

- Don't hail an occupied taxi. This will only confirm the taxi driver's view that most of his clients are idiots. It's not entirely the arm-waver's fault, though, because Parisian taxis' light signals aren't very clear. If a taxi is free, the white light on its roof is completely lit up. If it is taken, the tiny orange light below the white light is lit up and the white light is not. The problem being that, in daylight, both of these lights are practically invisible. Fortunately, France is introducing a new system, whereby the roof light will be green if the taxi is free and red if it's not. Though this might take some time to have an effect, because drivers are being allowed to keep their old white light until they have to buy a new car.

- It is also a given that if an unoccupied taxi driver doesn't like the look of you, he won't stop anyway. And that even if he does stop, he might wind down his window, ask you where you're going, and drive away if he doesn't want to go there.

- Don't step on to one of the pedestrian crossings that have no traffic lights and expect an oncoming driver to stop of his or her own accord. Stepping out in front of this car, even if it is some way off, will get you, at best, yelled at, and at worst run over *and* yelled at.

* For more on this annual phenomenon, see Chapter 3.

Warning: do not ask this Parisian 'Où est le Sacré Coeur?' When Parisians see tourists gazing blankly at a map of the city, they don't think, 'Huh, tourists,' they think, 'Thank God they're not going to ask me for directions.' If, in a dire emergency, you do need to ask, always remember to say 'Bonjour' first, thus avoiding a painful snub.

- Similarly, if cycling anywhere except in a cycle lane, always assume that you are invisible to car drivers, or that they want to kill you. Even cycle lanes are not always safe, because many of them share space with bus lanes. Bus drivers resent this, because *Bus* is written on the road in large letters and they assume that this gives them a monopoly. Taxis and motorbikes can also use bus lanes, and they see cycles as rivals for their hard-won privilege. And anyway, if you look closely, the cyclist painted in cycle lanes looks as though he's been squashed by a bus or taxi. In short, if cycling near any motor vehicles, prepare to die messily.
- Don't smile randomly at passers-by. You might think you're being friendly and showing how pleased you are to be visiting their city, but they will think you're either mad, laughing at them, or asking for sex. Of course, if you do want sex, all you have to do is smile at a passing Parisian male.

In your rented apartment or hotel

- In hotels, never complain that there are no tea- and coffee-making facilities in your room. Those who require an early-morning or late-night cuppa will usually need to come equipped with a kettle.
- Similarly, it's not worth complaining if your accommodation is gloomy or noisy. Any room or apartment below the second floor will probably be gloomy because almost every street in Paris is lined with six- or seven-storey buildings. Also, even with double-glazing, if you're right above the pavement, you may well have to listen to yelling drunks at night and the dawn chorus of clattering dustbins (they're plastic but still make a racket when slammed against a truck to be emptied and then dumped back on the pavement).
- If you're renting an apartment in a building occupied by

Parisians, don't say to yourself, 'Excellent, this entrance hall is empty, so there's lots of room to park the bike I've rented and/or stow the buggy rather than humping it up six flights of stairs.' In fact, the entrance hall is empty precisely because the residents who own apartments in the building have voted to forbid wheeled machines of any sort in their entrance hall. Leaving a bike or buggy, even for one night, will probably earn you an angry note from the old man on the second floor who's lived there for forty years and who tripped over a badly parked bike in 1982 and has needed an annual health-spa holiday ever since. If he hasn't got arthritis in his fingers, he might even let your tyres down.

Essential phrases for getting on with Parisians

Bonjour!

To be said in a loud sing-song way, so that rather than wishing someone a good day, it comes to mean anything from 'Hello, I'm not an enemy, honestly' to 'Yes, you're not hallucinating, I am here and you're going to have to stop yakking to your colleague and serve me.'

C'est à moi, en fait

'It's my turn, actually' – to be said with a calm, polite smile that proves beyond doubt that the wannabe queue-jumper is not going to be allowed to push in front of you. Try not to weaken and say, 'C'est à moi, *je pense*' (I think), because the queue-jumper can say, 'Non, je ne pense pas,' and carry on with their evil-doing.

Permettez-moi

Literally it means 'allow me', and strictly speaking should be said to accompany some polite gesture. However, it can be turned on its head when, for example, a Parisian grabs a visitor's *métro* ticket out of their tentative fingers and shoves it in the turnstile slot so that the dawdling visitor will go through and get the hell out of his life.

Après vous

'After you' – again, instead of its literal meaning, it can be used to mean 'Get through that door and out of my life.'

Pour qui il/elle se prend?

'Who does (s)he think (s)he is?' A confusing one, perhaps, but this is often said directly to someone who has got the better of you or is seriously trying to. In old-fashioned Parisian *argot*, to avoid the *tu–vous* issue, people used to talk in the third person. In black-and-white films, waiters asked strangers, 'Qu'est-ce qu'il veut, le Monsieur?' – 'What would the gentleman like?' So 'Pour qui il/elle se prend?' is a combination of a direct 'Who do you think you are?' and an appeal to anyone else in the vicinity to confirm that this other person is an idiot/snob/bastard, etc.

Franchement!

'Honestly!' – perhaps safer than trying to use the above vintage slang. To be huffed loudly if someone does anything to dent your Parisian sense of superiority.

Bonne journée/soirée, etc.

At the end of any transaction or meeting, as well as saying *au revoir*, Parisians usually wish each other a good day, afternoon or evening. In fact, despite their reputation for being unwelcoming, they will wish each other a good *anything*. A friendly waiter might wish departing tourists *bonne visite* (if he's received a decent tip), a hotel receptionist will say *bon séjour* ('have a good stay'). Once I even heard a woman wish her friend *bon dentiste* – the 'bon(ne) + noun' grammatical structure is so economical and flexible that this could have meant anything from 'I hope your visit to the dentist goes OK' to 'I hope you enjoy yourself on your date with the hunky dentist.' In short, it's a safe way of using your limited French vocabulary to the full, and winning Parisian friends. *Bonne improvisation!*

The sorely missed *pissoirs* were phased out in the 1980s, though many Parisian men pretend not to have noticed.

2

PAVEMENTS

Paris est la ville où les caniveaux sont les plus propres du monde parce que les chiens les respectent.
(Paris has the cleanest gutters in the world because the dogs respect them.)

ALAIN SCHIFRES, FRENCH JOURNALIST

IN MAY 2009, *Beaux Arts*, a monthly art magazine, published a survey entitled *Les Français et la beauté*. Amongst other things, the French were asked about the biggest 'source of beauty' in their everyday life.

Predictably, 35 per cent replied 'making love', but that was only the second most popular answer. The first was 'walking in the street', with 44 per cent of votes.

The conclusions are pretty catastrophic for the country's reputation. French buildings are more beautiful than French lovers? The curves of a passing Renault are more aesthetically pleasing than those on a French body? Even if this is over-interpreting the survey a little, the results do say something about the importance of street life in France, and particularly in Paris. In fact, walking around Paris is such an established tradition that it has its own art form. It's called *flâner*, a verb meaning to stroll aimlessly, and its artist is the *flâneur*, the man (women seem to be too busy to 'flan') who wanders the city streets in search of inspiration for his poems, paintings or travel books.

The concept of *flâner* was invented by the decadent poet Charles Baudelaire in the nineteenth century. When he wasn't writing verse or combating his *spleen* (a poetic combination of boredom, self-loathing and intoxicating substances), he was wandering the streets. Although by claiming this as an art form, in fact he was merely legitimizing what all Paris's gentlemen of leisure had long been doing – cruising in search of sex, with a waitress, perhaps, an impressionable off-duty servant, a married woman with a glint in her eye, or, failing that, a prostitute, of which there were many.

This fascination with *le flâning* (the French are bound to call it this one day) may explain why so many of the picture rooms in the Musée Carnavalet,* Paris's autobiographical history museum, are hung with street scenes. Men in top hats and ladies in bustles stroll along pavements, stream out of the theatre, and lounge on café terraces. There is even one painting of a *sortie de lycée*, with teenagers leaving school at the end of the day. Artists in every city paint street scenes, but in Paris it seems to have been an obsession. Life was, and is, *dans la rue*.

And even if you're looking for nothing more artistic than the chance to fill your camera's memory card with holiday snaps, walking is still an excellent way of getting around the city. Not only because Paris is so small that a day's footwork can take you through dozens of very different neighbourhoods, but also because there are so many uniquely Parisian things to discover on or alongside the pavements.

* For more on this museum, see Chapter 5.

What's in a *nom*?

When I first came to Paris, I was completely bemused by the road names. Although I could read the signs, I often had no idea which street I was actually in, because sometimes the smallest, simplest junction of two roads would have several signs telling me completely different things.

For example, at one street corner in the Marais, there are three blue enamel plaques – two on the left, one on the right – informing me that I'm in the rue Charlemagne. So far so good. But on the same walls, there are carved-stone signs suggesting that I might be in the rue des Prêtres. And on one side of the street, there's also a carved-out piece of wall where a name sign has obviously been taken down.

Meanwhile, in the small street leading off the rue Charlemagne/des Prêtres, there are more contradictions – the blue enamel plaques on either side of the street tell me it's rue du Prévôt in the 4th *arrondissement*, while a stone sign says it's rue Percée in the 12th. And on both sides there are hacked-out spaces where signs have been removed.

In all, then, at this one junction, within about 5 metres of each other, there are eight street-name signs and three mysterious spaces. The tourist or recent immigrant would be justified in wondering where the hell they were.

The same can be said if you sit outside the Bonaparte café in the street of the same name in the 6th. In front of the café, there are two modern-looking enamel plaques with street names, one above the other. The top one says rue de Rennes, the lower one Place Saint-Germain des Prés. Which one is it to be? Well, if you examine them very carefully, you can see that the rue de Rennes sign has what looks like two thin pieces of transparent sticky tape stuck in a cross over the name, as if this were enough to cancel it out.

Sometimes things are less contradictory, but just as bizarre.

There are often two identical street signs (or signs of different shapes with identical names) on the same wall. Take the small section of street just along the rue Charlemagne from the junction I mentioned above. Here, on one apartment building that is about 10 metres wide, there are three signs emphasizing that, yes, I am in the rue Charlemagne. Two of the signs are about 2.5 metres above ground level, and one much higher, about 4 metres up.

It's a similar scenario nearby, at the intersection of the rue du Roi de Sicile and the rue Pavée. On the corner of the rue Pavée, there are two blue enamel signs, set very close together just above head height, telling the passer-by twice, very legibly, what the name of the street is. In fact, the rue Pavée seems to have had an identity crisis at some time in the past, because if you walk along it, its short name is emblazoned at unnecessarily regular intervals until you get to the northern end where the system collapses with exhaustion, and there's a sign with missing letters.

The explanations on the signs about who a particular street is named in honour of are equally inconsistent. When it's a politician, like the totally forgotten Eugène Spuller in the 3rd, you get his full CV, telling you he was a local councillor, MP, senator and minister. A well-loved writer like Madame de Sévigné, on the other hand, merits nothing more than a *femme de lettres*.

Paris's street corners would seem to be suffering from a deep-seated identity crisis.

Signs of the changing times

The fairly obvious explanation for the jumble of repetitive and contradictory signs is that the city keeps introducing new rules about how its street names should be displayed, and doesn't always take the old signs down.

After the Revolution in 1789, for example, most street names that were too religious or royal were changed, and some of the old stone plaques were defaced. The rue de Turenne, for example, used to be the rue Saint-Louis, named after a thirteenth-century man who was both a king (Louis IX) and a saint, which might explain why his name has been crudely chiselled away.

Similarly, at its intersection with the rue de Thorigny, the rue Debelleyme has a barely legible stone sign indicating that it used to be the rue Neuve François, presumably named after King François I, who is now one of France's most fondly remembered royals, but whose reputation took a temporary nose-dive in the fiercely anti-royalist 1790s.

The reasons why there are so many street names scattered about at different heights throughout the city are pretty similar.

Ever since 1847, when the first complete register of house numbers was made, Paris has had its standard blue enamel street plaques, but it wasn't until 1938 that a city regulation defined the size, colour, design and positioning of the nameplates once and for all.

The rule is still in force today, and stipulates that 'public street names must be inscribed on a rectangular sign of at least 35 centimetres by 40 centimetres and at most 50 centimetres by one metre . . . The number of the *arrondissement* may be written on a semi-circular plate of 17 centimetres in radius situated above the street name.' The names too must be written in white letters on an azure background, 'within a bronze-green border decorated with shadow effects in black and white'. That last clause includes the instruction for four little dimples, one in each corner, *trompe-l'oeil* circles made to look as if they were the nails holding the sign up.

The rule says that these signs must be placed 'at the angle of two public streets, less than 2 metres away from the corner' and 'between 2 metres and 2.5 metres above the pavement', although they can be placed higher if they would otherwise disappear behind a shop or café awning. Many of the signs are exactly 2.3 metres up, hence the defacement of some old stone signs, like the one in the rue des Petits Champs in the 1st *arrondissement*, where a carved plaque has been partially destroyed by someone screwing on a more modern-looking blue nameplate at the designated height. The old sign now reads 'RUE DES PETITS PS', which is a cute idea – to today's Parisians that would read 'street of the small Socialist Parties' – but one that is the result of vandalism by a workman blindly sticking to the rules.

This French obsession with regulations can have bizarre consequences – for example, at the northern entrance to the rue du Prévôt in the Marais, a tiny alley too narrow for anyone wider than an average-sized American, there are two identical name plaques, one on either side of the street – so close together they could almost be a pair of earphones.

And in the rue du Parc Royal, the nameplates on either side of the road are at the standard height . . . the only problem being that they are therefore completely hidden by the pedestrian-crossing lights in front of them.

The multi-sign junctions survive quite simply because of municipal *laissez-faire*. Why bother to remove an old blue sign just because you're putting a new one up at a different height? And there's no need to chisel away an old stone street name because any fool knows that you're meant to believe the new blue sign.

There is flexibility in the system, however. These days, if a new building has, say, a glass façade that might explode into a million dangerous pieces if a workman started drilling holes in it prior to hanging up a heavy enamel street sign, the owners can use a lighter, adhesive plaque or even obtain permission to design their own. One of the most beautiful of these is the Art Deco mosaic in the rue Paul Séjourné (who was a railway-viaduct builder, by the way) in the 6th. There are many more, and if you come across one, it's worth taking time to admire it, because you can be sure that the people who put it there devoted quite a few hours to form-filling.

My favourite Parisian street nameplate, though, is one that has been hijacked as a playground for the city's acerbic wit. In the rue des Prêcheurs ('Preachers' Street') in the 1st *arrondissement*, some wag with a marker pen has crossed out the first R and changed the accent over the E to make it read *Pécheurs*, or sinners. And as if to rub in the anti-clericalism, someone at City Hall has ordered a sign to be placed just below the defaced word *Prêcheurs* declaring *Défense de déposer des ordures*, or 'no rubbish here'.

Writing on the wall

Quite often, I stop to read a plaque on a building that reveals a painful detail about its past. Scattered around the city, there are some 1,060 signs commemorating victims of the Second World War. There are signs indicating that people who had lived, worked or studied in that building were taken away by the Nazis. Schools are often marked with a plaque saying how many Jewish children were removed, and the sign will usually specify that it was French policemen or militia men doing the dirty work. All over the city, small plaques next to ordinary street doors will bear the name of a man or woman who was arrested, deported or shot – or all three – and the date when it happened. And on the anniversary of that date, the *arrondissement* will often arrange for a small bouquet of fresh flowers to be hung from a brass ring in the plaque.

Almost half of these plaques pay homage to people killed during the Liberation of Paris at the end of August 1944. In the centre of the city, and especially in the Latin Quarter, around the Hôtel de Ville and along the rue de Rivoli, there are beige marble plaques marking pretty well every spot where a Resistance fighter fell. At 1 rue Robert Esnault-Pelterie there's even a memorial to the only French tank destroyed in the street-fighting – yes, compared to most occupied towns and cities, Paris didn't see much heavy combat.

This in part was thanks to one of the most important figures in recent Parisian history: Raoul Nordling, the Swedish Ambassador who can be said to have saved the city by persuading the Nazi Kommandant, General von Choltitz, not to blow it up before surrendering. Nordling has a well-deserved plaque at the Lycée Janson de Sailly in the 16th.

Those buildings that did suffer in the fighting wear their battle scars with pride. If you look at the façade of the ultra-chic Hôtel Meurice, the old Kommandatur headquarters in the rue de Rivoli, or the Ministry of Defence in the boulevard Saint-Germain, the bullet holes have not been filled in. You can almost hear the machine guns strafing the buildings.

Although Parisians are justifiably ashamed of some things that went on under the Occupation, they don't want today's *flâneurs* to forget the city's proudest moment in August 1944.

'Excusez-moi, où est le . . .?'

Amongst the most prominent features of Paris's pavements are the *kiosques*. And as visitors to the city struggle to work out which street nameplate is actually correct, many of them assume that the kiosk selling maps, postcards and newspapers is a mini tourist-information office. Big mistake.

The *kiosquier* will almost certainly know the area inside out, because the kiosks in the centre of Paris are awarded by a city commission to the most experienced newspaper sellers, who have worked in the city's streets for years. Even so, he (and it's rarely a she) will probably not want to share his knowledge with a lost tourist.

Sales of daily newspapers are suffering because of the rise of the freebies, and Paris's 300 or so *kiosquiers* have seen their income fall drastically over the past few years. They're paid on a commission-only basis – they get 18 per cent of each sale, which is eroded away by the French tax and social security system to roughly 10 per cent net profit. Out of this they have to pay a rent for their kiosk of about 500 euros a year. And they earn nothing from the adverts on the sides of their kiosks, unless the poster is promoting a magazine that will boost turnover. They are generally not full of the joys of spring, even in spring.

Asking directions of a *kiosquier* is therefore a bit like asking Karl Lagerfeld to sew on a button or a lion tamer to catch a mouse. It's an insult to his vast knowledge of the neighbourhood and its inhabitants, and he has about a million better things to do to earn his living.

And rather like Karl Lagerfeld and lion tamers, the *kiosquiers* often have strong personalities. Standing alone in a cabin in the street from dawn till long after dusk breeds a special sort of person. The *kiosquiers* express themselves not only in the way they serve their customers but also through the positioning of certain lesser-known papers and magazines. The big-selling publications will obviously be prominently displayed, but look carefully and you might see more obscure publications sharing space with *Le Monde* or *Paris Match*. These will often be political, anarchist even, and are usually satirical, with the *kiosquiers* using their public location to take a swing at the establishment. My local *kiosquier* cuts out the most viciously anti-government cartoons and sticks them above the display of daily newspapers.

The *kiosquiers* are loners, like truck drivers, except that it is more difficult for them to take rest stops. They can't just lock up and take a toilet break (which, incidentally, is why so few women choose to do the job). A friend of mine once tried to buy a newspaper just after the morning rush, held out her money to the *kiosquier*, and was asked to 'wait just a moment'. Looking into the kiosk, she saw that the newspaper seller was taking a pee in an Évian bottle. Needless to say, she told him to keep the change.

All of which explains why it is probably best to ask a passer-by for directions rather than going for the obvious target. Unless, of course, you notice a big advertising poster for *Paris Match* revealing some huge scandal concerning Carla Bruni, Johnny Hallyday or another big-name celebrity. Then the *kiosquier* might just be in a good enough mood to point you in the right direction.

A clean machine

According to my city map, Paris has 5,975 streets. This means that it has twice as many pavements. Or more than twice, because some bigger roads also have gardens down the middle, or a wide central reservation where markets are held, with a pavement either side.

Paris employs approximately 4,950 workers to keep all these pavements clean by emptying bins, sweeping out gutters, spraying the ground, collecting bottles, picking up dumped furniture, clearing market-day debris, and generally making sure that the city's densely packed population doesn't turn Paris into a land-fill site.

According to city statistics, these workers sweep more than 2,400 kilometres of pavements every day, and empty the 30,000-odd transparent plastic sacks that have replaced the opaque green bins that used to hang on streetlamps until Paris decided that non-see-through bins were ideal hiding places for a terrorist bomb.

There are also some 380 green machines of various sizes and shapes sucking, sweeping and squirting rubbish off the streets and pavements. The machines come in a dizzying variety of models. There are, for example, the tiny one-person modules that crawl along like a hunched robot, sweeping up rubbish with twin brushes. Then there are the water tanks on wheels that allow a green-uniformed, hose-toting Robocop to stride along a street spraying Parisians' ankles.* There are also truck-sized vehicles that perform both of these functions simultaneously. All of them are cursed by Parisians for holding up traffic or soaking their new shoes, but without them the city would be uninhabitable.

I am always amazed by the scene when my local food market winds down at about 2 p.m. on Sundays and Thursdays. The crowds have dispersed, the awnings have been collected, the stallholders have packed up or abandoned their unsold goods. Meanwhile, a small army of green uniforms gathers and gets to work. The cardboard boxes are fed into a crusher. The wooden crates are stacked and collected. The non-recyclable refuse is swept by machine and human hand into piles and thrown on to waiting trucks. Less than an hour later, you would never even know that there had been a market, apart from the gleam of the still-wet tarmac on the square. The market itself probably hasn't changed much in a century or more (except for the presence of exotic fruit and non-native fish), but the clean-up is pure twenty-first century. And this goes on at over seventy outdoor food markets once or twice every week.

It's the same whenever there's a political demonstration – tens of thousands of militants will converge on Paris to march through the streets, scattering leaflets, water bottles, balloons, placards and food wrappings, and will do so for several hours, turning the boulevards into snowdrifts of litter. But as the last stragglers are chanting their way along the pre-arranged procession route, they will be followed by a full selection of the city's green machines and dozens of fluorescent-jacketed sweepers-up. The mess is cleared away even more quickly than it was made.

The old cliché is that the French never do any work, but I've

* For more on the ankle-spraying, see Chapter 3.

never seen people work harder than when they're cleaning up on the day of a general strike.

I pee therefore I am

Much of the mess on the streets comes from less honourable sources than a market or protest march, however.

I have probably written more than anyone on the subject of dogs doing their business on Paris's pavements. Even more shocking, to me at any rate, is that fact that Parisian men are just as active as the dogs. I'm not only talking about drunks, who have little control over any part of their body, let alone their bladder. I mean the sober adult bourgeois Parisian male, of almost any age, who will find a quiet corner, even in a relatively crowded street, have a quick peek over his shoulder to see if anyone in authority is watching, and unleash a stream of urine against a wall, a tree or one of the countless green-and-grey metal fences set up around roadworks and building sites. He will then zip up and leave the scene of the crime while his steaming river flows gently out across the pavement to wet the soles of unsuspecting passers-by. That *Le Parisien* commercial in Chapter 1 was no exaggeration.

Parisians have an excuse for this anti-social behaviour, as they do for everything else, and blame their bad toilet-training on the loss of the old metal *urinoirs* where men could pee in the street. These were called *vespasiennes*, after the first-century Roman emperor Vespasian, who introduced a tax in Rome to pay for the collection of urine (yes, trust the French to know a historical fact like that). The *vespasiennes* were introduced in Paris in 1834, though there had long been a law in the city against 'satisfying one's natural needs' in the street. Before the *vespasiennes*, the only public toilets had been barrels, 478 of which were placed on the streets of

Paris, probably making the city much more attractive to rats and flies than tourists.

The *vespasiennes* were purely stand-up toilets, some of them almost completely open to the gaze of the public. Others were more enclosed, either hidden away in the tall green columns covered in theatre posters, the *Colonnes Morris* (named after the printer who got the concession to paste up his posters there in the 1860s), or grouped in an open-air compound surrounded by a head-high metal partition.

Very quickly, the larger enclosed *vespasiennes* became gay hangouts, and, this being Paris, they inspired a minor literary genre, with writers like Jean Genet and Roger Peyrefitte telling stories of the encounters to be had there. The police also took a keen interest, regularly raiding them. During the Second World War, they were used as meeting places by the Resistance, but after the Liberation, the desire for a moral clearout turned against the *vespasiennes*, and they were slowly phased out. The only survivor I have seen is on the boulevard Arago in the 14th, outside the walls of the Prison de la Santé,* though temporary plastic *vespasiennes* are craned into the Bassin de la Villette during Paris Plages.

The *vespasiennes* were replaced in the 1980s by large, lockable *sanisettes* that you initially had to pay for, and that quickly gained a reputation for being used by tramps to sleep in and prostitutes for their quickie customers.

The result of demolishing all these traditional public places where men could relieve themselves for free without leaving the pavement was, predictably, the resurgence of the sly visit to a street corner. In desperation, the city's *sanisettes* have been made free of

* 'Health Prison', which was not called that because the wardens served organic food and taught Pilates. It was the site of Paris's last public guillotine, and two men were beheaded there (behind prison walls) in 1972. In fact, the prison is named after the street where it stands, which in turn owes its name to a seventeenth-century hospital.

charge, but queuing to use one is not a Parisian thing to do, and the complicated process of opening the cabin door is too much for some people (you often see tourists looking with glazed eyes at the long multilingual instructions).

All of which explains why there is a new police brigade interested in what goes on when men pee in public. It is the Brigade des Incivilités de la Ville de Paris, and as well as punishing litterers and errant dog owners, its eighty-eight members (no pun intended) can impose fines of up to 450 euros for *épanchement d'urine sur la voie publique* ('spreading urine on the public highway' – a wonderfully visual name for an offence), though the maximum fine is usually reserved for repeat offenders. According to a report published in the *Courrier International*, in 2008 some 56,000 square metres of Parisian pavement were soiled with urine every month. For those who have difficulties picturing 56,000 square metres, it is about equivalent to soaking the entire floor area of 500 two-bedroomed Parisian apartments in pee.

This story has two rather obvious morals. First, while out walking in Paris, it is highly unwise to tread in anything wet unless you're totally sure it's water.

And secondly, before the *sanisettes*, no one seems to have worried about where Parisian women were meant to pee.

Miscellaneous obstacles

Anyone who is planning to 'flan' around with their nose pointing up at the architecture should be warned – Paris's pavements are strewn with metal booby traps, many of them planted by the authorities themselves.

The most dangerous of these are the posts, painted dark brown or dark grey, that you often see lining the kerb. They look like elongated chess pawns, as if the city were playing a huge, and highly defensive, board game, and they can crop up at any moment, often in the middle of a wide pavement where you think you're safe. The Parisians call them *les bittes de trottoir*, a name they love because it is both correct and obscene at the same time. A *bitte* is a mooring post, a kind of stubby bollard that you tie boats up to. It is also a very rude name for a penis, and a *bitte de trottoir* therefore sounds like a sidewalk gigolo.

At first, from painful experience, I thought that the *bittes* were designed to trick pedestrians into cracking their kneecaps, thereby bringing in some welcome income for the city's medical system. They were, I assumed, related to the dark-brown cannonballs that are sometimes welded to the edge of the pavement in very narrow streets, and that were obviously meant to trip people up and/or smash their toes.

In fact, though, they are all to stop cars parking. Even though it's forbidden and drivers could get a sizeable fine, such is the outlaw spirit of the average Parisian driver that he or she would still park on the pavements if the posts or cannonballs weren't there.

So these booby traps are actually meant to protect pedestrians. Just try to remember that next time you are doubled up in pain after ramming your groin into a metal post that appeared from nowhere as you were walking along a crowded street.

Less dangerous than the *bittes*, but more decorous, are the endless numbers of metal skeletons lining the pavements – the remnants of bikes that have been locked to railings, lampposts and street signs and been cannibalized so badly that their owners can't be bothered to unlock them. Their metal carcasses are a sorry symptom of the Parisian lifestyle – as mentioned in Chapter 1, most apartment buildings have nowhere where you can park a bike without neighbours complaining. Anyone who owns a valuable two-wheeler will therefore carry it upstairs and park it in their apartment or on their balcony. The less valuable ones have to

Most Parisian apartment buildings forbid bicycles in their entrance halls. Bike owners live in constant fear of walking out one morning to find that their beloved two-wheeler has been attacked by predators.

survive on the streets, chained up all night outdoors, alone in a world of thieves, drunks and pranksters who will steal saddles, wheels and anything detachable – if they can't get the whole bike.

Canny owners paint their bikes ridiculous colours to ward off thieves in search of something resaleable, or use two or three locks to secure every moving part of the bike. But even these can fall victim to a bus or lorry that cuts a corner and squashes the bike against a traffic sign.

The result is that the streets are enlivened by the sight of rusted frames with no wheels, no chain, and no handlebars, abandoned bike skeletons that have been picked clean, like the bones of a hanged criminal in medieval times.

Sadly, these testaments to the strength of bike locks and the predatory nature of man have now become an endangered species. In March 2010, Paris passed a new rule decreeing that these *épaves* – the French word for shipwrecks – can be removed if there is sufficient evidence that they have really been abandoned, rather than just being left there by someone who wants to park their bike frame outdoors until they can afford wheels and handlebars.

Parisian council officials are doubly happy with their new scheme. Not only will they be cleaning up their streets, they have also been able to expand the French language. The job of freeing the skeletons is being given to a small army of *épavistes* – a new word coined specially for this endeavour.

Paris's urban jungle

Paris's pavements are lined with trees, the majority of them the same species of silvery plane tree that Napoleon Bonaparte planted along his marching routes across France. The second-biggest group are lime trees, though not, unfortunately, the type you can make *mojitos* with – these are *tilleuls*, the species that produce France's most insipid herbal tea.

According to City Hall, there are approximately 484,000 trees in Paris, most of them in parks, gardens and the Bois de Vincennes and Bois de Boulogne. Around 96,500 of them line the pavements, a stock that is renewed with 2,400 new trees per year, grown at the city's nursery out in Rungis, near the massive wholesale food market.

This doesn't mean that Paris is gradually being turned into a literal urban jungle (more's the pity), because many of them are to replace the 1,500 trees a year that succumb to disease, old age or pollution and get the guillotine treatment.

What's more, every one of the trees lining the streets – the so-called *arbres d'alignement* – has a microchip embedded in its trunk, with a record of its age, the vaccinations it has been given, and general notes on its health. They may not look like it as you walk past, but these trees are really robots with an electronic brain. It's all very Parisian – it looks natural and effortless but is in fact organized with scientific precision.

Less easily monitored are Paris's pigeons. Most Parisians hate them – almost as much as they hate the mad people who feed the 'flying rats', generally by emptying bags of breadcrumbs next to a bench and causing a fluttering, feathery riot.* Parisians know that there is a season when it becomes perilous to linger for more than a second under any one of those 96,500 trees lining the streets and gardens. When the plane trees are in fruit in autumn, the pigeons gorge themselves and let fly huge jets of lime-green poop that spatter the pavement and turn parked cars into Jackson Pollock canvases.

To combat the pigeon infestation – it is estimated that there are

---

* Feeding pigeons – or any wild creature (except one's children) – is illegal in Paris, and carries the same fine as letting a dog poop on the pavement: 183 euros.

A typical Parisian reaction to this scene would be 'beurk', or 'yuk'. Parisians call pigeons 'flying rats', though at least rats don't climb into trees and poop on your head. The city has recently introduced a pigeon contraceptive scheme, fortunately not involving condoms. For the unpleasant details, see this chapter.

80,000 or so pigeons in Paris, about one for every twenty-five people – the city is installing large pigeon coops in parks and gardens. The authorities have had to explain that they're not trying to increase the population by making life even cushier – on the contrary, these are 'contraceptive pigeon coops'. The first clutch of eggs is allowed to hatch, but when a female lays more eggs (and pigeons often lay six to eight clutches per year), these are given a good shake to make them infertile. The pigeons don't realize this, however, and continue incubating the eggs rather than immediately laying a new batch.

These pigeon coops also encourage the birds to poop in one place so that their droppings can be collected and disposed of, a new job so unpleasant that, rather than directly creating employment as it so often does, the city has outsourced the work to some unfortunate private company.

In the market for street entertainment

Two or three times a year, the pavements outside my building spring a surprise on me. I heave open the heavy *porte cochère* to find the way completely blocked by a jam of people selling or browsing at a *vide-grenier*.

Literally, this is an 'attic-emptying', though very few Parisians have attics. Many of them have *caves* (cellars) as well as wardrobes full of old clothes, shelves of books they'll never read again and toys that the kids have outgrown. This, in theory, is what a neighbourhood's *vide-grenier* should consist of, but of course Parisians are far too fond of bending rules to limit themselves to any theory, so in practice, the markets are a fascinating mix of private belongings and professional merchandise. They happen all year round (Parisians are naturally optimistic about the weather, and assume that Nature will obey their wishes), usually on a Sunday, and are always great places to pick up cheap pieces of Parisiana.

I went along to the most recent *vide-grenier* in my neighbourhood to see what kind of things might tempt a visitor to the city.

The first thing I noticed was the wide disparity between the stalls. Mine is a very mixed area, so the sellers ranged from families spreading out old sports shoes, PlayStation games and video-cassettes on a plastic sheet, to arty furniture sellers more suited to the Marais. There were also plenty of slightly roguish-looking *brocanteurs* (bric-à-brac dealers), postcard dealers (all French antique markets have at least one of those), stands selling a bizarre selection of old electrical parts, and one man in an *Aéroports de Paris* jacket selling suspiciously new-looking clothes.

But this *vide-grenier* was much more than a slice of Parisian street sociology. It was also a treasure trove for anyone looking for something unconventional but typically French to take home.

Here is a list, more or less at random, of *objets parisiens* that I saw:

An old gendarme's badge, a 1950s souvenir of the Sacré Coeur printed on a bit of varnished tree trunk, vintage black-and-white postcards of Parisian streets, alcohol jugs, trays and ashtrays (featuring Ricard and Pernod, of course, but also lesser-known brands such as Marie Brizard, Saint-Raphaël and Cusenier), complicated corkscrews (French engineers are constantly working on revolutionary ways of opening a bottle quickly to get at the contents), a 1960s Nescao tin with a picture of a hopelessly non-feminist French housewife, several old toy models of Citroën 2CVs, a book apparently claiming that the French single-handedly invented aviation, editions of *Paris Match* magazine from the '40s and '50s, with covers reporting on the death of Matisse, Princess Margaret's failed engagement to Peter Townsend (bilingual headline: *Sad Princesse*) and a 1949 edition predicting that *les mâles vont disparaître* ('men are going to disappear' – though they didn't say when).

My favourites, though, were the porcelain jug representing ex-President Mitterrand, which allowed me to ask, 'How much do you want for Mitterrand's head?', and a little lead statue of Napoleon, which I haggled for and eventually bought for 5 euros, telling the French antique dealer in my English accent, 'I'll take Napoleon off your hands . . . again.' For some reason, he didn't seem to think it was funny.

Say it with wordplay

The French love puns, and the streets of Paris are a perfect playground for messing about with words (as in the case of 'Sinners' Street' mentioned above). This is true on advertising billboards, of course, but there are also more permanent monuments to Parisians' verbal foibles on display, and these are the names they choose for their hairdressing salons.

Perhaps it is just the happy coincidence that the French know the English word 'hair', which lends itself to almost endless word games. They pronounce it the same way as 'air', and it's also like the French suffix '-aire' in *commentaire*, *commissaire*, etc.

So whenever you smell a waft of warm shampoo as you walk past a Paris shopfront, or see a perfectly coiffed man or woman smoking in front of their shop door, it is a good idea to look up at the sign. More often than not, it will contain a painful pun.

Here are just a few of the Parisian salons that you might stumble across while out 'flanning'. They are all real names:

Chambre à Hair – literally 'hair chamber', but sounds like the French for the inner tube of a tyre, which is a strange thing to want to look like.

Gram'Hair – another strange one, sounds like *grammaire*, or grammar. Specializes in coiffing schoolteachers, perhaps.

Besoin d'Hair – literally 'need for hair' but sounds like the French for 'need some fresh air'.

FM Hair – a clever, modernistic play on FM radio and hair, which sounds like *éphémère*, or ephemeral. Though come to think of it, that doesn't say much for the durability of their haircuts.

Post'Hair – sounds like the French pronunciation of 'poster', though surely it also sends out a disturbing subliminal message about baldness. What else is 'post hair'? A wig specialist, perhaps.

Hair du Temple – a pun on *air du temps* (spirit of the times) outside a salon in the rue du Temple, thus achieving a double-whammy play on words.

Diminu'Tif – a purely French pun. *Tifs* is a slang word for hair. *Diminutif* means diminutive, or small, and *diminuer* is reduce, so the name could be interpreted as 'reduce hair', presumably an allusion to cutting hair rather than making it fall out.

And finally, my two favourites:

Challeng'Hair – literally, 'hair challenge' but it sounds like the French pronunciation of 'challenger', a word they know. Appropriately, it deals in baldness treatments.

Volt'Hair – an electric-sounding play on the name of Paris's wittiest writer, Voltaire. A literary hairdresser – what more could you want? OK, Voltaire wore a wig in later life, but when a hairdresser's pun is in the offing, historical accuracy is neither hair nor there.

51

Paris Plages. Every summer, Parisians rush down to the banks of the Seine in the hope that former president Jacques Chirac will keep his promise to swim across the river.

3

WATER

Napoleon Bonaparte: *Je voudrais faire quelque chose pour les Parisiens.*
His Minister of the Interior, Jean-Antoine Chaptal: *Eh bien, donnez-leur de l'eau.*
(I'd like to do something for the Parisians. – Then give them water.)

A sinking feeling

PARIS IS a city of *eau*. Its motto is decidedly damp – *Fluctuat nec mergitur* means something like 'It might not be floating all that steadily, but it never sinks.' This is not because Paris is comparing itself to Venice or Atlantis – Paris's sandy river basin is not subsiding (at least, not according to estate agents). In fact, the motto refers to the very unseaworthy boat on the city's coat of arms, a kind of wooden banana with a pair of underpants as a sail and no visible crew members, which is floating precariously on a rollercoaster of waves.

This might seem a strange emblem for a city so far from the sea. The only waves you see on the Seine these days are when the river police are having a bit of fun with one of their speedboats. But until the nineteenth century, Paris was France's busiest port, and the city council was actually founded by river merchants.

These *marchands de l'eau* were so powerful in the early Middle

Ages that they persuaded King Louis VII to give them a monopoly on all merchandise coming in and out of Paris. A royal charter signed in 1170 states that 'No one may bring into, or take out of, Paris any merchandise unless he is a *marchand de l'eau de Paris* or in partnership with a *marchand de l'eau de Paris*.' Anyone breaking this rule lost their whole cargo, half of which would go to the King, and half to the *marchands*.

In 1246 the watermen went a stage further and formed themselves into the city's first ruling body, imposing their emblem – the banana-like ship – as Paris's official seal. And their legacy was further recognized in 1853, when Baron Haussmann,* the Prefect of the Seine region, made *Fluctuat nec mergitur* the city's motto.

Haussmann was only putting into words the Parisians' long and passionate relationship with water. It is almost as if they are former desert-dwellers, with a constant need to see water everywhere.

And in fact, this is not far from the truth, because their addiction seems to be a subconscious hangover from their ancestors' long battle to get clean drinking water. For most of its history, the city drew its water from the Seine, which lost its purity about 1,000 years ago. Long into the nineteenth century, there were pump houses beside the river, raising water to be distributed around the city via buckets or fountains. Some of the fountains were supplied by the springs in Montmartre and Belleville, the oldest of these being the Fontaine Maubuée, built in 1392 on a street corner that has since been demolished to make way for the Centre Pompidou. Which may be just as well, because the name *Maubuée* apparently came from *mauvaise buée* or 'bad mist', a reference to the inferior quality of the Belleville water.

Today, there are still dozens of these old fountains dotted around the city, some of them still working (and now providing

---

* For more on the Baron and his impact on Paris, see Chapter 5.

good drinking water), like the gushing spout at the corner of the rue de Charonne and the rue du Faubourg Saint-Antoine near Bastille, which must waste thousands of litres a day. No matter – the sight of running water is good for the Parisian soul.

The same goes for the Fontaines Wallace, the famous groups of green metal statuettes that provide a constant stream of drinking water, almost all of which goes undrunk. These were a gift to the city from a British philanthropist, Richard Wallace, the illegitimate son of a marquess who inherited his father's money and spent most of it on art (the Wallace Collection in London) and the rest on being kind to Parisians. During the Prussian siege of 1870–71, Wallace financed ambulances, and in 1872 he paid for the design and installation of the fountains that bear his name, even consenting to have them painted dark green so that they harmonized with the rest of the city's street furniture.

At the time the Fontaines Wallace were built, the city was still relying on systems put in place by Napoleon. In 1799, the average Parisian had access to only a litre of water a day. As a military man, Napoleon envisaged an effective but crude solution – digging canals to bring water close to the city. However, many Parisians were still reliant on water carriers who would sell drinking supplies in the street, most of it a bacterial soup pumped out of the Seine, which was also the city's main sewer. Predictably, disease was rife, and the cholera epidemic of 1832 wiped out an estimated 18,000 Parisians.

The hundred or so Fontaines Wallace were therefore literal lifelines, allowing Parisians to drink without fear of killing themselves. And many of them survive to this day – from the ornate towers with their four caryatids representing *bonté* (goodness), *simplicité, charité* and *sobriété** to the humble green taps in most of

---

* Looking at the four caryatids – for example on the fontaine outside the Chez Clément restaurant in the place Saint-André des Arts – I personally can't tell the difference between them. It is almost as if Wallace's designers hoped to convince Parisians that goodness was exactly the same as sobriety. Idealistic, to say the least.

Paris's public parks, where every Parisian child gets into the habit of drinking public water as soon as they can walk.

Drinking something alcohol-free was definitely a habit that Wallace wanted to encourage. After the Prussian siege, when water supplies were even less reliable than usual, the price of drinking water went up alarmingly, so that many people began quenching their thirst with wine. And unlike the toffs, they didn't have access to high-quality Champagne – they were quaffing vinegary gut-rot. It was no surprise that when the first Fontaine Wallace was connected up in August 1872, there was a small riot as people literally fought to get at the clean water.

Today, there are over 900 public drinking fountains in Paris, including three rather special ones that provide genuine French mineral water for free. The fountains in the place Paul Verlaine in the 13th *arrondissement*, the square Lamartine in the 16th and the square de la Madone in the 18th tap into a spring 500 metres below the city, and you can often see people filling up bottles to take home. The water is very soft (unlike Parisian drinking water), and is therefore said to give a purer taste to tea and coffee. These fountains also take the Parisian need for free drinking water to its logical French conclusion. They can't be content with plain clean water – they want *eau minérale*.

La vie est une plage

The Parisian love affair with water comes into full fruition in summer, during Paris Plage (Paris Beach), the festival started by Mayor Bertrand Delanoë in 2002. For four weeks, from around 20 July to 20 August, a sizeable chunk of the city's population can be seen streaming down to the river banks.

Before 2002, the city had turned its back on the river

somewhat. In the 1960s, most of the Right Bank was disfigured by a highway, and along the Left Bank, the *quais* are busy streets that force anyone trying to get down to the river to risk their life crossing three or four lanes of traffic. Both the Louvre and the Hôtel de Ville have cut themselves off from the river, whereas they used to be on its bank – the Hôtel de Ville was originally built on a square called the place de Grève (Sandbank Square) that was literally a beach.*

In fact, until Paris Plage, pretty well the only organized activities on the river were the *bateaux-mouches*, the expensive and infrequent Batobus river shuttles, one or two barge bars, dancing on the quai Saint-Bernard,† and the *bouquinistes*, most of whom now sell far more miniature Eiffel Towers than books. Riverside fun was almost all improvised – you would take a bottle of wine to the pedestrian parts of the embankment or picnic on the Pont des Arts. Some stretches of the *voies sur berges* were pedestrianized on Sundays, but it wasn't until Paris Plage that the citizens officially reclaimed full possession of the river from the car, albeit for only a few weeks in summer.

From mid-July to mid-August, palm trees spring up along the riverbank, while sandpits and pétanque pitches temporarily turn the riverside back into a sandbank. There is usually a swimming pool with aquagym and swimming lessons – all of them free. People can sign up for dance and aerobics classes and Tai Chi sessions, and try out sports like wrestling and fencing – again, all free of charge. And for those who prefer to do nothing, there are several hundred loungers and parasols laid out on artificial beaches (along with an

---

* *Grève* also means strike – it was on this sandbank that unemployed Parisian workers used to gather, or *faire grève*. Though they used to be hoping for an offer of loading or unloading work to come along – it wasn't until the nineteenth century that the word took on its modern meaning of the French workers' favourite negotiating tool.

† For a full account of these riverside dance sessions, see my novel *Dial M for Merde*.

equal number of security men to stop them being stolen). It really is a holiday resort for people who can't afford to, or don't want to, leave the city in summer. And Parisians flock there like migrating flamingoes.

The migration is spreading out from the city centre, too. I live near Napoleon's Canal de l'Ourcq, which was once one of France's main trade routes, and is now slowly emerging from decades of industrial and urban decline. In summer, people rent canoes and pedalos, there are one-euro boat trips up the canal to the suburb of Pantin, and a small marina has been installed. Part of the canal, along the Bassin de la Villette, has even been incorporated into the Paris Plage scheme, forcing the city to rename it Paris Plages, plural. Now, as on the banks of the Seine, for a month or so in summer, you can listen to concerts, battle for loungers, learn to line-dance and tango, refresh yourself in a cool mist spray, or dive in the canal and then get yourself vaccinated against Weil's disease, the potentially fatal illness caused by ingesting rat's urine.

The improvements made to this 800-metre stretch of canal have put a whole neighbourhood back in touch with its wateriness. Even the local firemen have been getting in on the act. I regularly see them testing their hoses, spraying an arc of water across the canal, and wetting anyone who strays too close to the opposite bank – especially if she happens to be good-looking.

In fact, the Paris Plage(s) scheme is not the first time since Baron Haussmann that city leaders have shown their attachment to water. During Jacques Chirac's time as Mayor of Paris from 1977 to 1995, and then as President of France from 1995 to 2007, Parisians jokingly called their tapwater 'Château Chirac'. In 1988, during his spell as Mayor, he promised to clean up the River Seine so completely that he himself would swim across it 'before the end of 1995'. This would not have been a good idea because of the strong current and the number of barges and *bateaux-mouches* constantly surging up and down the river, but it was an idealistic promise from a native Parisian that the city has never forgotten.

In 2004, during a presidential visit to a school, a pupil asked Monsieur Chirac whether he had done it yet. 'No,' he answered, 'because I'm not sure the Seine has been getting on too well since I left City Hall.' Joking aside, he admitted to the schoolkids that he shouldn't have made a promise he couldn't keep (thereby undermining the whole institution of electioneering, and setting alarm bells ringing across France's entire political landscape).

The Seine *is* getting cleaner, though, and apparently there are now twenty-nine species of fish swimming past the Louvre and under the Pont Neuf, none of which has legs and three heads. Even so, bathing in the river has been forbidden since 1923, and anyone jumping in these days will be fined for wasting river-police time, if they don't drown or poison themselves, that is.

Walking on water

At the end of January 1910, Paris's motto about not sinking was contradicted by the Seine itself, as the river rose 8.62 metres and burst its banks, partially submerging the city for thirty-five days.

An estimated 2.4 billion cubic metres of water (I say 'estimated' because I have no idea how much that really is) poured into the streets creating a filthy lake that engulfed not only the *quartiers* by the riverbanks, but also low-lying areas way 'inland', including much of the 8th and 9th *arrondissements*, almost up to the Gare Saint-Lazare.

The sewers and the *métro* were flooded, countless cellars were turned into swimming pools, and many ground-floor apartments had to be evacuated. The Eiffel Tower, built on a bed of sand, shifted 2 centimetres off the vertical, but with German efficiency, the canny engineer Gustave Eiffel (real name Bönickhausen) had

During the great flood of 1910, the phrase 'Do you need a lift?' took on a new, more hands-on meaning.

erected his tower on hydraulic pumps and it was easily righted.

As floods are meant to come around every century (according to the French, Nature works to a metric calendar), Paris has long been haunted by the fear of a repeat disaster in 2010. Engineers have built huge run-off reservoirs upriver, but these can only hold about 830 million cubic metres of water, leaving about 1.6 billion to gush onward to the capital if the river levels are the same as in 1910.

Paris has therefore resigned itself to getting its feet wet sometime soon, and has put in place a minutely detailed scheme to limit flood damage, aptly named the Plan Neptune.* Scientists say that it wouldn't be a flash flood – just as in 1910, the waters would take several days to rise to dangerous levels, so there would be time to mobilize all the city's workers, as well as 10,000 soldiers.

To ensure that radio programmes won't be interrupted (Paris wouldn't want to be without endless debates on the philosophical meaning of the deluge, or talk shows with politicians blaming each other's parties for the catastrophe), a 330-metre-long flood barrier has been prepared. It would be erected around the Maison de la Radio, which is by the river, near the Eiffel Tower. Meanwhile, the Maison's toilets, sinks and taps have been fitted with valves so that the studios won't be filled with river water and sewage (after all, journalists' voices would sound strange if they had to wear pegs on their noses).

Over at the Louvre, as the waters rose, 700 volunteers would start carrying works of art out of the basement storage areas and up to higher floors – the heaviest sculptures have already been moved.

And just to prove that the city does think about its people as well as its media and culture, it should be pointed out that the very first measure in *le Plan Neptune* is to evacuate all the homeless people who sleep on the riverbanks. Although that might only be to

* Neptune was also the name given to the seaborne operations during D-Day. Coincidence, or a symptom of how seriously Paris is taking the danger of flooding?

avoid having them float in through the windows of the Louvre.

Perhaps the most dramatic measure of all in Plan Neptune is that Paris's transport company, the RATP, plans to deliberately flood *métro* lines running alongside the river, presumably on the grounds that it's better to drain off clean water than dirty. Though of course the water would no longer be clean when the flood receded – someone would have to collect up all the dead rats, mice and accumulated rubbish. It is to be hoped that Plan Neptune includes a few pairs of rubber gloves.

Throughout 2010, the city expressed this obsession with flooding in a series of exhibitions about the events of 1910, and at each one Parisians could be seen studying maps of the flooded area to see if their current address was in there. I naturally did the same, and was relieved to see that I am currently out of danger. Until 2006, however, I was living near the Bastille, well inside the evacuation zone, and even back then, my next-door neighbour had started stockpiling sacks of plaster to block up his toilet, shower and all of his sinks. As soon as the sewers flooded, he said, the drains would overflow and our houses would be turned into fountains of *merde*. Fortunately, he didn't give his speech to potential buyers when I was trying to sell my place.

One of the flood-related exhibitions featured a collection of photos from a now-defunct newspaper called the *Journal des Débats*. The pictures showed that the streets of Paris, especially those around the river, have hardly changed since 1910. Apart from all the hats, long dresses and moustaches, the black-and-white photos could almost have been taken yesterday.

The traditional way of measuring the height of the Seine certainly hasn't changed at all in a century. Parisians still look to the statue of the *Zouave* (a French-African colonial soldier) on the Pont de l'Alma. Usually he stands well above the river on a plinth, gazing with blithe detachment into the oncoming current. If he has his toes in the water, the Seine is running very high and Parisians start to

Paris measures its floods by the height of the water flowing over the statue of the Zouave (French colonial soldier) on the Pont de l'Alma. Normally, he manages to keep his boots dry, but in the great flood of 1910, the Seine came up to his elbows. This picture shows a lesser flood in 1930 (being French, Parisian floods follow a metric timetable).

feel empathetic rheumatism. But in the stark photos of 1910, the rushing tide was over his elbows, and with his right arm crooked up towards his face, he seemed to be contemplating the imminent prospect of drowning.

To Parisians, the most worrying things about the exhibition were the obvious signs that the flood had lasted a very long time. A whole new way of life had sprung up in the city. The photos showed people being calmly ferried about in rowing boats with their shopping. There were also long, precarious walkways consisting of planks, doors and tabletops aligned on trestles. These had become the new pavements, running the whole length of streets and across squares. Improvised scaffolding was erected in front of buildings so that residents could climb through the first-floor windows and carry on with daily life – only the ground floor and basements were totally flooded.

The waste-disposal system had evolved, too – the exhibition showed some bizarre photos of men shovelling cartloads of rubbish *into* the river. The dumps were flooded, so domestic refuse was tipped into the Seine at the Pont de Tolbiac, a pretty stupid idea considering that this is upriver of the city, meaning that the waste flowed right through Paris and presumably straight back into the streets where it had been collected.

It wasn't all doom and gloom, however. One of the photographers of a century ago had found his 'you've got to laugh' picture. In a street at least a metre deep in water, someone had hung a sign outside a bar – *fermé pour cause d'inondation* (closed due to flooding). The name of the bar? *Le Café de l'Aquarium*.

And the exhibition's visitors' book showed that nothing can traumatize a French person so much that they will stop making bad puns. Someone had written *qui l'eût crue?* – who would have believed it? – a play on *cru*, the past participle of *croire* (to believe) and *crue*, meaning high water. And I'm sure that there are Parisian journalists out there just praying for another flood so that they can use the joke in a headline.

Did I just do that?

As well as riverboat trips, Parisians organize two very different sorts of water-themed tours of their city.

One of these takes visitors to admire some of the engineering work done by Baron Haussmann in the mid-nineteenth century. This would be understandable if we were talking about an aesthetically pleasing technological achievement like the Eiffel Tower, but less so (in my view, anyway) when the object of the guided tour is the sewers.

For an hour or so, starting from the Pont de l'Alma, visitors can wander through the tunnels, enjoying a truly multi-sensory experience. They can see, hear, smell, and if they're very clumsy, feel and even taste a generous sample of Paris's dirty water (and other waste matter, of course). The tour programme promises a visit to delightful-sounding places of interest such as the avenue Bosquet collector, the place de la Résistance storm drain, and a tunnel that carries the Left Bank's intellectual waste to the purification works.

The sewer walls all have road signs telling you where you are in the city, so an underground tour is rather like strolling through Paris, accompanied not by traffic and pedestrians but by *merde*.

The second type of visit is much more fragrant. Eau de Paris, the public water-supply service, organizes themed walking tours in different parts of the city. One of them takes visitors on a 2.5 kilometre stroll around the Left Bank, to see a seventeenth-century aqueduct and some of the old fountains. Another takes in the springs in the old village of Montmartre. There's also a guided tour of the best surviving Fontaines Wallace. (For more details about the tours, see the address list at the end of the book.)

Eau de Paris, by the way, is a relatively new organization created in 2009, when the city decided to take back control of its water supply, which had been in private hands since 1985. Other public services are being privatized, but Parisians couldn't bear to think of anyone else possessing their water.

Eau, what a beautiful morning!

All of the above would seem to explain the watery goings-on every time I walk out of my front door in the north of Paris before eight in the morning.

For a start, I am very likely to get a water cannon sprayed at me. This, I always feel, is a bit over the top. After all, my only misdemeanour is wanting to get a cup of coffee. But it is never the riot police who are trying to hose me back home again. It is a green-overalled city worker, gripping the long nozzle of a hose as if it was a small guitar, sluicing the previous day's cigarette ends, litter and dog muck into the gutter.

You would think that the residents of the neighbourhood would be grateful, but they often huff and moan at the cleaners, who have a habit of ricocheting a fine mist of watered-down detergent and assorted dirt particles on to the shoes and lower legs of anyone who gets in their way. Only when there are enough impatient pedestrians growling to get past will the cleaner turn away and squirt somewhere else, opening up a ten-second window during which people can scurry through to the wet-but-safe zone that has already been hosed.

After this trial by water, there is a second barrier at the corner of the street, which gets flooded every morning by a minor tsunami of floating jetsam gushing along the gutter on its way to the drain. The speed and depth of the torrent is often increased by a green-uniformed man sweeping it along, making sure than no paper, plastic bottles or leaves are left behind.

On some mornings, you have to be able to long-jump a couple

of metres to get from the middle of the street to the kerb with totally dry feet. And if you're half asleep and forget to leap, your shoes will be turned into shipwrecks.

Every morning, people on their way to work will complain about one or other of these watery obstacles. But if the streets were suddenly dry, they would complain even more, and then begin to worry that something in the city had gone profoundly wrong. They may be obsessed with the prospect of a flood, but they're even more scared of being deprived of their beloved *eau*.

346. PARIS — Station du Métropolitain - Place de la Bastille

Bastille's original *métro* station, by Hector Guimard. Today his designs are seen as architectural gems, but in his lifetime, fickle Parisians thought his Art Nouveau style outdated, and many of his *métro* entrances were demolished.

4

THE *MÉTRO*

On ne perd rien à être poli, sauf sa place dans le métro.
(You lose nothing by being polite, except your seat in the *métro*.)

TRISTAN BERNARD, FRENCH WRITER

PARIS IS proud of its underground rail system, and so it should be. Travelling beneath some big cities can be a slow, hot experience, like being stuck in a hammam with a crowd of grumpy strangers. But outside of rush hours and strike days, the Paris *métro* can whisk you from almost anywhere to anywhere in the city in under forty-five relatively painless minutes.

And it's getting even better, with old trains gradually (and on some lines very gradually) being upgraded and refitted, which is why I personally always choose the *métro* over the bus. If you don't have time to watch as a bus driver hoots at badly parked trucks, inches through roadworks, or terrifies cyclists, it's far better to travel underground.

I should stress that this chapter deals only with the *métro* itself, and not the RER (*réseau express régional*), the *métro*-like system that crosses Paris and stretches out into the suburbs. Parisians are inherently snobbish, and regard this system as a kind of slave ship transporting unfortunate chained-up workers away from their suburban homes and into the clutches of their cruel masters, with the cruelty even being doubled because in the evenings they're transported back again in the same horrific conditions. It is actually quicker to travel between some parts of Paris on the RER, but no true Parisian ever takes the option, presumably for fear of being mistaken for a suburbanite.

The light at the end of the *métro* tunnel

What few Parisians know is that their *métro* very nearly didn't get off the ground at all – or rather that it almost stayed overground.

In the mid-1800s, every major city in the Western world was trying to work out how to transport its residents and incoming commuters around the increasingly jammed streets. Paris was actually ahead of the game, because as early as 1852 it inaugurated an overground urban railway that skirted the edges of the city – hence its name, the *Petite Ceinture*, or little belt. At first, it carried only animals being sent to the city's abattoirs and freight, but gradually it was adapted to take passengers, and came into its own during the 1870–71 Prussian siege, when French soldiers were able to dash to defend different parts of the city on steam trains – one of the first examples of mechanized warfare.

The *Petite Ceinture* was taken out of service in the 1930s, but much of it is still visible. The raised gardens near Bastille, the Coulée Verte, run along a converted section of the old network. The Parc Montsouris in the south and the Buttes-Chaumont in the north are both crossed by stretches of unused railway, and the Flèche d'Or music venue in the 20th is in an old *Petite Ceinture* station.

Meanwhile, back in the nineteenth century, arguments about a bigger urban rail network raged on. London had opened its first city railway in 1863, connecting up its major train stations. New York, Berlin and Vienna followed, and even Budapest was jumping on the bandwagon. Paris was being left behind, and for a very Parisian reason.

From 1856, when discussions about a large urban railway network for the city began, to 1890, every proposal hit the buffers. Some of the ideas put forward by Paris's engineers were too insane to be taken seriously. One was a sort of funfair ride, with trains floating along on underground rivers. Another engineer called Arsène-Olivier de Landreville envisaged gigantic viaducts carrying steam trains above the Paris rooftops, thereby avoiding pollution from the smoke.

There was also a strong lobby for a straightforward over-ground train system, an extension of existing rail networks beyond the mainline termini and into the heart of the city, but none of the regional railway companies could decide which one of them would build and run the system, and continually opposed each other's projects.

Amongst the most futuristic ideas was a plan to get rid of steam trains altogether and use the largely untested technology of electricity. This daring project was put forward by Paris's Director of Works, Edmond Huet, in conjunction with the city's Chief Engineer, Fulgence Bienvenüe, who had already invented a funicular tram for the hilltop *quartier* of Belleville. Bienvenüe was also an expert at building sewers – an excellent blend of qualifications for designing an underground train system.

The difficulty was to get a decision. The existing railway companies were determined to manage the urban network, and entered into a prolonged power struggle with city officials who wanted control of their transport system. To cap it all, the national government was right-wing, whereas the city was *à gauche*, which created a whole new level of disagreement.

In the end, minds were focused by the appearance on the horizon of the 1900 Paris Exposition Universelle, which was to be a showcase for French innovation and technology.

Exhibits were to include one of the first moving walkways and a big-screen projection of films by the Lumière brothers. And as part of the Expo, the city was also organizing the 1900 Summer Olympic Games. Not only were millions of visitors expected, it was also hoped that many of them would want to travel from the main exhibition site around the Eiffel Tower to the sporting events out in the suburb of Vincennes, to the east of the city.*

It was therefore urgent to build at least one *métro* line, and finally, in 1897, Paris began to get its plans on track.

Rather predictably, the city opted for the project put forward by its own Director of Works – an electrically powered underground network (which, by now, wasn't that futuristic, because London had been operating an electric system since 1890). It was an idea that had one huge advantage as far as Parisian officials were concerned – it made interference from the railway companies impossible, because as well as being electric rather than steam-powered, the trains would run in tunnels that were too narrow for a conventional train.

The final barrier to building a Parisian underground was cleared in March 1898, when the national government voted through a law declaring that the project was 'of public utility', and thereby ceded control of the work to the city.

To prevent jealousy amongst French railway companies, the construction contract was given to an outsider, a Belgian industrialist and amateur archaeologist called Édouard Empain. He founded a company called the *Compagnie du Chemin de Fer*

---

* The 1900 Paris Olympics, the second modern Olympiad after the 1896 Athens Games, included the official sports of golf, ballooning, croquet, Basque pelota, polo, tug of war and cricket. The cricket gold was played for by only two teams – England and France – and the French team consisted almost entirely of British ex-pats. The match was played in Vincennes on 19 and 20 August, and won by England.

Métropolitain de Paris and, in October 1898, set Fulgence Bienvenüe to work digging.*

Sticking to a route that allowed him to dig along existing roads (he hadn't worked out how to tunnel under apartment buildings without making them fall down), Bienvenüe had soon turned the street running the whole length of the Louvre and the Tuileries into a gigantic trench. Work progressed with remarkable speed, though there were a few hold-ups – in December 1899, a tunnel underneath the Champs-Élysées collapsed, creating a crater 15 metres wide and 20 deep, swallowing up trees and lampposts, and fortunately injuring only two passers-by. And no one had foreseen the sheer quantity of earth that would be dug up. A flotilla of barges carried debris away down the Seine, and at night, the city's trams were requisitioned to pull wagonloads of earth out to dumps.

But on 19 July 1900, at 1 p.m., after only twenty-two months of work, Line 1 of the Paris *métro* was opened to the public and began to carry Expo visitors from the Porte Maillot, just beyond the Arc de Triomphe, to the Olympics at the Porte de Vincennes. The locals also started to use the *métro* straight away, and it was so popular that the three-carriage trains had to be lengthened to eight carriages – though, sadly, this slowed the trains down so much that the benefit was lost.

In any case, the project had worked, and Bienvenüe was commissioned to go ahead with the plan to build five more lines, including one, Line 4, that would require him to tunnel under the Seine.

This difficult and dangerous task was accomplished with two ingenious pieces of engineering. It was impossible to drill into the silty riverbank around Saint-Michel without damaging an existing overground railway line, so Bienvenüe pumped in ice-cold salt water and froze the ground solid. Even so, it took ten months of

---

* Not personally – Bienvenüe had lost an arm during a security inspection on one of his railways.

digging to complete 14.5 metres of tunnel through the silt, and this was without even starting to dig under the Seine itself.

For the actual river crossing, he put the work out to tender. More than thirty projects were put forward, and the most innovative and daring was chosen – a plan conceived by a company called Chagnaud, who had already built a three-tunnel *métro* interchange at Opéra. They proposed to sink a tunnel into the Seine that would be like a permanently parked submarine.

Starting in 1905, metal lengths of tunnel were constructed on the riverbank beside the Tuileries, and then simply dropped into the water and on to the riverbed. The water was pumped out of a hollow chamber built in underneath the length of tunnel; and into this chamber men were sent, via a chimney, to simply dig downwards beneath that section of tunnel until it was far enough underground and underwater. The crossing required two years' labour and five segments of tunnel. The horrific working conditions can only be imagined, and five men lost their lives digging in the fetid gloom. Line 4 was finally opened on 9 January 1910, just days before the Seine decided to show that it had not been tamed after all – the river broke its banks on 20 January, almost immediately flooding Châtelet station, and then gradually reclaiming the tunnels that had been dug through its territory. Line 4 had to close, and was not fully re-opened until April.

Art Nouveau grows prematurely old

Paris wanted everything to do with the 1900 Exposition Universelle to look spectacular. The Eiffel Tower had been built for the 1889 Expo, but now the Grand Palais and Petit Palais were to be constructed on the Right Bank of the Seine, and the new *métro* had to be just as impressive.

A competition was launched to find a designer for the station entrances. Twenty architects applied, but, typically for Paris, the job went to a man who hadn't even entered the contest. Hector Guimard was already known for his Art Nouveau houses, and had a highly influential fan – a banker called Adrien Bénard,* the Président du Conseil d'Administration (the equivalent of the CEO) of the *métro*. Bénard asked Guimard to submit some designs, which he did – glass and green-metal forms that were a stark, and highly modern, contrast to the classical columns proposed by most of the other applicants. Not everyone liked them, but Bénard's influence won the day, and when Line 1 opened, its first users must have been startled to have to descend into tunnels through what looked like a tangle of vines, guarded by towering twin lamps that resembled praying mantises. The jungle/insect metaphor was deliberate – Guimard said, for example, that the glass roofs of his covered entrances were meant to look like dragonflies spreading their wings. Today, his street furniture is one of the highpoints of any architectural tour of Paris. Difficult to imagine, then, that there were people who wanted to get rid of them almost immediately.

Some thought the entrances too erotic – the intertwining vines were too sensuous and the double lamps looked, one highly inventive critic said, like Fallopian tubes. Others felt that the designs were morbid, and that the green railings looked like stylized bones.

In 1904, a daily newspaper, *Le Figaro*, demanded that Paris get rid of 'these contorted railings, these hump-backed standard lamps that point out the *métro* stations like enormous frogs' eyes'. This was the same paper that, only five years earlier, had sponsored an exhibition by Guimard. The painful truth was that, like all extreme styles, Art Nouveau was going out of fashion almost as quickly as it

* Bénard later commissioned a dining room from Guimard, which is now on display at the Musée d'Orsay.

had come in, and at the turn of the twentieth century, modernists were sneering at its twee *végétalisme*.

Guimard's contract was terminated, no more designs were commissioned and when, in 1904, a prestigious new station was opened outside the Opéra Garnier, a classical stone entrance was chosen. Guimard's existing designs were used for a few more stations until just before the First World War, but Art Nouveau had officially fallen from favour.

These days, the *métro* may be very proud and protective of its Guimard architecture, like the beautiful gold-tiled entrance at Porte Dauphine or the open-top versions at Cité and Louvre–Rivoli, but almost half of Guimard's 141 station entrances have been destroyed, including two showcase pagodas at Bastille and Charles de Gaulle–Étoile. Fêted as a cultural hero today, during his lifetime Guimard was a victim of Paris's fickle artistic tastes.

A Parisian accident waiting to happen

One thing that the rational engineer Fulgence Bienvenüe probably did not bargain for was Parisians' behaviour when they were on the *métro*. And it was this behaviour that caused the *métro*'s first – and biggest – catastrophe.

It started with a technical problem. The first *métro* carriages were made out of wood, and the electric cables powering the engines passed right under them – a dangerous combination, especially if the system short-circuited, which it did on 10 August 1903, at Barbès–Rochechouart station on Line 2, causing a fire to break out underneath one of the carriages. Luckily, Barbès is an outdoor station, so the passengers were evacuated without any panic and the fire was quickly put out.

The following train was also evacuated, and began to push the damaged carriages through the tunnels towards the terminus at Nation, so that they could be taken out of service and repaired. Incident over, it was thought. The evacuated passengers got on the next train and continued their journey.

However, a few stops further on, at Ménilmontant, the fire started up again on the original damaged train. The driver of the train carrying the evacuated passengers was warned, and stopped at Couronnes, the station before Ménilmontant. Couronnes is an underground station, and the driver asked the passengers to leave the train yet again, and exit the station via the stairs.

At this point, one exasperated passenger demanded to know whether they were going to get a refund. The driver said he didn't know, and an argument began. Tempers flared, the passengers refused to leave until they were guaranteed a refund, and the stalemate was broken only by the arrival of a dense cloud of smoke that had spread back along the tunnel from Ménilmontant. In a panic, passengers began to flee along the platform, only to hit a dead end. Couronnes station has only one exit – via the stairs they had refused to climb, at the other end of the platform. Tragically, in an attempt to stop the fire at Ménilmontant, the electricity along the whole section of line was cut, plunging Couronnes into total, choking darkness. By the time the smoke cleared, eighty-four people had died of asphyxiation.

The technical lessons were learnt – wooden carriages were phased out, and the electric circuit for station lighting was separated out from that powering the engines. The only thing that hasn't changed since 1903 is that Parisians are still just as argumentative . . .

It's just not cricket (probably)

New York has its subterranean albino alligators, and Paris has crickets. Many *métro* users swear that they have heard the chirruping of these communicative insects, especially on Lines 3, 8 and 9 (not the others – it seems that, like many visitors to Paris, the crickets can't understand the signs at junctions telling them how to get from one *métro* line to another). I personally have never heard them – birdsong, yes, from sparrows that get in via overground stations, and the scurrying of mice and rats, but never the Mediterranean call of the cricket.

It is said that the insects migrated to Paris from the south of France, and originally took refuge in winter in *boulangeries*, where they would eat the wood used in the bread ovens. Then, in a piece of convenient serendipity, just when wood ovens were being converted to gas and electricity, the *métro* was built, and the crickets all hopped into the tunnels. Here they fed on discarded food, paper and cigarette butts, and managed to establish colonies on the three above-mentioned lines, said to be the warmest because they have no overground stations.

That, at least, is the gospel according to the LPGMP, or Ligue pour la Protection des Grillons dans le Métro Parisien. This cricket-protection league, founded in 1992, is campaigning for the creation of a subterranean auditorium in an unused *métro* station, where crickets would be able to breed and sing in peace. The league's 100 or so members also say that there are two vital conditions for the survival of the *métro*'s cricket population. First, there should be an official limit on the length of transport strikes, because the stations cool down if there are no trains running through them (a colony in Maraîchers station is said to have died out during the long strike of 1995). And secondly, the ban on smoking in *métro* stations should be lifted, because cigarette butts are an essential part of the Parisian cricket's diet.

So next time you see a passenger defying the no-smoking rule on a *métro* platform, and then flicking their cigarette butt down on to the rails, rest assured – it's probably just an animal activist trying to protect endangered insects.

Where am I going?

France is a pretty rational country, so it is appropriate that Paris's *métro* lines should be known by their numbers. The first six lines all do very basic, strategic things, linking up key points in the city. Line 1 runs east to west along the Seine; Lines 2 and 6 loop north and south respectively around the city limits; Line 3 heads out from Saint-Lazare mainline station to Opéra and République; Line 4 is a direct north-to-south route linking up the Gares du Nord, de l'Est and Montparnasse; and Line 5 connects the Gare d'Austerlitz to the Gare de l'Est. Subsequent lines seem to fill in the gaps.

Given this rational background to the *métro* map, it is strange that the line numbers are so unhelpful when you're trying to find your way around the city. The problem is that Parisians don't always use them when describing the best route from one station to another. Or if they do tell you which number line to take, it can get swallowed up in a mass of information. So if you ask for directions, it is essential to listen carefully not just for numbers but also for terminus names. A typical reply to 'How do I get to the Champs-Élysées?' might be 'Prenez la huit direction Balard, puis changez à Concorde et prenez la une direction La Défense et descendez à Franklin Roosevelt.' Rest assured, this is exactly what you want to know despite the fact that you have no desire whatsoever to go to Balard, Concorde or La Défense, and might not know why they're talking about an ex-President of the USA.

What the reply means is this: from here, take the Line 8 south

How to find your way (or not) in the *métro*. What if you don't want to go to Place d'Italie or Bobigny? Travelling on the *métro* requires an intimate knowledge of both the line numbers and their (ever-changing) termini.

towards its terminus, Balard, then change at Concorde station and look out for signs directing you towards Line 1's western terminus, La Défense. Take Line 1, and get off at the station called Franklin D. Roosevelt, which is on the Champs-Élysées.

It is a system with its own logic, the only problem being that Paris is a dynamic city and is continually extending its *métro* lines. If your map is out of date, or the person giving you the instructions hasn't realized that the line has been extended, the terminus might not be a terminus any more, and you could spend hours searching for a non-existent *direction*. It would surely be easier to say northbound, westbound, etc., as they do in London, but one thing I've learnt from living in France is that you must never tell the French that another country (especially *une nation anglo-saxonne*) does something better – you just have to adapt to the Parisian system.

Getting in line

Below is a run-through of the foibles and characteristics of Paris's sixteen *métro* lines. They vary a lot in character because of the different types of carriages they use, the routes they take and the people that use them, and all have a few memorable stations that are worth a visit.

Lines are identified by their numbers (1–14, with a 3*bis* and a 7*bis* tacked on) and current termini.

Ligne 1: Château de Vincennes – La Défense

A long, direct line that skirts along the north bank of the Seine and up the Champs-Élysées, it carries well-dressed commuters out to the office district of La Défense and tourists from Bastille to the Louvre. The oldest line, it was also one of the first to be upgraded, with fast-moving trains that aren't divided up into carriages. Trains are breezy, smooth and seem to sing as they speed into the tunnels. They also have automatic doors so you don't have to battle unlocking them.

FUN STATIONS

Bastille – its walls are decorated with cartoon-like tile frescoes depicting key events from the French Revolution. And just for a few yards, the line goes overground, with a great view along the canal basin towards the Seine.

Palais-Royal, because the entrance outside the Comédie Française theatre is unique – it looks like a crown made out of silver and multi-coloured precious stones, and was created in 2000 by the artist Jean-Michel Othoniel.

Ligne 2: Nation – Porte Dauphine

It sweeps around the north of the city, taking in some heavily ethnic areas – Chinese in Belleville, Sri Lankan at La Chapelle, African at Barbès, and white Catholic lawyers at Villiers. Heading east to west, there's a good overground section from Colonel Fabien to Anvers with views into some of the poorest apartments in Paris, then the line dips underground again, as though the city wanted to protect innocent travellers from the naughtiness above in Pigalle.

FUN STATIONS

Porte Dauphine, for its wonderful Guimard entrance, like a garden pavilion, and its period interior decor. In 1900, the station was used to try out a cream tile colour scheme that was later rejected in favour of the omnipresent white.

Barbès, an ironwork overground station overlooking the craziness of the cheap pink-and-white department store Tati.

Ligne 3: Gallieni – Pont de Levallois–Bécon

This line gets packed with the masses of commuters whose working day begins and ends with being squashed on to a suburban train at Saint-Lazare. The older Line 3 trains have been refitted and now feature bizarre holding-on poles in the aisles. Instead of a single pole from floor to ceiling, there is a sort of cactus structure that splits into three from waist height, giving triple holding-on space. On the ceiling, in the middle of this trio of poles, is a blue light that shines down the metal, making the whole thing look like some kind of teleporter. Touch the pole and you will be beamed instantly to Saint-Lazare, which, during rush hour, would be a welcome thing.

FUN STATIONS

Temple, because it is almost pointless. It emerges about 20 metres from République (where Line 3 also stops) and seems to serve only to take people to the door of the local Monoprix supermarket.

Réaumur–Sébastopol – not only does the station commemorate one of the few battles jointly won by the Brits and the French (the 1854–5 siege of Sebastopol in the Crimea), but also both Line 3 platforms are decorated with a collage of old newspaper articles, a reminder of the fact that this *quartier* was once Paris's Fleet Street. The front pages give a patchy version of recent French history – a 1912 boxing match, the 1936 Tour de France, a one-legged man taking up skiing, and the outbreak of the Second World War, followed rather quickly by 'Victoire!' in 1945. No mention of the Occupation except for the announcement of the 1944 uprising, which includes the outrageous French propaganda of the time: 'Paris has liberated itself . . . without support from Allied troops' (D-Day and the subsequent rout of Nazi forces in northwest France clearly didn't count as 'support').

Parmentier – the green trelliswork on the platform walls may make the station look like a garden in which the clematis have all died, but in fact the cross-hatching is meant to represent the threads of a potato net (potatoes are sold in net bags in supermarkets). This is a rather obscure homage to Antoine-Augustin Parmentier, whom the French claim as a pioneer in potato cultivation – which is why they call shepherd's pie *hachis parmentier*. In fact, Parmentier was the scientist who proved to sceptical Parisians in the 1770s that the potato wasn't poisonous, as was commonly believed. To win favour for his pet vegetable, he gave a plant to King Louis XVI, who wore the flower in his buttonhole. Fortunately, other Parisians understood that the tubers were meant to be eaten, and the potato has been a staple food in the city ever since.

Ligne 4: Porte de Clignancourt – Porte d'Orléans

The underground river crossing at Châtelet was one of Fulgence Bienvenüe's greatest technological triumphs, but these days the stations at Cité and Saint-Michel feel (and smell) as though you're in the very bowels of the earth. It's a highly useful dash from north to south, which means that its ageing trains are almost always jam-packed between the Gare du Nord and Montparnasse. The line also passes through some dodgy neighbourhoods, especially around the Strasbourg–Saint-Denis station, with its low-cost Chinese prostitutes.

FUN STATIONS

Saint-Germain des Prés, which hosts regular literary events, and has texts projected on to its curved walls and ceiling. This is why it's the only *métro* station without advertising billboards on the platforms.

Montparnasse–Bienvenüe – the station named after the *métro*'s creator is actually less fun than it used to be. In 2002, the long corridor leading to Lines 6 and 13 was fitted with the fastest-moving walkway in the world – 12 kilometres per hour. But there were so many accidents and panic attacks that it was taken out of service. As if to compensate, the corridor has now been decorated with literary quotations about the *métro*.

Ligne 5: Bobigny–Pablo Picasso – Place d'Italie

A good line for barflies (who will find all they need at Bastille, Oberkampf, and the Canal Saint-Martin near Jacques Bonsergent) and concert-goers (the Bataclan is at Oberkampf and the Zénith and Cité de la Musique at Porte de Pantin). At the Gare du Nord, heading north, there is a wonderful example of Paris's attempts at crowd control. The platform is painted with yellow arrows telling passengers where to stand to let people get on and off the trains. However, the arrows were all repainted after an apparent change of opinion, and if you try to follow them, you will end up doing a tango and falling under the train.

FUN STATIONS

Bastille – on the northbound platform (direction Bobigny–Pablo Picasso), you can see some of the foundations of the infamous prison that used to stand on this spot, the storming of which was one of the key moments of the French *Révolution*. Although, as you look at the historical stones, you might like to consider that the prison wasn't the notorious detention centre for political prisoners that it is made out to be. When it was liberated in 1789, it held only seven inmates – four forgers, two lunatics and a count who was accused of helping his sister run away from her husband. Not exactly revolutionaries.*

Quai de la Rapée, which is in the middle of nowhere, but just after leaving it, heading south, the train winds spookily around Paris's morgue and then performs an excellent overground river crossing, with a spectacular view towards Notre-Dame.

Ligne 6: Nation – Charles de Gaulle–Étoile

The mirror image of Line 2, it loops around the south, which is a much richer part of town. There are long overground stretches

---

* For the full story see my book *1,000 Years of Annoying the French*.

along the wide boulevards either side of Montparnasse, one of which allows you to see the 15th *arrondissement* without actually having to get off and be bored by it (though, to be fair, the area around La Motte-Picquet–Grenelle station is actually an oasis of liveliness). Line 6 also boasts two river bridges, one near the 'sewing machine' (as the hideous Ministry of Finance is locally known) and the other, the best hundred metres or so of the whole Paris *métro*, right next to the Eiffel Tower. When the Tower is flickering (on the hour, every hour from sunset till 1 a.m., or 2 a.m. in summer), it's a good idea to get off at Passy or Bir-Hakeim – the stations on either riverbank – and go back again for a second look.

FUN STATIONS

Passy and **Bir-Hakeim**, for the above reasons.

Saint-Jacques – it has a beautiful 1906 Art Nouveau brick and iron entrance, and its platform walls are covered in *pierre meulière*, the craggy, porous stone used to build Parisian houses in the nineteenth century.

Montparnasse–Bienvenüe (see *Ligne 4* above).

Ligne 7: La Courneuve–8 Mai 1945 – Mairie d'Ivry/Villejuif–Louis Aragon

Another line in need of refurbishment. Although its trains look relatively new and metallic, they groan and clank on metal wheels. Is it too cynical to say that the refit is considered less urgent because the northernmost section, from Gare de l'Est to La Courneuve, carries some of the city's poorest commuters? The line takes a very circuitous route, meandering its way across town like the Seine, looping along past the Pont Neuf and the Louvre, up to Opéra and through the most anonymous parts of the 9th *arrondissement*.

FUN STATIONS

Chaussée d'Antin–Lafayette – apart from the fact that it's the shopaholics' drop-off point (the Galeries Lafayette are just above),

THE *MÉTRO*

the ceiling of the Line 7 platform is covered in an immense Sistine Chapel-like fresco celebrating the American Revolution (or at least France's role in it). The Marquis de Lafayette, who joined Washington's army, ogles Liberty, represented of course by a beautiful woman. The fresco was designed in 1989 by French painter Jean-Paul Chambas.

Pont Neuf, which has decorations on both its ceiling and walls. The station is on the opposite riverbank to the Monnaie de Paris, the Mint, and features a large metal coin press, in front of a tile fresco of the press in use, as well as some gigantic 3D enamel reproductions of old coins that emerge from one of the advertising billboards and cross the ceiling to the other side of the platform, like bubbles in a miser's nightmare. There are also some glass cases containing small, life-size coins, which are probably replicas because no one has bothered to steal them. Another fun aspect of the station is that if you get off the *métro* here, you emerge right on the banks of the Seine, a pretty rare occurrence.

Ligne 8: Balard – Créteil Préfecture

A strange line that feels like a back-up for much of its length. On the long stretch between République and Richelieu–Drouot, it shares three stops with Line 9, and then shadows Line 12 at Madeleine and Concorde. At either end the line disappears into the dark depths of the 12th and the 15th *arrondissements*. This is because it was cobbled together out of other projects – originally it linked Opéra to Porte d'Auteuil in the far west, much of which has now been hijacked by Line 10.

FUN STATIONS

Opéra, simply because of its absurd exits. You hit street level in the middle of traffic islands in front of the opera house. Great views, but it can take ages to get off the traffic islands and on to the boulevard that you're looking for, and even longer to reach the opera house itself.

Bonne Nouvelle – if you try to read the name of the station written on the platform walls, you might think that the sign-writer was suffering from absinthe poisoning. However, the uneven lettering is deliberate, and is meant to evoke the Hollywood sign overlooking Los Angeles. (In fact, it was the person who had the idea who was suffering from absinthe poisoning.)

Ligne 9: Pont de Sèvres – Mairie de Montreuil

Another of the crowded lines, it ploughs through the office districts in the west and centre of the city into prime tourist territory (from Trocadéro to Alma–Marceau, the site of Princess Diana's memorial flame,* and on to the Champs-Élysées) and along the popular shopping route of the Grands Boulevards. It also goes out to the Parc des Princes (at Porte de Saint-Cloud), the home of Paris's football team, Paris Saint-Germain, whose fans are so violent that different factions kill each other rather than attacking the opposition. On home-match days, the western end of the line is jammed with blue-and-red scarves and distrustful expressions. The old trains have been done out with new paisley seats that seem unnecessarily hard – not that you'll get much chance to sit on one.

FUN STATIONS

Bonne Nouvelle, for its lettering (see Ligne 8 above).

Franklin D. Roosevelt – its Line 9 platforms are like a rundown museum of 1950s design. Its aluminium walls and glass advertising display cases were, half a century ago, the height of avant-garde. These days, the dusty relics are boarded up and ignored by the crowds of commuters. Above ground, things are still trendy –

* Which it isn't. The golden flame near the Pont de l'Alma is a life-size replica of the torch held by the Statue of Liberty that was presented to Paris by New York in 1989. The statue herself was of course given to America by France in 1886 to mark the centenary of the American Revolution. Yes, the French were ten years late, but it's the thought that counts.

the station's Line 9 exit takes you to Avenue Montaigne, which is lined with *haute couture* stores.

Porte de Montreuil – at the opposite end of Paris's social scale, this station is one of the access points for the massive flea market on a Sunday.

Ligne 10: Boulogne–Pont de Saint-Cloud – Gare d'Austerlitz

A posh people's line that goes through the Latin Quarter and out into the wilds of the 16th *arrondissement*, where it is used only by nannies, old ladies and rich schoolkids who haven't yet been given a Vespa. Like Line 9, it also ferries PSG football fans, so is to be avoided on home-match days. The line has one peculiarity – it splits into two after crossing the Seine, and has six one-way stations, three in either direction. It is a bit like a roller coaster – you can look across and see a platform on a lower level, but you can't get to it because it's a different station.

FUN STATIONS

Javel–André Citroën, because it takes you to the Parc André Citroën, where you can go up in a hot-air balloon and get a great view of Paris and the Eiffel Tower.

Cluny–La Sorbonne, which is decorated with ceramic facsimiles of the signatures of legendary French writers like Molière, Victor Hugo and Arthur Rimbaud. It's also fun for a bad reason, namely that the signposts towards Lines B and C of the RER are so confusing that the station is almost permanently haunted by lost-looking tourists.

Ligne 11: Châtelet – Mairie des Lilas

A cross between a bouncy castle and a roller coaster, it will shake, rattle and roll you up the hill from Châtelet to Belleville and beyond. There's no need to go to Disneyland Paris – this old, neglected line will give you all the thrills of the funfair. Its carriages are narrow and the seats so close together that if you travel any distance, you will soon be on knee-rubbing terms with the people sitting opposite and next to you. When entering this line at Châtelet, it's best to go underground at the place du Châtelet itself, because the Line 11 terminus is about a kilometre from other lines and you will spend so long wandering through tunnels that you won't need to visit the catacombs.

FUN STATIONS

Arts et Métiers, for its curved copper-plated walls, created in 1994 by Belgian artist François Schuiten to celebrate the bicentenary of the nearby engineering school of the same name. It feels like waiting inside a water pipe.

Porte des Lilas, because it inspired the character in Serge Gainsbourg's first hit, 'Le Poinçonneur des Lilas' (the ticket-puncher), and because it is part of Paris's cinema industry. If you see a movie scene filmed in a *métro* station, it will almost certainly be Porte des Lilas (even if the signs on the wall temporarily say something else). The station is regularly hired out to film producers, and has featured, for example, in *Paris, Je t'aime* and *Le Fabuleux Destin d'Amélie Poulain*. (See also Line 3*bis* below.)

Ligne 12: Mairie d'Issy – Porte de la Chapelle

A long, cosy line, apparently built so that the middle classes won't have to mix with anyone else. It winds in from the 15th, through the 7th and the posher office districts of the 8th and 9th, undergoes a quick culture shock at Pigalle, then heads for the chic part of the 18th behind Montmartre.

FUN STATIONS

Concorde, where excerpts from the *Déclaration des droits de l'homme et du citoyen* (France's 1789 declaration of human rights) are written on the curving walls, one blue letter per white tile. The ironic problem with this noble intention is that there is no punctuation, making it very hard to read what one's rights are.

Abbesses, which has one of the best examples of a Guimard Art Nouveau entrance. However, it was never meant to be there. It was moved from Hôtel de Ville station in 1974, even though the original managers of Line 12 had decided not to use any of Guimard's designs.

Porte de Versailles – during the Salon de l'Agriculture, Paris's immensely popular agricultural show held at the end of February, Parisians go there to see the cows, taste the sausages and watch the President perform. The rule is, if he's good with farmers, he's a good head of state. Sarkozy's first visit ended in a televised slanging match with a farmer. Chirac used to spend whole days out here discussing milk yields and techniques for force-feeding geese, and people still love him for it.

Ligne 13: Châtillon–Montrouge – Gabriel Péri Asnières–Gennevilliers/Saint-Denis–Université

Brings in commuters from the northern steppes of the 17th *arrondissement* and the well-off but not-too-snooty southern suburbs, and dumps them all in west central Paris. Some of the trains on this line have been fitted with an electronic list of stations that makes each name flash as you pull into the station, while a happy female voice tells you where you are. There's more standing room on these trains, which is good because the line has regular sardine moments between Montparnasse and Saint-Lazare. At its northern end, the 13 forks in two (at the aptly named station La Fourche) so spectacularly that if you are planning to visit the beautiful royal church of the Basilique de Saint-Denis, and stay on the wrong train, you will end up halfway to Brittany.

FUN STATIONS

Montparnasse–Bienvenüe (see *Ligne 4* above).

Guy Môquet (pronounced 'mockay' and not 'mocket' – *moquette* means carpet) – it's not exactly fun, but the station is noteworthy for the display case of photos and documents in honour of Guy Môquet, who was shot by the Nazis when he was only seventeen, one of forty-eight prisoners executed in reprisal for the killing of a German officer in 1941. Môquet is famous for the patriotic letter he wrote on the eve of his death, which is regularly read out in schools. The tragic irony is that he was only in prison because he had been arrested by French policemen for distributing Communist leaflets in the *métro*, at Gare de l'Est.

Varenne, which is close to the Musée Rodin, and appropriately decorated with sculptures on the platforms. As well as Rodin's famous *Penseur* (*The Thinker*), there is a cast of his wonderful sculpture of the writer Honoré de Balzac, who looks as though he regrets agreeing to be sculpted dressed only in his bathrobe.

Ligne 14: Saint-Lazare – Olympiades

The Parisians' favourite, this new line rockets across the centre of Paris in what feels like milliseconds. Young execs don't even have time to start a new game of phone Tetris between getting on at Saint-Lazare and shooting out into the squeaky-clean office district around the Bibliothèque Nationale. The stations are like glass tunnels, the trains are long and well ventilated and – best thing of all in Parisians' eyes – there are no drivers. The line is automatic, so there's no one to go on strike. The French like to say they're in favour of workers' rights, but if there was a referendum, everyone would vote to change the whole *métro* system over to driverless trains. Well, everyone except the transport workers, of course, who would go on strike in protest, therefore reinforcing the case for driverless trains.

FUN STATIONS

None, really. The trains are so frequent and fast that you never spend enough time in the stations to notice them. Oh, OK, Châtelet, because if you change from the old existing *métro* system on to Line 14, you have to go through what is quite obviously a narrow hole that was knocked through an old tunnel wall to connect the two networks.

Lignes 3bis (Gambetta – Porte des Lilas) *and* 7bis (Louis Blanc – Pré Saint-Gervais)

Dug so that people living in the centre of the 19th and 20th *arrondissements* wouldn't feel left out, these two short, link-up lines feel very toy-like, even though the carriages are much the same as on the other lines. The 7*bis* basically collects passengers up and takes them for a picnic at the Parc des Buttes-Chaumont.

FUN STATIONS

Botzaris on the 7*bis*, a little hole in the ground by the Buttes' metal fence from which you emerge with your picnic basket.

Pelleport, **Saint-Fargeau** and **Porte des Lilas** on the 3*bis*, which all have ceramic-tiled entrances in a more sober, post-Guimard style of Art Nouveau, designed by the architect Charles Plumet.

Singing the *métro*'s praises

Architects aren't the only artists to have been inspired by Paris's underground system. The *métro* has been celebrated in some of the most Parisian of French *chansons* – Édith Piaf sang a song called 'Le Métro de Paris', in which she compared a train to 'a gigantic glow-worm spinning its silver thread across the rooftops of Paris' (she seems to be confusing glow-worms with silkworms, but then she was an urban girl). Meanwhile, as mentioned above, Parisian crooner Serge Gainsbourg's first hit was set on Line 11.

The *métro* has also inspired some fascinating literature. Franz Kafka paid a brief visit to Paris in September 1911, and even though the network was only a decade or so old, he was perceptive enough to make some telling remarks in his diary. He talks about the 'unnatural indifference of the passengers', and notes that you can identify strangers to the city because they are the only people who stop at the exit to get their bearings rather than striding out and 'losing themselves straight away in the street life'. He also says how spooky it is to see lone passengers getting off at stations outside the city centre. A shame Kafka didn't stay longer in Paris – he could have written a great novel about feeling paranoid beneath the city, maybe having his hero turn into a giant Parisian cricket.

One of the most Parisian novels in French literature, Raymond Queneau's *Zazie dans le Métro*, uses the transport system as a central theme. The *métro* obsesses the young heroine, a provincial visitor to the city, as much as the Wizard of Oz enthrals Dorothy. Unlike Dorothy, though, Zazie doesn't suffer the disappointment of discovering that her idol is a fraud, because the poor young *provinciale* gets so entangled in her uncle's insane intrigues that she never actually sees the *métro*. According to literary critics, this is because Queneau is using the *métro* as a metaphor for an adult world that Zazie is not ready for (even though her uncle has just taken her to a gay cabaret club). Actually, the critics are right in a more literal sense, because anyone taking the Paris *métro* does need maturity to survive. It's a place with its own rules of behaviour and coded language, and, even outside rush hours, it requires a high level of self-assertion, elbow-sharpness, breath control and spinal flexibility.

The following section may help readers prepare for the experience that Zazie never knew . . .

The rules of life underground

Here are some dos and don'ts to avoid getting into a Parisian verbal wrestling match on the *métro*.*

- The first is, as in any city, to avoid certain lines during rush hour – that is, between about 8 a.m. and 9 a.m., and 5.30 p.m. to 7 p.m. The worst claustrophobia experiences are to be had on Lines 1, 2, 3, 4 . . . no, it's just better to try and avoid taking the *métro* at all between those times, or at least to be prepared for shovers, grumblers, sneezers, gropers and pickpockets if you do so.

- When trains are crowded and airless, especially in summer, I find it best to get on at the rear of the carriage. This way, with the windows open, you stand at least a small chance of gaining access to some oxygen. Further up the carriage towards the front, you might notice people passing out or frying eggs on bald men's heads. This is proof that the ventilation systems on Paris *métro* trains rarely work. The exceptions are Lines 1 and 14, which, as mentioned before, don't have separate carriages – they're long, metal snakes – and are therefore better ventilated.

- If you are standing on a crowded train, crushed up against the doors, and it arrives at a large junction, people are going to want to get off. They will probably start saying, 'Pardon, je descends,' even before the train has stopped. As soon as the doors open, you have to get out of the train, step to one side, and wait while hordes of impatient Parisians stream out of the carriage. Failure to do this can result in ruptured kidneys.

- In the standing areas of most *métro* carriages, there are so-called *strapontins*, fold-up seats. These are subject to fairly strict

* See also Chapter 1, 'Parisians', for a section on how not to annoy Parisians in other contexts.

rules of etiquette. They are only to be used when there is enough room for everyone to stand comfortably. At the slightest crush, the *strapontin* sitters are expected to get up. Some people play stupid and stay sitting, which can get them either moaned at or stomped on, and at the very least glowered at menacingly.

• Sometimes, a person who seems to be completely ignoring *métro* etiquette – sitting on a *strapontin* despite the crowds, listening to tinny music on a phone, smoking even – will not be admonished by affronted passengers. This is because they know that the person is trying to *choquer les bourgeois* and is best left well alone.

• If you get into a *métro* carriage and see that it is crowded except for one section of seating that is magically empty, it is usually not because a large group of friends have got off and no one has spotted the free seats. A more likely explanation is that the drunk sitting in the corner of the unoccupied area has just pooped himself.

• On fairly crowded trains, it is common for one place in the main seating areas of a carriage – the sets of eight seats – to be free. The problem is that there are two ways into these areas, so you might find yourself in direct competition with someone coming in from the other direction. The etiquette in these cases is to avoid eye contact and dash for the seat. If you get there first, it is only because you have won one of the many races for survival in Parisian everyday life. Of course, once you are seated, if you look up and see that the other person was old, pregnant, frail or beautiful, you can stand up again and make a great show of offering them your hard-won seat.

• The managers of the Parisian *métro* have obviously decided that passengers don't need to be warned to mind the gap when they get off a train. There can be a gap wide enough to fit half a baguette lengthways and they won't tell you. For example, at Cité, if you get off the rear carriage of a Line 4 train heading south towards Porte d'Orléans, there's a chasm between the métro door and the platform that could swallow up a slim *Parisienne*, but no warning. It really is necessary to keep your eyes on your feet when you get off a *métro* train, especially on to a curved station platform.

•   And when your *métro* journey is at an end and you want to leave the station, your troubles are not over. If you're exiting a station that has glass doors that you have to push open (rather than turnstiles or guillotine-like rubber gates), it is vital to push exactly where it says *Poussez*, or, if there's only a diagram, press right on the white hand on a green background. This pressure unlocks the door. Pushing anywhere else is pointless, and will have Parisians puffing down your neck within seconds, groaning at your stupidity.

After which, it only remains for me to say *bon voyage . . .*

Paris, a well-preserved historical city? Between the 1850s and 1870s, it was one huge building site as much of the medieval centre was demolished to make way for the boulevards.

5

HISTORY

La nostalgie, c'est le désir d'on ne sait quoi.
(Nostalgia is the desire for we know not what.)

ANTOINE DE SAINT-EXUPÉRY, AUTHOR OF *LE PETIT PRINCE*

MANY PEOPLE come to Paris to feel nostalgic. Often, this *nostalgie* is related to something they haven't experienced themselves – the glory days when everyone dressed like dandies or can-can dancers, the smoky café nights listening to Sartre explain how absurd everything is (except him, of course), the sound of jazz filtering up from basement bars, the sunlit summers when all you needed to fall in endless passionate love was a camp-bed in a Montmartre garret and a litre of cheap red wine.

Paris seems to be an ideal backdrop for reliving the perfect past. It still has the medieval Marais, the student-filled Sorbonne, the timeless waiters at the Café de Flore, the eternal banks of the Île de la Cité. It is so well-preserved that its nineteenth-century *grands boulevards* are almost banal.

Well, that is the cliché, anyway. In fact, Paris has suffered several waves of almost cataclysmic destruction. It's a miracle that the famous monuments survive. Even the Eiffel Tower came very close to being toppled – and not by invading enemies. It may come as some surprise to learn that throughout history, Paris has devoted a great deal of its energy to destroying its own architectural gems.

Most of this energy was expended during infighting by political and religious factions, who made a habit of knocking down each other's favourite buildings. But some of the most widespread damage was done coldly and calmly by the city's planners simply building over the past. And as we will see, if the modernizers' ardour hadn't been cooled in the late-twentieth century, tourists might now be nipping into the Louvre during a motorway coffee-stop, and taking monster-truck *mouches* instead of *bateaux* . . .

A carnival of history

Although Paris's past has been almost constantly violent, its history museum, the Musée Carnavalet, is a peaceful, intimate place, despite the fact that it is at the heart of the Marais, and its main entrance is just inches from the rue des Francs Bourgeois, a shopping superhighway for both Parisians and tourists.

The museum gets its name from its venue, the Hôtel Carnavalet. This is the former home of one of Paris's most celebrated writers, the Marquise de Sévigné. She wasn't an im-poverished aristocrat who was forced to move into a motel – in its original sense, *hôtel*, or *hôtel particulier*, meant an urban mansion. And Carnavalet is just that, a sixteenth-century city château, which the Marquise rented from the 1670s until her death in 1696. While there, she wrote her famous letters to friends and family, describing Parisian life and discussing the moral and religious issues of the day. The museum has a room dedicated to its former tenant, with three voluptuous portraits showing off her cleavage and coquettish curls. Some of her letters might be slightly prudish, but she was obviously a fun-loving lady.

Her old home was bought by the city in 1866 to be used as a history museum, and was renovated and enlarged using architectural gems salvaged from the vandalism then being inflicted on *Vieux Paris* by the city's greatest modernizer, Baron Haussmann (of whom much more in a moment).

Today, the museum may seem rather old-school (there are no interactive displays or smell-the-medieval-odours attractions), but it offers an excellent opportunity to stroll through several millennia of Parisian life, featuring not only the big names of history but also the forgotten everyday people.

Lunchtime at the Neolithic restaurant

Logically, the most forgotten people of all are the very first known Parisians. Recent excavations near the river at Bercy (now the site of a multiplex cinema and trendy food court) have unearthed traces of settlements dating back some 6,000 years, including long wooden canoes, and some smaller artefacts that seem to confirm all the stereotypes about food-obsessed Parisians. The Musée Carnavalet's collection of prehistoric tools consists largely of different-shaped blades for cutting and scraping meat. There are also several grinding stones, probably used for crushing herbs and spices, as well as a large variety of jugs and a selection of clay spoons, plates and even a ladle. Now I have seen a lot of prehistoric exhibits in my time, but never before spoons and a ladle. I was almost surprised that the archaeologists hadn't found a reindeer-skin apron and a tray, proving that the region once boasted a tribe of Stone Age waiters – ancestors of today's Parisian waiters, some of whom do have a certain prehistoric bluntness about them. And in case this idea seems too far-fetched, the museum also possesses a pair of wild-boar jaws with holes drilled through them, apparently so that they could be hung on a tree or palisade. Yes, in 4,000 BC the Parisians were already putting up restaurant signs.

Nothing, it seems, has survived to give us an idea of what happened in Paris between prehistory and the arrival of the Romans in 52 BC, probably because the Gauls torched their own village there to prevent the invaders capturing it. But we can guess what the site by the Seine must have looked like, because according to Caesar, it was then known as Lucotecia, a local word for bog. And the Romans kept the name, calling the place Lutetia.*

It is not certain exactly where in this tree-covered, silty bog the Gauls had their main settlement – on the Île de la Cité, some say, or near the western suburb of Nanterre.† But the Romans decided to build their city on higher ground, up on the Left Bank, centred around the hill now occupied by the Panthéon. And they brought the ultimate symbol of their civilization to the boggy riverside – the baths, les Thermes de Cluny, that still stand on a corner of the boulevard Saint-Michel. These weren't filled with bucketfuls of muddy Seine water, either – the Romans constructed a 26-kilometre aqueduct to link them up with much purer springs.

The Musée Carnavalet testifies to this quantum leap in sophistication. Gallo-Roman artefacts on display include a set of slim copper probes and scalpels that look much like the kind of instruments that a surgeon would use to nip and tuck modern flesh; intricate pieces of moulded plasterwork – reminders that the gypsum deposits in Montmartre are the origin of the name plaster of Paris; an effete-looking miniature bronze of the messenger god Mercury, who is sporting a winged hat that would be very much at home on a Jean-Paul Gaultier catwalk; and a ring-shaped earthenware drinking flask with inscriptions that show how the

---

* It wasn't until the fourth century AD that the city got its modern name, an abbreviation of the Latin *civitas Parisiorum*, or the town of the Parisi, the Gallic tribe who had previously governed the region.

† Which would have been appropriate, because it was partly the bogginess of the badly built university campus at Nanterre that sparked off the student riots in May 1968.

Romans were expanding the area's culinary horizons – on one side, the lettering reads 'Landlady, fill my bottle with beer' (the Gauls' crude brew), and on the other, 'Landlord, do you have spiced wine?' An indication, perhaps, that incoming Roman wine merchants were marrying local barmaids and setting up a new style of Gallo-Roman café.

Gladiators, lions and *pétanque* players

While much of Paris's history is thrust upon you – Notre-Dame, the Sacré Coeur and the Louvre, for instance – some of its finest historic sights are hidden away. One of the best examples of this is (or are) Les Arènes de Lutèce, in the 5th *arrondissement*.

At the end of the first century AD, the Gallo-Roman Lutetians built themselves a vast stone Coliseum outside their walls, about 500 metres south of the Île Saint-Louis. At its peak, the amphitheatre held 15,000 spectators, who came along to be amused either by theatrical shows or wholesale massacres of animals and gladiators. Even 2,000 years ago, Paris offered a wide variety of entertainment.

However, when Germanic invaders came visiting in the third century, entertainment suddenly became less of a priority, and stone from the amphitheatre was pillaged to shore up the city's defences. After this, the stadium fell into disuse. It was used as a cemetery, and then swallowed up when King Philippe Auguste built his city wall in the thirteenth century. A convent was subsequently built across most of the site.

What was left of the amphitheatre lay hidden for six centuries or so, even though the neighbourhood was still popularly known as *Les Arènes*, and Roman masonry was only stumbled upon in the 1860s, when a new street, the rue Monge, was ploughed through the area. The existence of an amphitheatre was noted by the builders, but apartments were constructed along its western edge and Paris's transport company bought the land to use as a tram depot.

The writer Victor Hugo and a protection committee, La Société des Amis des Arènes, were prompted to begin a vigorous 'save the Arènes' campaign. Hugo wrote to the *Président de la République*, Jules Grévy, in 1883, reminding him that: 'It is impossible for Paris, the city of the future, to abandon the living proof that it was the city of the past.'*

The lobbying worked, and after the convent was demolished, the half-excavated area became a public garden. However, it wasn't until 1917 that serious restoration was carried out, proof perhaps that by that time Paris was confident of winning the First World War and hanging on to its capital.

Today, this much-abused place has been absorbed into the city's everyday life. It is a half-hidden, half-forgotten park, almost invisible except from the apartments that overlook it, and accessible through entrances that seem specially designed to keep it a secret.

Standing outside the rue Monge entrance, the only sign that you are near anything Roman is a blank area of wall in an apartment building, and an archway decorated with a gladiator's helmet. A narrow passageway leads to what looks at first sight like a fairly typical Parisian park. An open area of gravel where local boys play football, a few green benches in fenced-off flower gardens, a terrace on which a dozen people are holding one leg in the air like dogs learning to pee against a lamppost – a Tai Chi class.

It is a million miles from the fully restored *arènes* in Arles, Nîmes or Orange. The amphitheatre is visible, though – the steps

---

* Interestingly, Hugo signed off his letter, 'Je vous serre la main' – 'I shake your hand' – perhaps a reference to Grévy's membership of the Freemasons. Hugo's father, General Joseph Hugo, had been a mason. In Paris, it's always easier to lobby friends of the family.

leading up to the top rows where the upper classes would have sat, out of reach of the blood and sweat of the gladiators, and the arcades from which big cats, armoured men and masked actors would have emerged, now put to modern sporting use as goals.

Apart from the shouts of the boys training to be temperamental modern footballers, the place is usually very peaceful these days, and remarkably empty. The small lawns up on the terraces are so little used that the park-keepers haven't even bothered to put up the notorious *Pelouse Interdite* signs, which usually make me want to laugh and cry. Laugh, because it seems absurd to erect a sign saying 'lawn forbidden' on a lawn. (What's it going to do, apologize and stop growing?) And cry because the sign means more than just 'keep off the lawn'. It is saying 'no fun or relaxation here'.

In the Arènes, however, lawn-based lazing is legal, and on a dry day it is a great place to lie down, stare up at the sky and wonder how this amphitheatre, one of the oldest vestiges of the ancient city, can be so rudely ignored.

Not that it's always so peaceful. Modern Parisians have their own version of the blood and drama of the gladiatorial arena – *pétanque* tournaments. Almost inevitably, the amphitheatre's gravel floor has been adopted by a *pétanque* club, the Amicale Bouliste des Arènes de Lutèce. The club has met there since the end of the Second World War, and regularly evicts the young footballers to take over the arena for its tournaments, at which point the stadium rings out once more to the clash of metal on metal and the groans of the vanquished.

No respect for history

In the third century, the Romans left their mark on Paris in another, even more memorable way. It was after they beheaded Saint Denis, the man who introduced Christianity to the region, on high ground to the north of their city that the place of his execution was named 'martyr's hill' or Montmartre.

From then on, things went rapidly downhill for Paris. In the fifth century the city was seized by the Franks, and then snubbed by the greatest Frankish King, Charlemagne, who set up his capital in Aachen. The Vikings regularly came pillaging, and soon all that remained on the Left Bank of the Seine was a clutch of convents, presumably with heathen-proof gates.

However, in the tenth century, Paris again became a capital, albeit of the tiny realm governed by the Kings of the Franks, and this elevation in status was the cue for some impressive refurbishment. The ancient cathedral on the Île de la Cité, which probably dated back to the fourth century, had survived the heathen onslaught and was one of the biggest in Europe, some 70 metres long, with five colonnaded naves decorated with mosaics. It must have risen above the hovels on the boggy island like a shiny new pair of wellingtons in a muddy puddle.

So what did the Bishop of Paris, Maurice de Sully, do in 1163? Well, Maurice was the son of a humble woodcutter, so it was perhaps inevitable that he should decide to hack the old cathedral to the ground. This lack of respect for history was not unique to Paris, of course – practically every ancient cathedral stands on the ruins of an even more ancient church. Sully commissioned a new cathedral – Notre-Dame – in the gothic style that was all the rage at the time. And thus it was that for the next two centuries, the centre of Paris was a gigantic religious building site.

This huge project was just one sign of the way Paris was flourishing. Despite the murderous civil wars caused by *les Anglais*, which the Parisians helped to end by sending out some of their clergymen to prosecute the troublemaker Joan of Arc,* Paris

---

* For more details of Paris's role in the martyrdom of France's teenage patron saint, see my book *1,000 Years of Annoying the French*.

gradually established itself as the capital of a rich and stable nation, one of the power centres of Europe. It also began to assume its modern identity as a travel icon.

There is evidence of this double status in one of the most fascinating parts of the Musée Carnavalet, devoted to the Renaissance. Here, the democratic mix of exhibits works wonderfully: in the same room, you have the portrait of a glum-looking Mary Queen of Scots – who grew up in Paris and became an unhappy teenage Queen of France by marrying the short-lived King François II – and a party scene, with a drunken man groping a lady in front of a backdrop of Notre-Dame and the old city, a sort of Breughel on a dirty weekend in Paris. This latter picture looks as though it's a pre-photography version of a 'Your Face Here' portrait – you no doubt paid the artist to have your portrait set against a stock background. In this case, the silhouette of Notre-Dame must already have been famous enough for people to want to boast about getting drunk in front of it. Stag and hen parties are nothing new, it seems.

The sixteenth-century rooms at Carnavalet also hint at the way Parisians turned their blossoming city into a bloodbath. There is a glowering portrait of Catherine de' Medici, the mother of three Kings of France and the reputed instigator of the St Bartholomew's Day Massacre in 1572, when 15,000 Protestants were killed in the space of twenty-four hours. In the portrait, Catherine's eyes are as dark as her widow's weeds, her expression as stony as if it was a marble sculpture instead of an oil painting – enough to turn anyone into a Catholic.

Which is exactly what happened to her son-in-law, King Henri IV, who was so terrified by the massacre that he renounced his Protestant faith. In the museum, he is commemorated in the most bizarre fashion of all – a narrow corridor is dominated by hunks of a massive statue of Henri that used to stand on the Pont Neuf. It was hacked to pieces by a revolutionary mob in 1792, and the

Carnavalet somehow obtained a giant boot, an arm, a hand, and an amputated horse's leg.

And it is the museum's Revolution section that is the most fascinating, because these turbulent years are presented from the point of view of an ordinary Parisian citizen of the time. There are banners that were waved during meetings and demonstrations, obviously home-made, because one of them misspells the key word *liberté* as *libeté*. (But then, education for all was one of the revolutionaries' key demands.)

There is also a collection of portraits of officials in revolutionary uniform. It was obviously a shrewd move at the time to have oneself painted this way, as proof of one's patriotic zeal. And what is intriguing about the pictures is that most of them are very primitive, suggesting either that the sitters were too poor to pay a decent artist, or that all the good portrait painters had fled the country with their best clients, the *aristos*.

Political events also inspired a rash of revolutionary knick-knacks. The museum has an inkstand with the catchy slogan *unité et indivisibilité de la République*, a plate showing *le patriote satisfait* (the well-fed patriot) and – eerily – some intricate ivory working models of the guillotine. The weirdest exhibit, though, has to be a watch that tells 'revolutionary' time, with a day of 10 hours divided into 100 minutes of 100 seconds. It's surprising that the idea didn't catch on – with each revolutionary hour lasting the equivalent of 2.4 of our hours, the Parisian's legendary two-hour lunchtime would have lasted the equivalent of 4.8 modern hours. Definitely worth revolting for.

The objects commemorating the end of the monarchy are just as down-to-earth. There is a recreation of Louis XVI's cell at the Temple prison, with furniture that was spirited away by sympathizers after his death and donated to the museum later. He had a decent enough bed, a bookcase, and even a miniature billiard table – probably for his son Louis-Charles, who died in prison aged ten, after three years of incarceration.

The museum even has Louis XVI's prison laundry list. In two weeks, he sent out seventeen shirts, eight pairs of stockings, two *caleçons* (underpants or perhaps trousers), seven items of miscellaneous linen and three sheets to be washed. It doesn't seem excessive, except when you remember that the only fresh linen many of the other prisoners got was a scarf to hold their hair out of the way when the guillotine blade came down on their neck.

Paris shoots itself in the foot (and elsewhere)

Immediately after the Revolution, Paris lapsed into a period of pleasure and violence, often with the two of them combined.

The most famous piece of architectural masochism was demolishing the Bastille, of course. Though this was a cleansing act, because the notorious prison was a symbol of aristocratic oppression – although, as mentioned earlier, it was almost empty on 14 July 1789 – many of its previous inmates had been locked up for nothing more damning than inconveniencing an *aristo*.

More dubious, perhaps, was the wholesale destruction of ancient buildings just because of their religious connections. A whole series of paintings at the Carnavalet show triumphant post-revolutionaries pulling Paris's churches to pieces stone by stone. Notre-Dame survived (albeit with decapitated statues) only by proving itself useful as a food depot and being adopted by the newly atheist Parisians as a church devoted to the god of Reason.

The only building of note to attract the attention of the city's post-revolutionary painters figures in a twee little oil sketch of a mass in the Chapelle Expiatoire. Smartly dressed Parisians stand or kneel, facing a statue of a very sexy-looking Marie Antoinette in a negligee. The artist was obviously a fan of hers.

The Chapelle Expiatoire was built in 1815, and it seems strange to see the former royal anti-heroine being hero-worshipped on canvas so soon after both her head and her régime were toppled. But as early as 1815, after Napoleon Bonaparte's spell as a self-elected Emperor, the royals had returned, and it was Louis XVIII who commissioned the Chapelle as a mausoleum for his brother Louis XVI and sister-in-law Marie Antoinette, on the site where their bodies were buried after execution.

Amazingly, the building came through the whole of the turbulent nineteenth century unscathed, and it can still be visited today. It is an eerily peaceful place despite its location a stone's throw from boulevard Haussmann. The gardens leading to the Greek temple-like mausoleum are lined with twin rows of graves, which have always been empty. They represent the King's body-guards, the Swiss Guards, about 600 of whom were massacred when Louis was arrested in the Tuileries Palace in August 1792 (yes, the Tuileries gardens used to contain a Renaissance palace, built by Catherine de' Medici – it was another victim of the Revolution).

Inside the Chapelle, the tombs of Louis XVI and his wife are said to be situated exactly where the bodies were discovered, which must be why the marble statues do not reunite the couple. Marie Antoinette is with the Virgin Mary, while nearby an angel seems to be holding the resurrected Louis' head in place. The chapel's visitors' book is also worth a peek – it's full of drawings of fleur de lis (the royal flower) and *vive le roi* inscriptions. The 1789 Revolution and all the subsequent insurrections have never killed off French royalism completely.

Becoming the City of Light

The nineteenth-century rooms in the Musée Carnavalet bear testament to the climate of violence that reigned in Paris for decades after Louis XVI lost his head on the square named after him (now the place de la Concorde). Contrary to what the French like to believe, their Revolution wasn't simply a bit of political debating, a few thuds of the guillotine and then *liberté, égalité, fraternité* for ever more. There were rebellions and/or coups d'état in 1799, 1815, 1830, 1848, 1851 and 1871, as well as various lesser outbreaks of violence that took their toll on the cityscape.

Whole walls at the Carnavalet feature nineteenth-century paintings of well-known buildings like the Louvre and the Hôtel de Ville being bombarded, almost always by Parisians, as well as more intimate scenes of martyrdom on the barricades – one victim of the 1848 uprising is writing a slogan on a half-demolished wall in his own blood.

However, the greatest destruction of the city wasn't caused by political upheaval – ironically, the demolition of most of Paris's medieval core was done in an attempt to save the city from itself.

It was in the mid-nineteenth century that Baron Haussmann, the man who gave his name to a boulevard and a whole style of Parisian achitecture, tore down so many medieval houses, churches and palaces that he gave Paris its nickname, the *Ville Lumière* or City of Light – there is a theory that the name is a reference, not to quaint streetlamps or philosophical enlightenment, as is often suggested, but to the sun shining through the gaps that Haussmann smashed in the ancient pattern of streets.

Georges Eugène, aka Baron Haussmann (in fact, he had no right to the title), was a native Parisian, the son of one of Napoleon Bonaparte's military attachés. He was also, some would say, the city's biggest vandal.

He was the Préfet de la Seine (Paris's chief administrator) from 1853 to 1870, and the man entrusted with a mission to remodel the city along rationalist nineteenth-century lines.

In fairness, much of the destruction he unleashed was well meant. During Napoleon III's enforced exile in England, the French Emperor fell in love with Victorian London.* He saw a grandiose city that had been reconstructed and much expanded in the centuries after the Great Fire of 1666, and began to think that he could do the same thing to Paris, but without all the smoke. He therefore conceived a grand plan entitled *Paris embellie, Paris agrandie, Paris assainie* (Paris beautified, enlarged and cleaned up), making trebly sure that people knew which city he was talking about.

Napoleon III's promise was to bring air, light and clean water to the Parisians. He also had a secret ambition, which was to make it more difficult for the city's rebellious populace to barricade the streets, as they had done in 1830 (when King Charles X was booted out) and 1848 (when King Louis-Philippe was forced to flee). Napoleon III also thought it would be useful to have wide roads linking the city's various army barracks, so that troops could move about freely to crush uprisings.

Haussmann, a politician and friend of the Emperor's Minister of the Interior, was chosen for the job, apparently because of his total lack of nostalgia. He was a great lover of straight lines, and quickly set about smashing them through the old city with no regard for the treasures that got in his way. He destroyed about half the buildings on the Île de la Cité (it was almost literally a stroke of luck that Notre-Dame was not in the way of the three new streets he drew across the map of the island), and even

---

* Napoleon III was also inspired to rebuild Paris by a stay in Southport, on the northwest coast of England, and some say that Paris should therefore be nicknamed the Southport of the South.

knocked down his own birthplace in the Faubourg Saint-Honoré.

To his credit, before launching his campaign of destruction, Haussmann had the old city preserved for posterity by a photographer. Le Baron commissioned one of the first exponents of the new art form, a Parisian painter called Charles Marville, to take hundreds of pictures of the neighbourhoods that were about to be toppled or built over. Though Haussmann wasn't just being a romantic – he also got Marville to photograph his work in progress, like the piles of bricks that were to become the avenue de l'Opéra, and the similar mounds of rubble that would be cleared away to create the place du Carrousel, the roundabout that now lies between the Louvre Pyramid and the Tuileries.*

The Musée Carnavalet's collection of paintings records the trauma that the destruction caused. One picture shows a row of old buildings that look like bodies with their ribcages torn open, the victims of Haussmann's charge through the Opéra district. A beautiful model of a gothic tower set into the fabric of an ordinary residential house is a poignant record of a corner of the place de l'Hôtel de Ville that was sacrificed so that the large square could be made squarer. Vast areas were redeveloped during this Haussmannian frenzy – it is estimated that about 20,000 buildings were destroyed, and around 40,000 built (many of those in the outlying areas annexed into Paris to increase the number of *arrondissements* from twelve to twenty).

Haussmann was interested in the details as well as the general destruction. He dictated strict rules about the style and height of the buildings that would line his new streets – they were to be 20 metres high, with the different storeys of adjoining buildings closely aligned, and their façades had to be similar in style, even if they

---

* Some 350 of these pictures of pre-Haussmann Paris, alongside new photos of the same spots today, are reproduced in a book called *Paris Avant/Après: 19e Siècle–21e Siècle* by Patrice de Moncan.

were designed by different architects. All of which explains the uniformity of so many of Paris's streets today.

The Haussmann era was also a turning point in the city's social history. Before he began his clear-out, apartment buildings were a cross-section of Parisian society – shops on the ground floor, their owners on the first, the rich bourgeois on the second (known as *l'étage noble*), lower middle classes on the third and fourth, workers on the fifth, and servants, students and the miscellaneous poor at the top.

After Haussmann, these distinctions disappeared. The new buildings were posher, with people of similar (mainly middle) class on every floor except the ground (still for shops and businesses) and the top, which was now reserved for the *chambres de bonne* or maids' rooms. It was the beginning of the gentrification that has steadily evicted the poor from all but the far reaches of the city's outer *arrondissements*.

Haussmann did some good works – he created large 'English-style' parks – Monceau, Montsouris, and the Buttes-Chaumont. He laid out the Champs-Élysées, and built the Gare de Lyon and Gare de l'Est. More importantly, he renewed the water-supply system and oversaw the construction of the sewers, replacing the centuries-old system of simply dumping everything in the fetid unpaved lane in front of medieval houses, or sluicing it off into the Seine, from where the drinking water came.

Predictably, such huge changes weren't made without whiffs of financial wrong-doings, and the Prime Minister Jules Ferry was moved to publish a pamphlet called *Les Comptes Fantastiques d'Haussmann* – Haussmann's Fantasy Accounts, a neat pun on *Les Contes Fantastiques d'Hoffmann*, Hoffmann's Fairy Stories. And it was amid allegations of overspending and dubious dealings that the Baron lost his job in January 1870 – just months before Napoleon III himself was deposed after an ill-advised Prussian war. All of which was followed in 1871 by yet another round of riots and barricades that even Haussmann's boulevards couldn't contain.

A Parisian nightmare

Fortunately, Haussmann's destruction work inspired literary creativity – Émile Zola, that tireless transcriber of social changes, wrote a novel called *La Curée* (which could be translated as *The Feeding Frenzy*). It features a speculator who makes a killing out of Haussmannian insider trading, buying up land and buildings that he knows will be compulsorily purchased at a good price by the city.

But perhaps the most interesting book inspired by the great clean-up is an early example of sci-fi, a story called *Paris Nouveau et Paris Futur* by Victor Fournel, a writer and journalist who, like Zola, spent much of his time documenting life in his city. Fournel's books include *Les Rues du Vieux Paris*, in which he describes not only the streets but the people who lived in them in the Middle Ages, and *Les Cris de Paris*, a record of the calls used by street peddlers and buskers.

Given his feel for history, it is not surprising that Fournel was horrified by Baron Haussmann's plans to remodel Paris with the wrecking ball, and in 1865 he wrote *Paris Nouveau et Paris Futur* as a nightmare vision of how the city would look in a hundred years' time. He foresaw Paris in 1965 stretching unbroken halfway to the sea. Fournel predicts 'a century of hard work, a furious obsession for building and a delirium tremens of demolition' that would produce 'a typical capital of modern civilization ... at its centre, a square one *lieue* [about 4 km] across, off which radiate 50 boulevards, each 50 metres wide, lined with buildings 50 metres high, a long series of gigantic cubes containing an equal number of equal-sized apartments'.

These boulevards, just like Haussmann's, are tools of military oppression – in the centre of the main square, Fournel envisages an enormous army barracks topped with a lighthouse to shine along the boulevards, preventing disorder.

The city would be a giant wheel with spokes 15 kilometres long, Fournel says. It would be perfect for tourists, who 'wouldn't need a guide – they could just go out of their hotel, turn left or right, walk around the circle and, in the evening, arrive back at the hotel.'

Piling on the irony, he predicts that the city would at last get rid of 'gothic monstrosities' like Saint-Germain l'Auxerrois (the old church opposite the eastern façade of the Louvre). Meanwhile, Notre-Dame could be modernized so that it looks presentable, and other monuments like the Hôtel de Ville and Invalides would be displaced so that they stood in alignment with the new boulevards.

Fournel's dream ends when he is shaken awake by his concierge and warned to leave the building, which is about to be demolished to make way for the boulevard Saint-Germain.

But, even if he meant to exaggerate, he did get a few things uncannily right. For a start, he gives a vivid description of armies of workers being transported into the centre of the city by train. Rush hours today at Saint-Lazare and the Gare du Nord are far worse than his nightmares. And even more accurately, Fournel's *Paris Futur* seems to be an exact model for the post-war French new town, a concept so soulless that it has turned many of the city's poorer suburbs into drug-dealing, rioting no-go areas. In a way, his nightmare vision of the future is actually more humane than these real *banlieues* because, being a typical Parisian, Fournel couldn't resist imagining that his futuristic boulevards would at least have plenty of cafés.

Paris exposes itself

The 1889 Paris Exposition Universelle brought more light to the city. The exhibition was a hymn to modernism, with electrically illuminated fountains, floodlit galas and glowing glass pavilions. The Expo site was spread along the largely empty banks of the Seine to the southwest of the old city, and featured some spectacular architecture. In front of the École Militaire there was the enormous Galerie des Machines, the grandest of Paris's Art Nouveau glass palaces, bigger and more striking than the Grand Palais. It was flattened in 1909 so that the army could reclaim its parade ground, the Champ-de-Mars. And the centrepiece was, of course, the Tour Eiffel, the world's tallest tower until it was knocked off its pedestal by the Chrysler Building in 1930.

There are famous photos of the Tower at different stages in its construction, but the Musée Carnavalet has one of the earliest paintings of Paris's new tourist attraction, made shortly after its completion in 1889. It is a night-time scene showing the Tower as a giant beacon, attracting admirers in a procession of river cruisers and a hot-air balloon. Even the crescent moon seems to be smiling down on it. Strange, then, that the Eiffel Tower was almost immediately declared by a committee of Parisian artists to be a 'useless, monstrous tower in the heart of our city' and came very close to getting the chop when its management contract ended in 1909.

It's almost as if the city planners were as frivolous as the newly emerging *haute couture* designers – they just couldn't bear to see last year's buildings any more.

The end of a century

In the brief spell between the end of Haussmann and the time when the *métro* builders would start ripping up his boulevards to lay underground railway lines, Parisians had a brief opportunity to get out and enjoy themselves without inhaling too much demolition dust.

The end of the nineteenth century was the *Belle Époque*, and the mellow mood is reflected in the Musée Carnavalet's gallery of *fin de siècle* paintings, in which crowds of Parisians promenade up and down their airy new boulevards. Apart from the fashions, the beards and the horses, the street scenes are very similar to modern Paris – the trees lining the pavements already have iron sheaths protecting their trunks and the benches look like the ones you can still see today – wide green slats of wood set in a grey iron frame.

Café tables dominate the landscape, and the museum takes you inside one of the old *grand boulevard* brasseries. A private *salon* has been salvaged, a beautiful Art Nouveau boudoir with carved, plant-inspired furniture, including a very inviting couch. This was where a Parisian gentleman or well-to-do tourist would entertain his lover or paid companion, cajoling her from table to divan with seductive words and a few *coupes de Champagne*. A thick velvet curtain ensured total privacy, and the room even had a back door for a discreet exit. Yes, in the 1890s, the Parisian culture of adultery was part of the city's architecture.

And this is the great thing about the Musée Carnavalet – thanks to the quirkiness of its collection, it manages to conjure up the atmosphere in the city at each period in its long, turbulent history, from the time when Paris was little more than a small settlement on a riverbank to the days when it became the most sophisticated, seductive city in Europe. Spending a couple of hours wandering through the museum, you will be able to feel the direct link between those Stone Age men and women making their earthenware plates and the secretive lovers enjoying a crystal *coupe* before stretching out on their velvet couch.

The (n)ever-changing city

After a century of almost constant devastation, you'd think the city would have wanted to savour its surviving architecture. But no, the one constant about Parisians seems to be that they can't resist abusing their own skyline.

Miraculously, the First World War and even the Nazi Occupation swept over the city without doing a great deal of damage. In 1914, the fighting came within a few kilometres of Paris before its taxi drivers rallied to the national cause and ferried thousands of troops out to the front line, where they valiantly held off the invaders and accidentally invented trench warfare. There were occasional air raids throughout the Great War, and artillery shelling, including bombardments by Grosse Bertha, the giant cannon firing from over 100 kilometres away. In all, about 500 Parisians were killed by bombs and shells, though compared with the way the rest of northeastern France was flattened, Paris suffered relatively little architectural damage, except for the destruction of the *métro* station at Corvisart, and a large hole in the roof of Notre-Dame des Victoires church in the 2nd *arrondissement*.

For most of the Second World War, things were much quieter – the city surrendered without a fight, and it wasn't until 1944 that the *Ville Lumière* came close to having its lights put out once and for all. This was when Hitler famously ordered his Governor of Paris, General Dietrich von Choltitz, to destroy the city before it was liberated – 'Paris must not fall into enemy hands,' the Führer said, 'or, if it does so, only as a field of rubble.' The General had his troops torch the Grand Palais, but, as mentioned in Chapter 2, disobeyed

For a short period in September 1914, it was actually easier to get a taxi in Paris. You just had to put on a uniform and say, 'Take me to the Marne.' And for the only time in history, Parisian taxi drivers were happy, because they were paid what was on the meter for the fifty-kilometre trip to the battle front.

the order to set off explosives under Paris's key monuments. Choltitz was probably acting in self-defence rather than expressing a fondness for architecture, because if he had flattened the city, he wouldn't have survived very long after the French caught up with him. Even so, Paris breathed a sigh of relief when it was liberated almost intact, with most of the scarring limited to the Grand Palais, some bullet-spattered streets, and its conscience.

Bizarre, then, that after the two World Wars, the city set about mutilating its historical centre once more. In 1963, a scheme was announced to 'renovate' (that is, demolish) an immense segment of the unfashionable Right Bank, from the Seine up to the Gare de l'Est. In 1968, the demolition balls began to swing, smashing down the crystal palaces that had housed Les Halles, Paris's vast food market. A major chunk of the Marais was also destroyed, along with its priceless medieval staircases, stone fireplaces, carved beams and other period features that get estate agents excited.

In their place, Paris was given the underground shopping mall that has rather blasphemously hijacked the name Les Halles (which is a bit like calling a new motorway Leafy Lane); the plastic city called the Quartier de l'Horloge (a complex of apartments and photocopying shops that is very central but cheap to live in because everyone hates the buildings); and the multi-coloured modernist toaster that is Beaubourg (or the Pompidou Centre as tourists call it. Rightly so, because it's its official name.)

I personally like Beaubourg, and am consoled by the fact that Les Halles sits astride road tunnels that syphon traffic away from the Louvre and spit it out several hundred metres to the north, but all in all, with a bit of self-respect, the Marais could have remained about twice as big as it is today, and Les Halles shopping centre would have been housed in nineteenth-century market halls.

Not only this – throughout the 1960s, Paris tried to out-Haussmann Haussmann and slice motorways through its surviving medieval streets. The *Plan autoroutier pour Paris* was a scheme dreamt up by road planners who were apparently upset that Paris got in the way of their nationwide motorway network. They therefore drew up plans to channel high-speed traffic straight through or under the city.

True, it would have been great for truck drivers to be able to admire the place des Vosges in the middle of their Calais–Bordeaux marathon, and coach parties wouldn't have had to stop to visit Père Lachaise cemetery – the guides would have been able to point out the most famous graves as the tourists cruised by on their way to a toilet break at the Tuileries services, followed by a high-speed drive through the legs of the Eiffel Tower.

If the *plan autoroutier* had been implemented, Paris would have had not only the *périphérique* around its borders and an inner ring of *grands boulevards*, it would also have been criss-crossed by eight four- or six-lane highways, with both banks of the Seine being converted into trunk roads.

In the event, only the *périph'* and part of the riverbank road were built. Which is why today, if you mention *les berges* (the banks) *de la Seine* to a Parisian, they will picture not cobbled walkways and a stroll along the Île Saint-Louis but charging traffic. The Right Bank is a honking highway from opposite the Eiffel Tower pretty well all the way to Bercy on the southeast edge of the city, and the Left Bank was only saved thanks to the intervention of President Giscard d'Estaing in the 1970s.

To the city's residents, this constant demolition is all a bit traumatic. It's as though there's a permanent threat hanging over Paris's neck, like some giant municipal guillotine – who knows when someone will unveil a plan to turn Notre-Dame into a multi-storey car park or flatten Montmartre to create a city airport?

For me, though, it is this constant spirit of change that is the unchanging thing about Paris. Life itself stays the same – it is only the setting that changes. Take La Coupole, for example, the classic brasserie at Montparnasse with its wonderful Art Deco murals that are a monument to Parisian café culture. In the 1980s, the owners plonked a glass-fronted tower block on top – architectural vandalism par excellence, you might say. But the brasserie's interior, and the life going on inside it, didn't change at all. Today, you can sit and eat oysters beneath the jazz-age frescoes and not care how many modern storeys are piled up over your head.

You can't say the same of Les Halles and Beaubourg, of course, but even they have matured and been sucked into Parisian life. Students queue to study and chat each other up in the Beaubourg library, while the pedestrian streets around Les Halles are where suburban kids come to escape their depressing new towns, and the underground shopping centre now houses the second-biggest cinema complex in the world,* with a dozen screens, over 3,000 seats, and 120 staff. Similarly, there were howls of protest when the Louvre courtyard was 'desecrated' with a glass pyramid in 1989, but these days it's impossible to imagine the museum without its futuristic entrance. The Pyramide du Louvre was one of President Mitterrand's departing gifts to the nation, and he definitely wouldn't have said that he was ignoring Paris's history by commissioning the shockingly modernist building. On the contrary, he was writing himself *into* that history.

So, *oui*, Paris is a beautifully preserved historical city, although by no means as well preserved as it could have been, and is, one could argue, much more interesting for it.

To redeem themselves for their past acts of destruction, though, it seems that the powers-that-be want to restore some of Paris's lost beauty, because there are now plans afoot to reclaim the riverbanks from the cars. At last, the wheel may actually be turning the other way.

---

* The biggest is in Korea. South, of course.

It's behind you . . . Many visitors come to Paris to meander from the Eiffel Tower to the Louvre to Notre-Dame, and ignore them completely.

6

ROMANCE

L'amour ne meurt jamais de besoin, mais souvent d'indigestion.
(Love never dies of want, but often of indigestion.)*

NINON DE LENCLOS, SEVENTEENTH-CENTURY WRITER AND COURTESAN

Amour glamour

ROMANCE IS, of course, a matter of personal taste. One person's favourite love song will send another diving for earplugs. Couples who met during a blizzard probably find it highly romantic to spend the occasional evening sitting with their feet in buckets of ice cream. That's the great thing about romance. It's completely personal.

Most people, however, seem to agree on one thing – that Paris is inherently romantic. There's something about the combination of riverbank sunsets, snug restaurants, effortless elegance and affordable Champagne that strikes a chord in almost everyone's heart.

When we look at Robert Doisneau's famous photo of a couple snatching a kiss on a Paris street, something subconscious convinces us all that if we could only be walking past the Hôtel de Ville right now, we too would feel the urgent need to grab our loved one and clamp ourselves to their lips. Like the tousled young guy in the photo, we might even take the cigarette out of our mouth to do so.

---

* Advice, perhaps, for couples planning a romantic candlelit dinner in Paris.

Doisneau snapped hundreds of Paris street scenes, some of them impromptu, others less so, but it's no coincidence that 'The Lovers' is his best-known photo. Their clinch seems to sum up the city in one primal gesture.

It doesn't matter that the picture was posed – Doisneau took it in 1950 as part of a photo report for *Life* magazine, and pragmatically chose the Hôtel de Ville as a backdrop that would be easily recognizable to foreigners. So it's art, not life, but who cares? It is an image created by someone who loved the city and what it stood for, and it's brilliantly acted, too – the male model is squashing his nose against his partner's face so passionately that she hangs almost breathless in his arms.

And the background to the photo is perfect – the heat of the embrace is set against the dull, damp weather and the disapproving glance of a lady passer-by (who was not posing), while behind the couple, an office worker, buttoned up tight in his overcoat, a beret clamped over his knitted brow, suddenly seems to have realized what is missing from his life – romance. The lovers, meanwhile, turn their backs on the dullness around them and live the Parisian dream. And we all want to be right there, right now.

What is it about Paris that does this to people? Is it the sheer density of kissing couples per square kilometre, or the almost infinite number of viewpoints where you can stand with your loved one and gaze out across glittering lights? Or is it simply expectation – you're almost obliged to feel romantic in Paris the same way that you laugh before a famous comedian even opens his or her mouth?

Well, yes to most of those rhetorical questions, but they aren't the only reasons for the city's success as a venue for canoodling.

The city that can't fail

Like a well-chilled glass of Champagne,* Paris is almost always capable of hitting the mark, whatever your tastes in matter of the heart.

To get us in the mood for romance, all most of us need is some period decor (interior or exterior), soft lighting, tasteful music (which is why, for me, the accordion is a no-no) and time to stroll, sit or loll while exchanging *mots d'amour* with the love of your life (or of that evening).

You also need to feel classy. A romantic evening or weekend doesn't work if there's anything fake or sordid about it, and genuine class is something that runs through Paris's veins. Everything about the city feels authentic, not just a bunch of elements packaged together and marketed at the tourist hordes. The waiters are real, rather than seasonal student workers, and their aprons are the same shape and size as they have been since the nineteenth century. The restaurants aren't converted warehouses – they're traditional eating-houses, often decorated exactly as they were in the *Belle Époque*, or the *Années Folles* of the 1920s, and probably frequented by as many locals as visitors because the food will be genuinely French. Your dinner may not always be candlelit, but no matter – it will feel as if the candles are there, glowing like the flames of your love (and in French, even cheesy metaphors like that don't sound hackneyed). In short, your romantic *soirée* in Paris won't be just a night out on the town, it will be an occasion, a *tête-à-tête*. After all, Champagne is practically local produce.

And these essential ingredients are available all over the city, at places that have been listed in endless guidebooks. What's more, the

---

* Official perfect temperature for a Champagne toast – about 8 degrees centigrade, for those who are prepared to be unromantic enough to poke a thermometer in the bottle.

best-known sites usually work a treat. The Sacré Coeur on its hilltop is a wonderful viewpoint; a bench on the riverbank can afford a timeless view of Notre-Dame; and when the Eiffel Tower starts its shimmering light display,* the couples on the balcony of the Palais de Chaillot at Trocadéro can't help but go 'ooh' and snuggle just a little closer.

But the best-known lovers' dallying spot has to be the Pont des Arts, the pedestrian bridge that crosses the Seine at the eastern end of the Louvre. It has been a romantic meeting place ever since it was built in the 1980s, and was officially consecrated as such in the clinching episode of *Sex in the City*, when whatsername, the spindly blond narrator, finally gets it together with whatsisname, the tall, stuffy rich guy.

For couples wanting to gaze at romantic Paris, it's an ideal location. First of all, the gaps between the slats in the boardwalk mean that anyone with vertigo will cling more than affectionately to their partner as they look down into the rushing Seine. Then there is the absence of traffic – no danger of getting run over as you kiss. And, from the centre of the bridge, the 360-degree view is perfect. To the east, there is the pinnacle of Notre-Dame, the Pont Neuf and the weeping willows on the triangular square du Vert Galant (literally: Lusty Smooth-talker Square), where the amorous King Henri IV used to meet his mistresses. To the south is the domed Institut de France, its two neo-classical wings spread like tentacles pulling everyone into the embrace of French culture. Stretching away to the north is the whole riverside façade of the Louvre, and away to the west, beyond the twin golden splashes of the statues on the Pont Alexandre III, is the tip of the Eiffel Tower, which, as mentioned above, sparkles with unfailing regularity like an explosion in a diamond factory – a guaranteed canoodling moment.

Granted, on a crowded evening, it can feel like queuing up for

* On the hour, every hour from dusk till 1 a.m., and 2 a.m. in summer.

A modern version of the lovers' knot on the Pont des Arts. Apparently, the etiquette is for lovers to attach a padlock (preferably engraved with their initials) to the railings, and then throw the key into the Seine, thus sealing their union for ever. It is considered impolite to say, 'I'll keep a key just in case.'

a bed in a love hotel – you're not exactly the only ones aiming to enjoy a private romantic tryst. And the bridge is such a popular picnic spot that the city has now hung unsexy green plastic bags every 10 metres along the railings, as well as forbidding the consumption of alcohol there.

This hasn't killed the mood altogether, though, and many couples come prepared to perform the bridge's trademark love ritual. The thing to do is to attach a small padlock to the wire fencing and then throw the key into the waters below (making sure there are no *bateaux-mouches* passing under the bridge), thus sealing your love for ever and leaving your own permanent memorial in the city of romance.

Personally, I have my doubts about the padlock as a symbol of *amour* – do you honestly need to keep your loved one in a relationship by means of a lock and key? If so, why not handcuffs (much sexier) or, if you want to get really modern, an electronic tag? And many of the padlocks have names either engraved on them or written in marker pen, but what happens if the couple separate – can they never return to the bridge for fear that their new love will see the old symbol of 'eternal' togetherness, or does one of them sneak back with a hacksaw and remove the evidence?

But this is just cynicism, and the number of love locks is growing steadily on the Pont des Arts (and other, more exclusive, bridges), so it looks as though optimism has won the day, as of course it should do where romance is concerned.

Yes, we canal

There are some less well-known, but equally romantic, spots for an arm-in-arm stroll in Paris. My favourite is in the north of the city, at the Bassin de la Villette.

At first sight, this canal basin has one or two minor disadvantages. First, it is near Paris's least romantically named square – the place de Stalingrad. This is the problem with countries like France that have had a lasting revolution – they tend to give their streets and squares highly unpoetic names – National Uprising Avenue, Victory of the People Boulevard, Decapitation of the Royal Family Gardens. And in Paris, this effect is heightened because of its traditional solidarity towards Communist republics, including the old USSR.

Coupled with the problem of the name, the Bassin de la Villette used to be a drug dealers' hangout. There is still a very small community of crackheads living by the waterside, but they keep themselves to themselves these days, no doubt because they have seen the way the social tide is turning (yes, even by a canal, there can be tides), and know that they will be moving on soon.

These days, on a warm evening, the area is perfect for a lovers' stroll, mainly because of the lighting. At the southernmost end of the basin, twin industrial glass buildings have been turned into cinemas decorated with multi-coloured neon artwork. On one side, the MK2 Quai de Seine is lit up with simple lines of blue and white that turn the dark sheen of the water into a star-encrusted Van Gogh night sky. Opposite, the MK2 Quai de Loire is even more colourful. It sports two glowing child's faces, and the building's metal columns are all lit a different shade – purple, pink and red.

Looking further along the basin, you see another twin-set of industrial buildings. One, now a waterside students' residence, has retained its stone walls, but the other has been covered in a chain-mail of walkways and balconies that pulse with ever-changing neon colours like some kind of giant metal squid. As soon as dusk falls, the building begins to flow through the spectrum, changing tone every few seconds, and lighting up the whole of the canal basin at its widest point so you almost feel as though you could walk across the silk carpet.*

The southeastern bank of the basin, the Quai de la Loire, which catches the sun for longer in the evenings, has become *the* place to be on summer nights. Picnics on the bank of the Seine? Old *chapeau*. These days, you pack up your wine and glasses, not forgetting your corkscrew, buy a few baguettes and delicacies to drape or smear on them, and then stake your spot on the cobbled stones of the canalside between the cinema and the students' residence. Here, you can drink a toast while looking out over the second-best (but most colourful) mood lighting in Paris, and listening to the laughter of the people behind you playing *pétanque*.

Yes, the stretch of gravel running alongside the basin has been re-discovered by a new generation of *boules* players. Stroll along here any evening between May and September and you need to watch that your feet don't get bombarded by large lead balls. And if you haven't got your own *boules*, it doesn't matter, because the bar halfway down the *quai*, the Bar Ourcq, lends out *pétanque* sets, and even has deckchairs for people who have forgotten their picnic blankets.

In short, the Bassin de la Villette has it all – soft mood lighting reflecting on the water, Parisians being *très parisiens*, and the opportunity to drink lots of wine. Romance quotient: 100 per cent.

What's more, after your stroll, you can go into one of the cinemas and see a French film. It will almost certainly be about love. You might not understand the dialogues, but that doesn't matter because if you've seen one French love story, you've seen them all. The dialogue goes something like this:

'*Je t'aime*.'

'I love you too, darling.'

---

*Not that this would be a good idea – one thing to bear in mind, even on the most love-crazy of evening walks, is that this is urban canal water and, as such, is seriously dirty. The poor fools who strip off and dive in on hot summer nights are risking a highly romantic bout of *turista*, skin disease or worse.

'But why did you sleep with that other woman?'

'My love, it's because you're so perfect that I had to shag someone else to prove to myself that you're real.'

'Oh Pierre, you're so poetic.'

'Yes, and what's more I wrote, directed and starred in the film, so I'm an all-round pretty amazing guy. And you do realize that, as a French actress, you are contractually obliged to get your kit off, so why don't you start stripping while I have a quick smoke?'

Of course it won't always be like this – if it's a thriller, the guy will have a gun. But in any case, it'll be French, meaning you'll almost certainly get a naked love scene, as well as picturesque views of Paris to try and sell the movie to American distributors, so your evening's romance quotient is bound to soar to dizzying heights.

Romance closer to home

The Bassin de la Villette is a bit of a trek out of the centre of Paris, so those visitors who want to stay central might prefer a more attainable venue for their romantic stroll.

There is, for example, the Palais-Royal, right opposite that other former royal palace, the Louvre. Not very original, some might say, but it is a peaceful spot just a few steps from the mad rush of the rue de Rivoli, a place to linger and whisper sweet nothings or, *pourquoi pas*, sweet somethings – Paris has always been a philosophers' city, so there is no reason for lovers' whisperings to be inane.

And these gardens were designed for Parisians who wanted to come and speak freely about love, life, politics and any other deep

---

* Here, the King was inadvertently showing how out of touch with everyday life he was – French shopkeepers traditionally close on Sunday afternoons and Mondays. No wonder the Parisians cut his aloof head off.

† This was more than a decade before he legalized French brothels.

The Paris effect. Before their stroll in the Palais Royal gardens, this couple hadn't even held hands.

things that excite them. The arched galleries around the square were built in the 1780s for King Louis XVI's brother, the Duc d'Orléans, who owned the palace and its park, but didn't want to live there any more. So, just like a modern property speculator, he decided to maximize the value of his centrally located land by erecting some shiny new apartments and shops around the edge of the gardens. The King is said to have scoffed at his brother, saying, 'So you're opening a shop? Does this mean we'll only see you on Sundays?'*

After the Revolution, the Duc d'Orléans actually became a member of the new, more democratic parliament and diplomatically changed his name to Philippe Égalité. He even voted in favour of Louis XVI's execution. This didn't save his royal neck, though, and he in turn was guillotined in 1793.

His gardens, however, had already taken on a lusty life of their own. They had become a popular strolling place because the Duke, a bit of a stirrer against his brother even before the Revolution, had declared the Palais-Royal off-limits to police. Parisians could come here to speak and act without fear of repression, and they did so *en masse*. The arcades housed fashionable shops, cafés and gambling clubs, and the gardens and the discreet galleries had quickly become a notorious cruising zone for prostitutes.

And it was here, on 22 November 1787, that an eighteen-year-old Frenchman experienced one of the most amorous moments of his life, which he recorded in some detail in his diary. The young Napoleon Bonaparte, then a recently qualified artillery officer, was up in Paris and feeling depressed, so he went for an invigorating walk at the Palais-Royal. Just a stroll through the gardens, you understand – he wasn't looking for a temporary *amoureuse*. It was a chilly night, though, and after a while he turned towards the warmth of the cafés. In the arcades, his eye was drawn to a rather attractive girl. He knew she was almost certainly a prostitute, and, as he assured his diary, he 'detested prostitution',† but the girl seemed timid compared to most of her brazen colleagues, and possessed a soft voice and pale cheeks, so he struck up a conversation with her. He told her that it wasn't good for a frail young *mademoiselle* to be out all hours in the cold, asked her where she was from (Brittany) and how she lost her virginity (to an army officer), and then took her back to his hotel to lose his own.

These days, the hookers have all gone elsewhere, but if you find yourself strolling through the Palais-Royal gardens in search of tranquillity, it is touching to think that the amorous adventures of one of France's greatest leaders began here. Later in life, under the weight of responsibility, he would become famous for telling his Empress Josephine 'not tonight', but something about the atmosphere at the Palais-Royal meant that on that November evening in 1787, he could think of nothing else but the joys of female company.

Martian fields

Another romantic strolling place in central Paris also has Napoleonic connections. The teenage Bonaparte was a student at the École Militaire, which is still a military college today, and he almost certainly performed manoeuvres on the former training grounds in front of the school, the Champ-de-Mars (named, of course, after the god of war).

The fact that this was where generations of French officers practised ordering their troops to march into hails of musket fire and cannonballs isn't inherently romantic, of course, but today, these 780-metre-long gardens are a sort of strollers' driveway towards the Eiffel Tower. At any time of day, and especially at night, as you walk from the École Militaire, the sheer proximity to the Tower gradually becomes breathtaking. Even at the start of your walk it looks huge, but as you head right up to its splayed legs, pretty well every bolt of the magnificent metal latticework becomes visible, while its sloping sides curve away to the pointed summit. In such a low-rise city, the effect is mesmerizing – you really need a glass of Champagne afterwards to get over it.

This in itself is the stuff of a romantic evening, but the Champ-de-Mars goes further than that.

It was the main site of the 1867 Exposition Universelle – this wasn't the expo for which Eiffel built his landmark (that was in 1889), but it was the show at which the *bateau-mouche* was first introduced into Paris. This age-old venue for Parisian snuggling was given its first outing during the Expo, after a boatbuilder called Michel Félizat was commissioned to bring thirty or so specially built sightseeing vessels up from his workshops in the Mouche area of his home city, Lyon.

And one of the most famous visitors to the 1867 Exposition, who therefore certainly came walking in the Champ-de-Mars, was Paris's greatest-ever romantic, the future King Edward VII of Britain, or Dirty Bertie as he was known to his friends (and no doubt to many *Parisiennes*) when he was still just a prince.

Bertie was so fond of organizing romantic getaways in Paris with his mistresses – and, it should be added, his wife – that at one point the French secret police was having him followed to make sure that he was only meeting up with politically 'safe' lovers. And every time he received an official invitation from Paris to come for a state visit, he was on the boat almost as fast as you could say *RSVP*. We can be sure, then, that it was a very cheerful Prince Bertie, with a pronounced romantic glint in his eye, who came to the Champ-de-Mars in 1867.*

He was back at the Champ for the 1878 Expo (to see the recently invented telephone and the head of the future Statue of

* For more on Edward's amorous outings to Paris, and their far-reaching geopolitical implications, see my book *1,000 Years of Annoying the French*.

Liberty) and yet again in 1889 to admire the Expo's spectacular entrance arch, aka the Eiffel Tower and, of course, to revisit the Folies-Bergère and his private room at Paris's most luxurious brothel, Le Chabanais.*

What Edward didn't get was a chance to wander through the Champ-de-Mars gardens, arm in arm with his loved one *du soir*, as the Eiffel Tower's 20,000 lightbulbs explode into shimmering splendour, filling the whole night sky in front of them. This intensely romantic experience, provided courtesy of France's excellent electricity network, is reserved for modern lovers . . .

A room with (or without) a view

On my first trips to Paris as a penniless student, I never bothered to book a room. In those days, there were no cheap on-line reservations, and no websites to help you choose. The thing to do was to emerge from the railway station and find somewhere afford-able that looked as though the plumbing might work. Preferably a place that had locks on the doors.

It all felt incredibly romantic, mainly because Paris was the only capital city in Western Europe where a penniless student could afford to sleep somewhere other than a youth hostel, campsite or railway-station bench. Cuddle up with your girlfriend in a hotel double bed? Only millionaires could afford that, surely?

Looking back with slightly less fuzzy hindsight at my first forty-franc (about six euros) room near the Gare du Nord, the lack of windows and fire escapes was potentially lethal, the slimy green patch on the wall was probably not an abstract oeuvre left behind by a Dadaist painter, and it really wasn't that convenient to share a

---

* For more on the *bordels*, see the next chapter.

bathroom that was about half an hour's walk away along dingy corridors littered with drunk students.

Luckily for visitors, many of those old hotels have now been revamped to attract better-off clients. This means that Paris's accommodation is gaining in style (and price), but is also creating new dangers – it is, for example, becoming essential to make sure that you don't book a hotel so boutiquey that you can't work out how to sit on the chairs or turn the lights on.

Despite all the guidebooks and travel websites, however, choosing a hotel in Paris can be difficult. In any part of the city that takes a visitor's fancy, there will be dozens of hotels, many of them in the same price bracket. But more than the neighbourhood, it's vital to check up on the exact location of the building and its different rooms – on a large or small street, near a junction with traffic lights, above a café, overlooking a street market. All of these can ensure that you will be seeing (and hearing) more of Paris by night that you might have planned.

Many visitors think it's romantic to open their window in the morning and gaze down on a typical Paris street scene. But often they are heading for disappointment – instead of seeing a flour-encrusted *boulanger* carrying a fresh batch of baguettes to the corner bistro, or a concierge throwing out an artist's used paint tubes, early-morning street voyeurs are more likely to see office workers dashing for the *métro*, a green-clad street cleaner brushing out the gutter, or, of course, a dog owner taking the mutt for a spot of surreptitious pavement polluting.

Guests who have been given a room on a lower floor will probably have opened the window before dawn to ask the binmen if they could possibly fit padding on to the wheels of the dustbins, or to try and identify the whirr-hiss, whirr-hiss noise, like a motorized python, that wrenched them from their sleep. It will probably be a little street-cleaning vehicle with a rattling engine and high-power water hose – a guaranteed dawn wake-up call.

Even those who have chosen a hotel room on an upper floor in a quiet street, with good double-glazing to deaden the noise of midnight revellers, can find the Paris experience disappointing if the only thing romantic about their room is that it's so small they can't actually get out of bed.

Below, therefore, are three of my favourite romantic hotels, which take all this into account, and should provide something for all tastes.

A night in the Cinquième Dimension

The Hôtel des Grandes Écoles is for people who believe that romance blossoms against a backdrop of medieval history, with a whiff of literature and maybe even a touch of Latin. The hotel is in the 5th *arrondissement*, just behind the Panthéon and a stroll away from the Sorbonne and the École Polytechnique. James Joyce once lived next door, and Ernest Hemingway used to drink and write (probably in that order) in the nearby place de la Contrescarpe.

The hotel is set in a courtyard so long and deep it almost amounts to a private road – no danger of clattering binmen at dawn. It's a very rare location in the dense old city centre. As you wander in from the street (the rue du Cardinal Lemoine), you see a low pinkish building that looks like a country house imagined by Renoir. The cobbled entrance opens out to reveal a walled garden, where a second, matching pink house appears amongst the trees.

The hotel (three buildings in all) used to be a *pension de famille*, a lodging house providing term-time accommodation for students and teachers at the Sorbonne and the Polytechnique. They were all evicted when the owners sold up in 1964, and the place was converted into a hotel.

Today, it is a real family affair (the owners live *in situ*), and feels like a country inn. The furniture is a warm, wooden hotch-potch of new and Louis-Philippe style, the wallpaper is somehow tastefully riotous – in one wing, the rooms are papered with Toile de Jouy, a traditional style of wallpaper, here with illustrations of an early balloon ride over a rustic scene. The story ends badly, with the balloon punctured and some yokels poking at the rip in the fabric, but this shouldn't spoil the romantic mood, because the hotel possesses all the ingredients for a sublimely peaceful lovers' weekend.

The rooms all look out on to the cobbled private lane or the walled garden, so opening the windows should bring you nothing more stressful than birdsong and rustling leaves. You can even ask for a top-floor garret room if you need to get that impoverished young-Hemingway-in-Paris feel (though he probably didn't have a fitted bathroom).

And there are three other things about the hotel that ought to guarantee a romantic Paris experience. First, there is no air-conditioning, which not only limits the noise, it also reduces the number of aircon-loving guests who shout all the time because they're used to conducting conversations against a backing track of rattling machinery.

Second, and most importantly for people who have come to Paris to get away from it all rather than to see as many portraits of Louis XIV as possible, breakfast is served, either in the dining room, the garden or in bed, *until midday* – paradise for those with an early-morning appetite for something more than a croissant.

And finally, for couples who are at a stage in their relationship where it is better to avoid all possible sources of argument, there are no TVs in the bedrooms. This is wonderful news, not only because French TV is generally abysmal, but also because it means that there is no danger of the day ending in a decidedly unromantic argument.

Readers will probably recognize the male and female voices in the following bedtime dialogue:

'Big European match tonight, darling, mind if I just watch the football highlights before . . .'

141

'Before what?'

'Uh? Where's the remote control?'

'I said: before what?'

'Oh, yes. Well, before, you know, darling . . .'

'Before you fall asleep snoring and I have to switch the TV off for you?'

'No, dear, we're in Paris for a romantic weekend, so naturally . . .'

'. . . you're going to spend it watching Real Madrid play the Harlem Globetrotters?'

'No, darling, the Harlem Globetrotters are a basketball team – oh I get it, you were joking.'

'And so are you if you think anything remotely sexual is going to happen after you've spent half an hour watching football.'

'Five minutes, no more, I promise . . . er, darling, why are you putting on that pair of thick pyjamas?'

Yes, some TV remote controls might look like sex toys, but they can kill your love life stone dead.

Royale romance

Pigalle is a lot less sedate than the Latin Quarter, but somehow it can actually feel romantic to stroll past the massage parlours and girlie bars with your loved one, thinking how great it is that you don't need to descend to drinking fake Champagne with a girl who'd prefer to be at home in the Ukraine studying to become an architect.

The Villa Royale is right at the steamy hub of Pigalle – the hotel overlooks the semicircular place Pigalle with its Théâtre X and its Ciné X. A few yards away is a street of girlie bars with names like Les 3 Roses, Soho Bar and (this is no joke) Dirty Dick.*

* I'm sure Dirty Dick is just a language problem – they thought it sounded like an American saloon. It reminds me of a Parisian friend who wanted to teach *pâtisserie* baking in Miami and planned to call her website *French Tarts in Florida*. I must admit that I now regret warning her not to.

The hotel is not exactly secluded – it's for lovers who want to be in the thick of the city – but the rooms on the higher floors only let in the noise like a backing track to the Parisian romantic comedy you're creating.

Appropriately, the Villa Royale goes for the boudoir look. The décor is all gold and red velvet, a sort of Moroccan baroque, which is actually a good description of French Romantic art, and the tented lobby wouldn't be a bad setting for one of Delacroix's orientalist paintings.

The rooms don't have numbers, and are named after famous people, most – but not all – of them French. Guests can opt for someone classical, like Debussy, Bizet, Victor Hugo and Renoir, or quintessentially Parisian like Édith Piaf, Maurice Chevalier and Serge Gainsbourg. You can even boast that you've been in Catherine Deneuve's bedroom, and not many men can say that nowadays. (You can also overnight in Madonna's – no comment.)

Not that the rooms necessarily reflect the artists they're named after – the *chambre* Édith Piaf doesn't have a tiny bed, for example, and the Gainsbourg doesn't smell of cigarettes. They're all snugly perfect for a winter hideaway, with plush wallpaper, gothic lamps, sheeny curtains and kitsch walnut and velvet furniture – yes, it all has a very *bordel parisien* feel to it, except that you won't be kicked out after an hour, and there's no danger that the police will burst in and demand to see your *carte d'identité*.

The beds are big enough for 360-degree antics (except, perhaps, for basketball players), and so are some of the bathtubs – the Catherine Deneuve room comes with a king-size jacuzzi. 'Her' bathroom even has a view of the Sacré Coeur, if you don't mind people up in Montmartre ogling you through those tourist telescopes.

A true-love hotel

A few years ago, the sultry ambiance of Pigalle became even hotter when it was announced that the people behind the very trendy (or *ultra-tendance* as the Parisians like to say) Hôtel Costes and Café Beaubourg had created a Tokyo-style love hotel in Pigalle – an artily decorated place called the Hôtel Amour where you could rent a room by the hour.

As far as I know, no hotel in Paris had advertised such a service since the brothels closed in 1946. The city's hotels haven't needed to, because lovers wanting an afternoon or evening of intimacy simply go to any of them, and book a room for the night. The fact that they're not there at breakfast time won't bother the staff in the slightest. It just means less work for them clearing tables.

But with the Hôtel Amour, Paris seemed to be making a statement. Illicit love was going to set up its official head office (if that's not a gruesome pun) just a couple of hundred metres south-east of the Place Pigalle.

I didn't really become interested in the place until I started doing the research for this book, and wondered which chapter to include this hotel in – 'Romance' or 'Sex'? I decided to call up and make an appointment to have a look around.

The hotel's voicemail was as erotically charged as you'd expect.

'Pour joindre le restaurant tapez un,' a naughty-sounding woman purred, 'pour joindre l'hôtel, tapez deux, et pour joindre les serveuses, tapez ... mais pas trop fort.' (To translate the risqué message: 'To reach the restaurant, hit one, to reach the hotel, hit two, to reach the waitresses, hit ... but not too hard.')

Anywhere except Paris, they'd get raided by feminists. Here, though, apparently anything goes. I set up a meeting with the PR man for a few days later at 1.30 p.m., the time, he told me, when the cleaning ladies go into the rooms. Would they be contractually obliged to dress up as French maids, I wondered. Surely not.

On the appointed day, around lunchtime, I emerged from the

métro at Pigalle, and turned south, the bright neon of the Sexodrome erotic supermarket flashing red in my peripheral vision. I passed the tired-looking Théâtre X, its neon distinctly less flashy, and walked down the rue Frochot, where the Play Lounge and Dirty Dick's were closed and shuttered, and headed down the hill, past the corner café where an old fur-coated prostitute used to hang out. I know this not because I was a customer, but because when I used to play in bands, I would often come to the guitar shops in the neighbourhood to buy strings or get my bass repaired.

Next left, and I was in the rue de Navarin, and from a good fifty metres away, even in the early afternoon I could see the pink *Amour* sign protruding from the left-hand streetline, a beacon for lovers in search of a place to get undressed.

The entrance to the hotel didn't look furtive or sordid at all – the reception area was in a corner of the ground-floor brasserie, where hip Parisians (the men unshaven, in jeans and dark pullovers over a white T-shirt; the women sporting ponytails and equally dark pullovers) were having laid-back business lunches. No huddling couples waiting for a room to be free. The waitresses, too, looked very normal – young girls in everyday streetwear.

The hotel's PR man, an equally hip, equally unshaven young Parisian, greeted me cordially and offered to show me some rooms. He'd specified that most of them would be unoccupied at that time of day. Lovers, I presumed, catered for their food appetites before their sexual ones.

As we went up the narrow stairs, he explained that the building used to be a *hôtel de passe*, one of the places where streetwalkers would bring their clients. Almost all of these had since lost that trade, he said, and settled down into a seedy existence of just being a cheap, badly decorated hotel, which was what this was before the Amour people refurbished it.

And refurbish it they certainly have, with classy, knowing eroticism. Most of the bathtubs seem to be right in the bedrooms.

From bath to bed and back again (with, presumably a quick towel rub in between) could be a dance of the seven oils. Large, strategically placed mirrors add to the effect. Several of the rooms have erotic photos – featuring no pornography, but plenty of nudity. One also has a glass bookshelf of vintage French photography magazines and racy novels – lots of oiled and pouting women on show there.

The *crème de la crème* of eroticism, though, had to be the room with 200 disco balls on the ceiling. Close the black curtains, turn on the lights, set the balls revolving (the disco balls that is) and you're in your very own sexy cabaret show. The bath is, of course, at the foot of the bed, which stands on a raised plinth like a stage on which guests can play out their very own sex film.

So, I ask, how much an hour is this room? I resist the temptation to add 'with and without the S&M waitresses'.

At which point the modern reality of Paris catches up with me.

'Oh, the rooms aren't rented out by the hour any more, or for the afternoon,' I'm told. 'We got raided a couple of times by the *Brigade des Moeurs* [Paris's vice squad].'

'Why?' Surely the Parisian police weren't cracking down on adultery and premarital sex?'

'Prostitution. They were afraid it would turn back into a *hôtel de passe*. And anyway, we're doing so well now that we don't need the hassle of renting out rooms just for an afternoon.'

For a few moments, I feel as if my fantasy world has collapsed. But then I realize that this doesn't really matter at all.

'Your customers are still mainly lovers, though?' I ask.

'Yes. Lots of Parisians book it for their wedding anniversaries, or just for a romantic night alone without the kids. There are no TVs and no phones, so people can be together with no outside disturbances.'

So, in fact, it is still a love hotel, and a love hotel in the true sense of the word, a place more geared to *amoureux* than *amants* –

the French, typically, have two words for lovers. *Amants* are people who have sex together, *amoureux* are those who are (also) in love. And in the Hôtel Amour's rooms, you're more likely to find *amoureux* enjoying some sexy romantic seclusion, secure in the knowledge that they don't have to get dressed and back to the office an hour later. How much more romantic can you get?

Where to go for a *verre*

Pretty well any half-decent café or bar in Paris will be a great venue for a romantic drink. But if you want to make it very special, there's only one place to go – the Ritz. A bit of a cliché, but like so many clichés, it is one because it's so irresistibly true.

Even if you don't care that this is the hotel where poor Princess Diana had her last drink before falling victim to a piece of spectacularly bad Parisian driving, the Ritz has just that level of effortless chic to make anyone feel a little bit royal. And anyone can go there. All you need to do is dress up a little (though a tie is not *de rigueur*) and wander in, saying a friendly *bonsoir* to the doorman and any staff you might meet, as if you have every right to be there. Which, of course, you do – all the bars in Paris's posh hotels are public places where it is perfectly acceptable to drop in for a glass of wine or even a simple espresso if you just want to check out the decor and use the ultra-classy loos.

And surprisingly, a glass of the house Champagne at the *bar du Ritz* is actually pretty good value. It will be about double the price of a *coupe* in a normal restaurant, but you get so many bowls of excellent snacks – the most delicious roasted-nut mix in Paris, for example – that if you're a light eater like me, afterwards you'll hardly be able to manage dinner (not that you need to explain the economics of all this to your loved one, of course).

The bar itself is very snug, but as soon as the weather is warm enough, I like to sit outside in the garden amongst the kitsch sculptures and the parasols. The only problem is that this is a rich person's hotel, and some rich people have to show how comfortably off they are by trying to asphyxiate everyone with a cigar-shaped tube of donkey droppings. But that is just a personal whinge, and even I am capable of pretending that I can breathe normally if it means preserving the romantic atmosphere that seems to come naturally when you combine luxurious surroundings with your loved one and a glass of chilled Champagne.

Oh, and one final thing. If you want to look as though you belong, it's best to know where you're going. The Ritz has several bars, but the one I'm talking about is very close to the entrance, almost immediately on the left as you go in. If in doubt, just ask, *Où est le jardin?* – preceded by a friendly *bonsoir*, of course.

The perfect Parisian dinner date

Paris is very good at serving up romantic restaurants, even if it doesn't always realize it. Practically any decent restaurant has most of the necessary ingredients, although it probably won't bill itself as a lovers' retreat. Below are a couple of my favourites.

Braque's brasserie

My first suggestion is a classic but, like the Ritz, no worse for that, because it is a quintessentially Parisian experience.

La Coupole, for me, is the best of the big Parisian brasseries. Not because the food is spectacular (except for the high-rise shell-fish platters, which are a spectacle in themselves), but because Paris wouldn't be the same without it. When it was announced that the building, in the heart of Montparnasse, might be pulled down, an old friend of mine was in a panic – 'Where will I go for my birthday dinner?' he kept saying. 'And where will I eat oysters at Christmas?' He probably wasn't the only Parisian saying that kind of thing, because people like Picasso, Braque and Édith Piaf used to be just as addicted to the place.

In the end, though, as mentioned in Chapter 5, the brasserie wasn't demolished – it was simply covered over with a sort of concrete marquee – a few floors of apartments were built on top, leaving the restaurant intact, so that today it must look pretty well exactly as it did back in the 1920s. Except, of course, for the lack of smoke.

It's a huge place, a football pitch of old brasserie benches, with racks behind your head to store your jacket and bag, saving space to cram more people in. But for some reason, the immensity of the *salle de restaurant* and the fact that you're likely to dine elbow-to-elbow with strangers doesn't detract from the romanticism. For a start, there's no music and the high ceiling provides excellent acoustics, so you can actually hear what your conversation partner is saying without yelling or lip-reading. And the atmosphere is always cosy rather than cramped, with diners eyeing their neighbours' plates as they decide what to order. The Art Deco murals on the thirty-odd columns help, too – they were painted by pupils of Matisse and Fernand Léger, and some of them depict rather suggestive scenes of semi-naked dancing.

Watching what's going on around you is always entertaining – the waiting staff are brisk but friendly, and as professional as they come. They're divided into ranks, like an orchestra. At the bottom of the prestigious heap you have the guys in long white aprons and waistcoats – these are the violinists who carry the weight of the melody, and they sway between the tables holding giant trays of food at shoulder level. Above them are the people in black suits and

bow ties – soloists who take orders and banter with the customers.*
And conducting the whole symphony (and a place this size needs
several conductors) are the maître d's in their shiny suits, chic and
commanding, forever flitting about checking that everyone is
getting what they came for.

As a place for a romantic dinner, it's not an intimate venue, but
couples seem to go there to get a loving buzz. It's like a short trip on
a classic ocean liner – it's a communal experience, but you have
your own snug cabin. And, of course, it's best known for its seafood,
so it's the perfect place to order the ultimate, stripped-down
romantic menu – a couple of dozen oysters and a bottle of
Champagne. And if that doesn't get your Parisian hormones going,
nothing will.

Love in the *maquis*

Perhaps you prefer your romantic rendez-vous with a little less of an
open-space feel, and you may also be looking for somewhere less
conventional, which is where my next address comes in.

First, though, a couple of warnings . . .

The restaurant in question is located near the second least
romantically named square in Paris – République.† And not only is
it near an unromantic square, it also has a rather banal name – the
Café Restaurant Le Temple. It's right opposite Temple *métro* station,
and should not be confused with the *Tabac* of the same name a few
yards nearer République.

To make things worse, this Temple was the prison mentioned
earlier, the place where Louis XVI and Marie Antoinette were held

* This banter includes trying to explain what all the dishes are to anyone who can't
read French. There may be plenty of tourists here, but there's no English menu –
it's French through and through.
† The first, for those who didn't read the earlier part of this chapter, being
Stalingrad.

before they were taken to Concorde to have their heads cut off. *Pas très romantique.*

Luckily, the restaurant has not opted for a dungeon theme – it's a Corsican place. If you're meeting a *Parisien* or *Parisienne* (and a hearty slap on the back to you if that's the case) the Corsican theme could be another potential risk to the romantic ambiance – to Parisians, Corsica is less a rugged green jewel in the Mediterranean than the home of people who like to amuse themselves in the winter by blowing up holiday homes. Best to check first whether your date, or one of his or her relatives, has recently lost a beach house to high explosives.

The decor might at first sight be a little off-putting, too. One of the collages on the wall features a pair of gun-toting Corsican hunters apparently lying in wait for Parisians, and the rest is a riot of kitsch. Almost every surface is covered in fake panther skin – seats, lamps, the ceiling, the walls, everything. I even happen to know that down in the loos, the soap dispenser, hand dryer and toilet-brush holder are painted in panther camouflage, as if they had been designed by someone with a synthetic-fur fetish.

Those surfaces of the restaurant that aren't devoted to the worship of the nylon panther are covered in zebra skin or pictures of Marilyn Monroe. She is on posters and photos pinned to the wall, as well as featuring on all the coffee cups.

All of this might sound a bit gaudy to people who think of Paris as a place where everyone wears dark-blue Chanel suits and eats croissants with their fingertips, but most Parisians much prefer kitsch to chic. The real Paris is colourful and over the top, like the Art Nouveau interior of the Galeries Lafayette, the older *métro* stations with their lurid green vegetable-matter entrances, or the Centre Pompidou.

The tables at the Café Restaurant Le Temple are very close together, and to squeeze the woman on to the *banquette*,* you virtually have to redecorate the place, pulling out the chair and table and making sure the neighbours don't have glasses or condiments too close to the edge of their table, so that you avoid a messy sweeping-off accident.

In this place, though, the density of tables is compensated for by the fact that they're divided off into small panther-skin booths. You are sitting very close to your neighbours, but you're separated from them by a small partition. It's as close to intimacy as you'll get in most Parisian restaurants.

The food here is simple French, but with a little something extra from the islands (and not only Corsica) – salmon in a coconut sauce, for example, or scallops served in a *cassolette* (a sort of fish stew). They also do an excellent version of an old favourite of mine, the *salade de chèvre chaud*, or goat's-cheese toasts with a green salad.

So if you're sure your partner will not be put off thoughts of love by fake zebra skin, Marilyn Monroe, Corsican cowboys and quirky food, this is an offbeat place to try. And quite frankly, worse things can happen than ending a romantic evening with a little game of 'I'll be Marilyn, you be the Corsican cowboy' (or vice-versa, of course).

Say it with *fleurs*

And there we have it. For romance, Paris is a city that can't fail. You just have to let it do its magic. And to press the point home, I will

---

* In France, the rule is: *les femmes sur la banquette* – that is, women on the bench, referring to brasseries with bench-like seating along the walls. Even if there is no *banquette*, the ladies must face into the restaurant. This is so that the woman will be the sole centre of the man's attentions, or to put it more bluntly, so that the man will be gazing only at his lady love and not at every other woman in the restaurant.

finish with a single telling statistic – in the Paris *Pages Jaunes*, there are 641 florists listed. In the London *Yellow Pages*, there are 707. But London is approximately seventeen times bigger than Paris (1,706 square kilometres as opposed to only 105 square kilometres). What's more, sit in any restaurant in Paris and your dinner will almost certainly be interrupted by a man trying to sell you a rose. Frankly, if you can't get the romantic mood right, you don't deserve to be in Paris.

But if you do press the right buttons, and the ambiance does end up *amoureuse*, it is only natural that your thoughts might turn to another subject, which will be discussed at length in the following chapter . . .

The Crazy Horse, or 'crezzee orrsse' as the French call it, is the most Parisian of the cabarets. Its dancers are all the same height and have the same distance between their ... but you'll just have to read the next chapter to find out.

7

SEX

After dinner, he [James Bond] generally went to the Place Pigalle to see what would happen to him. When, as usual, nothing did, he would walk home across Paris to the Gare du Nord and go to bed.

IAN FLEMING, FOR YOUR EYES ONLY

THERE'S AN old Parisian joke about the shutting-down of French brothels in 1946. When the fancy *bordels* closed, their furniture and fittings were all sold off at auction, and according to the joke, the parrot at one of the fanciest establishments, Le Chabanais, went up for sale along with the mirrors, beds and bathtubs.

The bird is bought by a pet-shop owner, who puts it on display with a warning that it is an excellent speaker, but prone to use bad language because of all the shady people it was associating with in its previous home.

No one wants to buy the foul-mouthed creature until one day a housewife, Madame Dupont, comes into the shop and says she's looking for a talking parrot to keep her company. The shopkeeper says he only has the one, and he's selling it at a discount because it swears so much. Madame Dupont decides to buy it all the same, and puts it on a perch in her living room.

'What a shitty dump,' the parrot squawks. 'The Chabanais was much smarter.'

Things get even worse when Madame Dupont's teenage daughters come in from school.

'Cheap whores,' the parrot squawks. 'The tarts at the Chabanais were much classier.'

And then Madame Dupont's husband arrives home.

'*Merde alors*,' the parrot squawks, 'you here, Monsieur Dupont?'

Yes, Parisians like to think of their city as a *ville chaude*, a horny town, the kind of place where even a respectable family man has a secret sex life. Sex is meant to be everywhere – not just in massage parlours and swingers' clubs, but just a smile away if you happen to meet the eye of the right person in the street.

When I first came to Paris, I took this erotic omnipresence for granted. I was living in an apartment that looked out into a narrow courtyard, and the place just opposite was shared by three girls who used to wander from bathroom to bedrooms completely naked. What's more, they were allergic to curtains. I thought that this was a completely normal part of Parisian life, and after a while, I hardly even paid attention when a freshly showered *demoiselle* went flitting across my eyeline. Whenever friends came over from the UK to visit, they'd gasp and ask me if I'd seen the nudie show opposite, and I would nonchalantly tell them, of course, this is Paris.

As soon as the girls moved out, though, I found out how wrong I was. The next occupants were a young couple who immediately put up thick curtains, and scowled at me if I was looking out of my window and dared to nod or smile across at them, even though I was usually fully clothed.

Parisian friends regularly tell stories about sexy goings-on in their neighbours' apartments – yelps coming through the walls or ceiling, a pair of splayed female legs poking up above a window sill, or silhouettes in a bathroom window performing a shadow play of stand-up fornication. But these, it now seems to me, are only symptoms of the sheer density of population in the city. Glancing in a neighbour's window or inadvertently eavesdropping through thin walls are inevitable features of city life.

Even so, Paris still loves to think of itself as a sexier place than anywhere else, capable of making non-Parisians blush with its openness about *l'amour*. In a recent article for the *Sunday Times*, Paris's resident philosopher and socialite, Bernard-Henri Lévy, wrote: 'I am always working, but I do have time for a little pleasure as well. For me, the greatest pleasure in life is making love. You're blushing? I'm sorry.' Yes, he was convinced that his non-Parisian readers were so prudish that they would be shocked by this startling confession that he enjoys shagging.

Don't get me wrong, Paris is sexy, but its real charm is that it thinks it's so much sexier.

Tonight, Josephine

If Paris sees itself as such a sex machine, it's because it is, in all fairness, a very experienced lover.

In the court of French Kings, sex was a perfume that hung permanently in the air. Louis XIV insisted on *le droit de seigneur* over any lady who caught his attention at Versailles. His successor, Louis XV, was notorious for his willingness to drop his silk breeches. And scattered around these depraved monarchs like so many silk cushions were the indolent, tax-exempt aristocrats, who had little to do apart from adopt the Kings as role models and bed each other's spouses, servants and relatives.

Things didn't calm down much after the Revolution, either, because the survivors were so happy to have made it through the Terror without being separated from their heads that they indulged in a frenzy of physical gratification. The young Napoleon Bonaparte first met his future wife Josephine at a chic Parisian party, where she, like all the other society ladies of the time, was dressed in a low-cut, almost transparent, gown that was split at the side to reveal pretty well all her curves as she danced. She was a serial mistress, but no one thought less of her for that, and a few years later she became Napoleon's Empress.

The *Empereur* himself wasn't much of a Latin Lothario – he was more of a practical man. He legalized France's brothels, the *maisons de tolérance*, as a way of making sure prostitutes were under medical supervision so that his soldiers weren't distracted in battle by itchy diseases. And ironically, it was this clinical measure that provided the last building block for Paris's reputation as a capital of copulation.

During the nineteenth century, the city's medicalized sex factories evolved into a whole subculture that attracted well-to-do young men from all over Europe and the newly rich continent of America. It became *très chic* to nip to Paris for a weekend or stop over on one's tour of the great European capitals and, after a quick peek at the architecture and a dash around the Louvre, indulge one's less artistic instincts in a high-class whorehouse. And these weren't dark places where a man would sneak in, his collar turned up, and quickly choose the recipient of his paid attentions. The expensive *bordels* were often brightly lit temples of the senses, riotous cabarets with music and dancing, cafés where the female drinkers were all semi-naked and available.

And, like that other great royal role model, King Edward VII of England, who spent much of his youth undressing Parisian prostitutes,* in later life these satisfied customers would return to the city with their wives, and mentally relive their wild days as they drank Champagne in more decorous establishments. And at the

---

* For the full story of his amorous adventures in Paris, see my book *1,000 Years of Annoying the French*. Though for Edward it was less about annoying them than seducing them, both sexually and diplomatically.

end of the evening, back at the hotel with wifey, the men could almost imagine they were with little Brigitte or Marie-Rose, or one of the other girls they'd toyed with at the *maison de tolérance*. A Victorian wife would probably be surprised to see her staid, respectable husband looking so relaxed, and (as long as she didn't suspect why he had that wistful look in his eye) would no doubt be delighted at his ardour. Arriving back home, couples would whisper to their friends: 'Marriage in a rut? Love life gone off the boil? Go to Paris, *tout de suite.*'

And of course it wasn't only married couples who were taking up bed space in Paris. Parisian hotels were so used to playing host to the unmarried that no hotelier would bat an eyelid if a couple signing in didn't seem able to agree on what their name was. Pigalle was full of *hôtels de passe* where prostitutes brought their clients, and even less lugubrious places were not too conscientious about who was renting their rooms. This was how Paris became a bolthole for adulterers and illicit lovers who were afraid of damaging their reputations if they flaunted their philanderings at home – a trip to Paris was a journey to an oasis of immorality, with the added bonus that the city always had a sheen of romance. Taking your lover to Paris has always been so much classier than ducking into a motel or trying to convince some dragon of a seaside landlady that you really are Mr and Mrs Smith.

Paris would still like to think of itself as a kind of Western Bangkok, where unfortunate citizens of less erotic countries can come and lose their inhibitions. Coaches stop at Pigalle so that tourists can get a thrill by wandering past the explicit photos outside the lapdancing clubs and hostess bars. A whole section of the rue Saint-Denis, right in the centre of the city, still has scantily dressed prostitutes in doorways. There are also several well-known swingers' clubs, openly advertised in ordinary listings magazines, where free-loving Parisian couples go to have sex with perfectly respectable strangers. At one of them, it is rumoured, a soirée not so long ago got off to a slow start because, as the manager explained, 'We're waiting for Monsieur le Ministre.'*

The Parisians would love to trademark the brand *Sexe*, or at least get an *appellation contrôlée* on it. I can hear the ads now, spoken by a modern Brigitte Bardot – 'Sexe de Paris, ze only real sex.'

But times are changing. The prostitutes are being edged out of the rue Saint-Denis, which is getting so clean that a far-from-daring friend of mine has even rented an apartment there for her student son. The street, for long a no-go area for property investors, is being targeted as one of the last ungentrified pockets of central Paris. Even Pigalle, the nerve centre of Paris's sex industry, is changing – nostalgic residents complained bitterly when a sex shop recently closed down and was replaced by a health-food supermarket.

In fact, Parisian sex has become so endangered that it now has its own museum . . .

A trip down memory boulevard

The section of the boulevard de Clichy between the *métro* stations Blanche and Pigalle is dotted with sex shops (many of them looking decidedly jaded) and lapdancing clubs, and if a male walks along the north side of the boulevard, day or night, every 10 metres or so he will be approached by a man or woman who steps out from a velvet-curtained doorway and invites him to come in and check out the girls. Personally, though, I've never seen them pull in any punters. Well, no one sober, anyway.

The area is also home to a much more successful place that sells sex toys, pornography and 'intimate' jewellery, and attracts

---

* I should add, for legal reasons, that he is not a minister at the time of writing.

both male and female customers day and night despite the fact that it has no one outside touting for business – it's the Musée de l'Érotisme, and it's so respectable that it figures in the city's museum listings, alongside the Louvre and Napoleon's tomb at Les Invalides.

Hoping to get an insider's view up the skirts of Pigalle, I made an appointment to talk to the museum's curator, Alain Plumey. He is a diminutive, shaven-headed, pale-skinned sixty-year-old, dressed like someone who might sell second-hand books at a flea market. He is, however, a retired porn actor. In the 1970s and early 1980s, Plumey did his stuff in 129 hard-core movies with typically descriptive French titles like *Suce-moi, Salope* (Suck Me, Slut), *Cuisses en Délire* (Delirious Thighs), *Blondes Humides* (Wet Blondes) and *Déculottez-vous, les Starlettes* (Panties Off, Starlets).

I must admit that even I feel a tinge of nostalgia when I read those titles. Not that I've seen any of the films. No, before the internet and DVDs killed off Paris's porn cinemas, the listings magazines used to publish the names of new X-rated releases, and they were often hilariously explicit, especially when translated literally into English – my all-time favourite was *Il y a la Fête dans Mon Cul – There's a Party in My Arse*. It's an image to make anyone's eyes water.

But Plumey is not at all what you might expect of an ex-porn star. No open-chested shirt, gold medallion and leather trousers for him. When he speaks, however, there is no mistaking which industry he is working in.

'I got into porn acting because I wanted to have lots of sex,' he told me. 'I've always been fascinated by sex. When I was a kid, there was a permanent funfair along the middle of the boulevard, and I used to crawl under the awnings to watch the girls in the striptease tents. They were often purple because of the cold.'

This part of Paris, he said, has been associated with sex since the reign of François I, King of France from 1515 to 1547. Apparently François used to venture outside the city walls to visit the convent at Abbesses. As Monsieur Plumey put it, 'The mother superior was the biggest pimp in Paris, and used to rent out the nuns. And at that time, the windmills in Montmartre were all brothels. The millers used to provide girls to entertain the farmers while they were milling the grain. That's why we have the phrase to enter a place *comme dans un moulin*, meaning to be able to walk in freely and feel at home. The windmills were open to anyone who wanted to have a girl. Then later on, in the eighteenth and nineteenth centuries, rich people built *folies* here, outside the city walls, to meet up with their mistresses in private.'

Folies were elegant country houses, often hidden behind discreetly planted trees, that became notorious venues for orgies, and served as models when Paris began to build its most luxurious brothels in the mid-nineteenth century. Even after the rapidly expanding city made the *folies* too urban to be discreet, the lower classes maintained the area's erotic reputation with cheaper *bordels*, girlie bars and streetwalkers. The Folies-Bergère can-can show is a reference to the former rendez-vous houses, just as the Moulin Rouge harks back to the hospitality provided by millers.

In the nineteenth and early-twentieth centuries, though, despite all the cheap sex on sale, the atmosphere in Pigalle was far less seedy than today, Plumey told me, because it was much more open.

'The brothels were often run by dangerous criminals, but they were rogues who excited the ladies,' he said. 'And the *filles** were everywhere, they were a part of life. Back then, no single working-class woman could support herself on her meagre salary, so they were all looking for a *gentil monsieur* [kind gentleman] to supplement their income. Part-time prostitution was the norm. And there was no shame involved – artists and writers celebrated the

---

* In French, *fille* can mean prostitute. When talking about a girl, strictly speaking one should say *jeune fille* – young girl – to make it completely clear she's not also a hooker.

prostitutes. They were Picasso's and Renoir's models. Picasso's painting *Les Demoiselles d'Avignon* was a group of Montmartre hookers. He painted it just up the road from here at the Bateau-Lavoir. And some of the most popular songs of the time were about prostitutes – the singers used to come out on to the boulevard, busk and sell the sheet music. People would take it home and sing the song around their piano.'

My own grandparents used to buy a lot of songsheets, and I've tried to picture my proper, white-haired grandad singing about ladies of the night while my granny nibbled fruitcake. But no, it doesn't compute. And somehow I couldn't picture respectable middle-class Parisians doing the same thing in the early-twentieth century, either, especially if Monsieur wanted to hide the fact that he was a client of the ladies in the songs. Here, I felt, the Parisian romanticism was kicking in. After all, alongside the chic brothels, France also had its notorious *maisons d'abattage* (knocking shops), where, right up until 1946, the girls would cater for eighty or ninety clients a day. Even if a girl worked a twelve-hour shift, it would mean seven or eight men an hour. Not idyllic by any standards.

Plumey is too young to remember the golden (and not so golden) age of legal prostitution, but he did recall the old theatres, where, instead of waiting to be lapdanced on, customers would go to see a sexy review – an explicit version of the Folies-Bergère and the Moulin Rouge shows. These cabarets have all died out now, killed off by the big, and then the small, screen.

In the 1970s, porn cinemas were doing a roaring trade in Paris, thanks to the lack of censorship. In France, this encouraged totally above-board producers to fund typically French films, featuring, say, a *châtelain* (chateau owner) and his maid, or a perverse husband and wife. That was when Plumey began acting in them. At first the settings were all provincial, so he also started to write scripts featuring Parisian characters like café waiters, delivery boys and gendarmes. These were filmed in Paris and were, Plumey told me, very lucrative, 'Because I knew how to write to a budget and my wife was a *monteuse*.'

At this point, our conversation was interrupted for a while because of a slight misunderstanding. I assumed that *monteuse* (literally, a female 'mounter') was some kind of porn-movie stunt-lady. An understandable assumption, surely, because one of the movies in Plumey's filmography is *Les Monteuses*, the story of a young man who has a bewitching flute that causes girls to go wild and straddle the nearest male every time it is played. (And Mozart thought *his* flute was magic.)

But it turns out that the word *monteuse* also means female film editor. Madame Plumey was able to help her husband in the cutting room, not because she was one of the female leads in his movies.

Anyway, Parisian films like these helped maintain Pigalle's reputation because they were shown in the neighbourhood's porn cinemas, and received an even wider audience when the sex shops started up, and began to sell the videos.

However, these shops, like almost every sex-themed place on the boulevard and in the surrounding streets, are looking run-down these days. Plumey believes that this is because Paris itself is getting less sexy.

'France used to be *une grande nation copulatrice* [a nation of great copulators],' he said, 'but now Parisians are tired and too materialistic. More and more men are becoming premature ejaculators or impotent. And the women are getting greedy – these days, you have to be rich to make a conquest. And people are more conservative. Even the porn movies shown on French TV are censored because they're for the general public. There are things you can't show any more.'

I asked whether this was why Plumey opened his museum in 1997, a place of titillation rather than gratification.

'Yes,' he said, 'and that's why we get so many women visitors. Women enjoy foreplay and aesthetics. Men are into direct, immediate action, they're brutes compared to women. And we get lots of older people, too, couples.'

'And lone men?' I ask, remembering my one previous visit, when I was researching a scene for my novel *Merde Actually*, and wandered around alone, feeling very self-conscious and voyeuristic.

'No,' he said, 'we don't get many lone men.'

And with that, he announced that he was going to leave me to visit the museum on my own again . . .

Sex costs extra if you wear glasses

This time, because I was researching a book about Paris, I spent less time admiring the collection of ethnic erotica. The museum contains hundreds of sex-related objects from around the world, such as Mexican water jugs with the most startling handles and spouts, and Japanese engravings that seem to have been commissioned by men in need of some highly unrealistic flattery.

Instead I lingered in front of a 1932 cartoon that depicted Pigalle's racy image in the inter-war years – it was a street scene, in which all the characters had suddenly been seized with the urge to have an orgy. The passengers of a passing bus had all leapt on one another. Meanwhile, a male pedestrian was fondling a sailor, a woman was enjoying herself with a pig that had escaped from a butcher's van, and even the two horses pulling a cart had begun to do it doggy-style. Clearly there was something very special in Pigalle's air back then.

The museum also houses several of the risqué songsheets that Monsieur Plumey mentioned. They feature coy pictures of smiling ladies, and have titles like 'Les Marcheuses' (The Streetwalkers), 'Le Pensionnat des Demoiselles' (The School for Young Ladies – a fantasy about soldiers being billeted with a dormitory full of schoolgirls), and 'La Rue de la Joie' (The Street of Joy), a song that includes the poignant lines:

> *Pour se faire aimer*
> *On veut se donner*
> *Hélas on ne peut que se vendre.*

In other words – 'To be loved, we want to give ourselves, but alas we have to sell ourselves' – a myth that probably wore thin at the *maisons d'abattage*.

The most interesting part of the collection, though, deals with the old brothels, and includes publicity shots of the girls on offer at one establishment, most of them completely naked except for their shoes or the occasional scarf or necklace – the customers had to know what they would be getting for their money.

There are photos of the luxurious interiors of chic Parisian brothels like the Chabanais, the Sphinx, the One-Two-Two and the Quatorze (brothels were often known by their street numbers, because name signs were forbidden). The decors were as elaborate as film sets – an Egyptian room, a cruise-liner cabin, a medieval chamber, and even a kitchen with apron-only 'helpers'. Every fantasy was there to be bought, and it was all legal. These photos weren't sneak peeks behind the scenes, they were promotional literature – like a pre-1946 version of today's brochures for spas.

And talking of the 1940s, the Musée also has some revealing documents showing which Parisian brothels were allocated to the Nazis during the Second World War. A leaflet in German informs officers that three of the top-class establishments – at 12 rue Chabanais, 6 rue des Morillons and 50 rue Saint-Georges – were reserved for them, and tells them their nearest *métro* stations. However, the text spends even more time warning the soldiers that after each visit they have to go to one of the *Sanierstellen* (health offices) for a check-up, and need to get a receipt from the

Before Parisian brothels became illegal in 1946, they attracted almost as many tourists as the Louvre. Though you weren't allowed to touch the Mona Lisa. Here, prostitutes in a luxury *bordel* wait for rich clients.

prostitute they have just visited so that her health record can be updated, too.

The most intriguing insight into the sexual past, though, was a frame displaying a prostitute's notebook, written in 1942. Each page was a record of the day's business, and she had listed all her customers and the prices she charged them. The teacher had to pay 40 francs, the *beau garçon* only 30, while the *chanteur* (singer) got a special deal – 27.50. This wasn't her lowest price, however. The *petit Juif* (small Jew) paid 25 francs, as did the *aveugle* (blind man) and the writer (a poorly paid profession, obviously). And she even gave student discounts, charging the *étudiant* only 20. Her highest prices were for the *grand gros* (tall fat man), who was made to pay 45 francs, as was the louche-sounding *type à lunettes* (guy in glasses).*

In any case, the girl's services all came pretty cheap – using the official conversion tables provided by France's economic-statistics institute, the INSEE, I calculated that her highest price, 45 francs, would have been the equivalent of around 15 euros today, the price of a salad and a glass of wine in a cheap Parisian café. Even if she got tips, or deliberately recorded lower prices so her Madame didn't take such a big share, it looks as though the massive supply of sex for sale kept the prices very low. All of which explains her high tally of punters per day – fifteen or sixteen was about average, which wasn't *maison d'abattage* standard, but still meant she was having sex with 100 men a week. After reading her notebook, any romantic notions about what went on in Parisian brothels go flying out the window.

* As a short-sighted person myself, I felt obliged to go and ask Monsieur Plumey about this discrimination against spectacle-wearers, and he said the man probably had 'special tastes'.

Parisian sex today – strip but no tease

The streets of nineteenth-century Paris might have been paved in prostitutes, but it was of course rare to glimpse more in public than a stockinged ankle or a hint of *décolleté*. To see larger expanses of bare female skin, men would have to go to a brothel or, for less hands-on action, to one of the theatres or cabarets. This was when the Moulin Rouge, the Folies-Bergère and the Lapin Agile grew up, and kept starving artists like Toulouse-Lautrec in food and absinthe by commissioning them to create advertising posters.

Here, can-can dancers would show underwear and even a bit of thigh, cleavages would be allowed to breathe, and risqué songs would add to the atmosphere of mass titillation.

Meanwhile, rich gentlemen would catch the eye of the dancers – or was it the other way round? – and in between dances, presents would be offered and promises made, and the girls would make appointments to supplement their income.

You can still go to these cabarets today, though the Lapin Agile has transformed itself into a *chanson française* music club, and the other two have become big-time tourist shows, giving visitors to Paris an evening of can-can, feathers and *ooh-là-là*. The Lido, on the Champs-Élysées, is a more modern version, with men and women putting on a Vegas-style extravaganza of long legs and occasional glimpses of bare curves.

These days, however, the club that keeps Paris's history of choreographed eroticism alive is one of the newest of all – the Crazy Horse, founded in 1951 by an 'insatiable admirer of women' called Alain Bernadin, who clearly didn't give a damn about belonging to the Moulin-Lapin-Folies tradition because he named his club after a Sioux chief and opened it a long way from Pigalle, near the Champs-Élysées.

The club attracts far more Parisians than outsiders, many of whom go along to see the regular guest stars who come to bare all on stage. Recently, Pamela Anderson, Dita van Teese and an actress called Clotilde Courau (better known in French celeb mags as the wife of the grandson of the last king of Italy) have slapped on the all-over body make-up and attracted big crowds.

If you ask a Parisian what goes on at the Crazy Horse, he or she might not have been there, but they'll know that it's all about naked-ness. The girls on stage are famous for wearing more square millimetres of covering on their feet than on the rest of their body put together.

And so it was that I convinced my Parisian feminist *amoureuse* to spend an evening ogling naked female flesh. *Vive Paris*, I thought – there probably aren't many cities where the feminists would do that without taking along some spray paint to graffiti the girls.

The Crazy Horse (or *le cray-zeee orrss* as the French call it) is just opposite the Chamber of Agriculture and the Paris head-quarters of Givenchy and Yves Saint Laurent – sex, fashion and food, the heart of the Parisian consciousness.

Inside, the decor is plush velvet carpeting, muted lights and black woodwork – very illicit-feeling. A staircase leads down into the basement, and emerges in a surprisingly small theatre with tight rows of cabaret tables facing a tiny stage. It's clear that the audience is going to get very close to the girls indeed.

I look around at the audience and am surprised. Next to us are a middle-class, middle-aged couple – the type of people who sold me my bank loan and washing machine. There are also small groups of young women, pairs of businessmen getting some R&R, and what looks like a daughter and her parents – checking out career prospects, maybe. Most of them are in slightly formal evening wear, and only one couple have come wholly dressed for the part, with the woman in a silky pink corset.

On the wall by the stage I notice a large plaque of names, similar to the one at the British Embassy that lists the ambassadors to Paris. This is slightly different, though. It's a roll of honour of past dancers – names like Lady Pousse-Pousse, Diva Novita, Vanity Starlight and Venus Océane. Not their real names, of course – traditionally, a Crazy Horse dancer's name is given to her by the show manager or artistic director after her first night on stage. The girl can refuse it once, but has to take the second name offered. Most of them apparently accept the first choice.

The music starts, and is typically Parisian. Not accordion, you understand – these days, you mainly hear that played by Eastern European buskers on the *métro*. No, this is '60s French rock'n'roll, what they call *yé-yé*.

The curtain opens on a very un-Parisian scene – a row of naked female Grenadiers, marching on the spot and saluting. It's a clotheless version of the Changing of the Guard at Buckingham Palace. They have the black-fur busbies, but there any resemblance with English soldiers ends. Their uniform is a flimsy framework of jacket that reveals their bare breasts, and they are wearing nothing down below except what looks like a strategically pasted rectangle of black silk to protect their modesty. Not a very practical outfit for standing around outside the Palace.

After a few minutes, the curtain falls and the tableau changes – now it's a silhouette dance in coloured shadow, a Parisian version of the credits of a James Bond film. Next comes a solo dancer miming to a song that suggests, rather unconvincingly given her almost total nakedness and willingness to point her buttocks at perfect strangers, that she's a 'good girl'.

And as the show progresses, I realize that the girls in fact do almost no stripping. And although having young women shake their smooth, shapely naked buttocks at me for an hour or more is not a neutral experience, the dances are not at all pornographic. The girls are somehow too perfect, too doll-like, for sexual thoughts. The show is an almost abstract use of the female body, even in the slightly fetishist sequence where we see only legs and high heels.

The dancers also look so alike that there's no way a spectator can fixate on one of them, as the rich gentlemen at the nineteenth-century clubs used to do. This is a deliberate policy. The dancers are chosen according to strict physical criteria, and two measurements have to be exactly the same – the distance from nipple to nipple and from navel to pubis. Only guest stars are ever allowed to break the mould.

In the final tableau, all ten or so of the girls dance around the glittering letters D-É-S-I-R, miming to a bilingual song that talks rather erotically about Champagne flowing between one's fingers, and then the show is over, the lights go up and the audience files out into the foyer to buy souvenir T-shirts and spangly knickers.

I wonder what my partner thought of it all – as a feminist, she might say it totally dehumanizes women, and accuse me of taking her to see the public enslavement of her gender. Relations might be frosty for the next few days.

We cross the street towards the Chamber of Agriculture and, nervously, I ask her opinion. She reflects for a moment, and then says that the show was much classier than she'd expected. 'And I'd really like to know how that girl took off her stockings without taking off her shoes.'

It's a conclusion that says as much about Parisian sexual politics as it does about the city's erotic cabaret.

Où est le sexe?

Where, then, does this leave Parisian sex?

The city cherishes its reputation for being completely un-inhibited and free-speaking. Deep down, it still thinks its theme tune is Serge Gainsbourg's song 'Je T'Aime, Moi Non Plus'*, which

---

* The song's title is actually a cruel putdown: 'I love you – neither do I.'

contains a chorus that can be hilariously translated, rather like one of the old French sex films, as 'I come and I go, between your kidneys, and I restrain myself.'

The song's orgasmic gasps and groans are not just the sound of Serge's posh new English girlfriend Jane Birkin expressing her surprise at how turning herself into a Parisian sex kitten has launched her career, it is also Paris saying, '*Bonjour*, everybody, listen to us shagging.' And as Bernard-Henri Lévy's previously quoted outburst in the *Sunday Times* shows, Parisians still have a tendency to think they're the only ones doing so.

In fact, though, as we've seen in this chapter, sexually speaking, Paris has changed a lot in recent years. Pigalle is gradually shedding its seedy skin, and even though the Crazy Horse plays on the old showgirl reputation, it has turned its shapely back on the sordid pornographic side of the city's history.

Of course, Paris's peep shows, sex shops and swingers' clubs still exist, as does the prostitution – you can find women, men and everything in between hanging out on pavements all over the city if you know where to look – but these days the explicitly sexual stuff has pretty well all been marginalized.

There are still plenty of erotic things to do here, but nowadays, more often than not, the explicit sex is left up to your imagination. Just as, in my chapter on Romance, the Hôtel Amour gave up trying to be a love hotel and turned into a true-love hotel, Parisian sex has stopped being seedy and has gone mainstream. It's still naughty, but these days the naughtiness is also nice – romantic, even. The hardcore has gone soft.

Though it's probably best not to destroy Bernard-Henri Lévy's world by telling him so.

During the Prussian siege in 1870–71, Parisians were forced to forage for food and eat 'siege game'. Rat salami became something of a favourite.

8

FOOD

Le dîner tue la moitié de Paris et le souper tue l'autre.
(Dinner kills one half of Paris, and supper the other.)

CHARLES DE SECONDAT, BARON DE MONTESQUIEU,
EIGHTEENTH-CENTURY SATIRIST

PARISIANS HAVE a hands-on, in-your-face, almost sexual rapport with food. It has to be seen, touched and felt as well as tasted. They need to be absolutely certain that it's fresh – alive, even. Hence the shellfish stands in the street outside restaurants – the oysters, crabs and lobsters to be eaten in the brasseries are often displayed outdoors on the pavement, and the poor man (it's almost always a man) responsible for opening up oyster shells and pulling off crabs' claws has to work in the open air even in winter, just so that passers-by can ogle his wares.

The same thing goes for the food markets, where all but the poshest stalls let you squeeze and sniff your oranges, avocados, fennel and bananas before you buy them. Even in supermarkets, only the softest fruit like strawberries will be under plastic – everything else is on display to be fondled by potential customers.

My favourite description of Parisian food is in Émile Zola's novel *Le Ventre de Paris* – 'The Belly of Paris'. The story is set in and around the food markets at Les Halles at the end of the nineteenth century, and begins with the hero, Florent, an escaped political prisoner, arriving in the city just before daybreak. He has hitched a ride with a woman coming in to sell her vegetables, and awakes, starved and exhausted, to the first rays of dawn: 'The sun set the vegetables on fire,' Zola writes. 'He [Florent] no longer recognized the pale watercolour hues of twilight. Now the swollen hearts of the lettuces were burning, the carrots began to bleed red, the turnips became incandescent.'

No one, not even the poutiest celebrity chef, ever wrote about turnips like that. Here is a writer who wants to have sex with a vegetable. And in Paris, that's probably legal.

Brain food, or food on the brain

It's a miracle that Parisians stay relatively slim, because food is never far from their thoughts. By a linguistic accident, even their word for 'slim' looks edible to English-speakers – it's *mince*.* Not that Parisians are snackers and grazers – their thoughts are usually focused on regular mealtimes.

These mealtimes are often spent talking about food. At a French dinner party, it is not considered polite to discuss what you are eating – apart from complimenting the chef, obviously. It is, though, very much the done thing to recall other great meals you have eaten. This may seem bizarre, like describing a torrid night spent with someone other than the person you are currently making love with, but in fact it is seen as a way of paying homage to what you're eating. The food is so good that your taste buds have over-loaded your brain with images of sumptuous meals from your past, and you have to express yourself.

---

* The French word *mince* doesn't mean English mince, though – that would be *viande hachée*.

Logically, lack of food is therefore a double deprivation – nothing to eat and nothing to inspire you. This probably explains why the 1870–71 siege of Paris by the Prussians has stayed in the city's folk memory for so long. It wasn't just the shelling, the fighting and a subsequent revolutionary uprising – there was nothing to eat. And unlike in 1940, there was no way of getting relatives to bring in the odd hunk of bacon or bunch of carrots from the country. The city was cut off. Things were made even worse because at the beginning of the siege, in September 1870, the optimistic Parisians carried on eating more or less as normal – no one dared to introduce any rationing. Food was not too difficult to obtain because there were still farms and smallholdings in the closest suburbs, and Parisians had been warned of the likelihood of a siege, so many of them had got in plentiful stocks of food.

Gradually, though, as winter set in, supplies dwindled and stomachs started to rumble. Restaurants began to serve wolf burgers and rhino drumsticks as the zoo animals were slaughtered. The poor had to sacrifice their cats and dogs, and even vermin became a delicacy. In the Musée Carnavalet, Paris's history museum, there is a gruesome painting of a street butcher during the siege. All he has on offer is rat – at the time, *ratatouille* was no joke.

There is also a glass flask on display containing a real piece of bread baked during the siege. It is made of flour mixed with wood shavings, the latter perhaps being appropriate. After all, a *baguette* is a stick.

But Paris being Paris, even during a siege it managed to fight off depression by turning privation into a gastronomic experience. Rats, mice, pigeons and anything caught in traps became known as 'siege game', and they weren't just boiled up and eaten – they were prepared. Rat salami became something of a favourite.

And although a famous Christmas 1870 menu served at the Café Voisin in the posh rue Saint-Honoré, based almost entirely on zoo animals, was only available to the rich, there is something admirable about it, like the musicians on the *Titanic* going down playing their instruments. The six-course meal included such delicacies as elephant consommé, roasted bear ribs, antelope pâté, kangaroo stew, camel 'roasted English style' (that is, without sauce) and, just to add the common touch, cat accompanied by a side dish of rats. No doubt conversation during the meal was about simpler foods from less turbulent times – a roast chicken, a fresh apple, real bread.

This ability to eat their way through a crisis is still much in evidence today. Parisian workers, like all of their fellow French citizens, are under siege. Globalization is chiselling away at their jobs-for-life cosiness, employment laws are being tightened so that it is easier to fire inefficient workers and harder to go on strike (until 2004, some employers still had to pay employees for their strike days), retirement ages are being raised, and everyone agrees that it's *la crise*. A friend of mine teaches at a journalism school in the 10th *arrondissement* and regularly sends students out to do vox pops. One of the most popular subjects is asking passers-by what they usually do at lunchtimes (yes, social issue number one for Parisian journalism students – lunch), and recently, to my surprise, lots of people have been complaining that they just get a sandwich and eat it at their desk. *C'est la crise*, they say.

But I don't think the students have been getting a representative sample. Logically, people wandering about alone at lunchtime are more likely to be getting a takeaway than going to a restaurant. And if you go to any office area in Paris – behind the Champs-Élysées, for example, on the *grands boulevards*, at the Bourse or in the north of the Marais, the cafés are always crammed with workers enjoying a sitdown meal with their friends and colleagues. They may not take two hours for lunch like they did (or claim to have done) in the past, but they'll be feasting on the *plat du jour* or even the whole three-course menu of *entrée, plat, dessert*. Since it's *la crise*, more of them will be drinking water from the carafe rather than having wine, or they will opt for just two courses – most restaurants and cafés offer a choice, *entrée/plat* or *plat/dessert* for a reduced price. But they'll be there, day in day out, lunching their way through the economic siege.

No doubt talk at table will be at least partly about their working conditions, but they're French, after all, and no conversation between French colleagues – even during a well-cooked, efficiently served lunch in a Parisian café – is complete without a whinge about how hard life is. The people tucking into that camel 'roasted English style' back in 1870 probably said much the same thing, although they were being bombarded by Prussians, so perhaps they had more of an excuse.

In the market for a market?

The market that Zola described in his novel *Le Ventre de Paris* was knocked down at the end of the 1960s and replaced with the homeless persons' toilet and underground big-brand shopping hell that is Les Halles today. The food stalls were deported to Rungis, seven kilometres south of the city, near Orly airport, which is still one of the biggest and most varied food markets in the world.

Fanatical foodies would drool over a visit to the immense market at Rungis, but everything interesting happens there before dawn (the fish market, for example, is only open from 2 a.m. to 7 a.m.), all buyers need a membership card, and they can only buy in bulk. So unless you're in the market for a whole cow or half a ton of potatoes, it's not a practical place for visitors.

But this doesn't matter, because at their best, the street markets in Paris itself are every bit as droolsome as Zola's descriptions.

To get the full market experience, it is wise to avoid the posher parts of town, where you're not allowed to touch anything, and head to an *arrondissement* numbered over nine (except the 16th).

My favourites are the big market in the 12th at the place d'Aligre, between Bastille and the Gare de Lyon, which combines cheap stalls with an upmarket covered hall, and my own local market in the 19th, at the rue de Joinville, reputed to be the cheapest in Paris.

The Joinville market takes place every Sunday and Thursday, and its hundred or so stalls push Parisian small-shop specialization to the limit. There is a trader selling only onions (red, white and shallots) and two types of garlic. The herb sellers display nothing but different types of wet green leaf – parsley, chervil, marjoram, sage, coriander, mint. Another stand sells only dates (wrinkly or smooth) and raisins, which rise up from the table in three glistening golden mountains. The mushroom man is just as specialized – he deals only in grey button mushrooms from his farm in the Aisne, a hundred-odd kilometres northeast of Paris. He sells out every time, and by the end of the morning his stall consists of nothing but a stack of empty wooden crates, a handful of unsold mushrooms and a huge smile.

The three or four cheese stalls all have a hundred or so varieties on offer, including adulterated kinds for those who think the French are fanatically purist – goat's cheese coated in golden sultanas, or a soft, whitish variety covered in dried papaya. Cheese is probably the only product that's more expensive at the market than in the nearby supermarkets, which may be why there are rarely queues in front of the *fromager*. At one of the stalls, I once heard a lady seller, impatient at the lack of custom, start to call out 'Allez, mangez, régalez-vous, on est là!' – 'Come on, eat, enjoy yourselves, we're here,' which sounded almost like a call to cannibalism.

At food markets in Paris's poorer neighbourhoods, there are two zones – one selling higher-priced, top-quality merchandise and a second, in the case of Joinville squashed up against the back wall of the church, where people go to buy irregular cucumbers, fennel bulbs that have been amputated to take off the rotten bits, mottled (though perfectly edible) bananas, and dirt-cheap strawberries that will be fine for lunch, but by dinner time they'll have mutated into a cross between a summer-fruit smoothie and Roquefort cheese.

The crowds in the cheap section of the market are worse than anywhere else. People shove through with shopping baskets, crushing feet, while the street lamps become roundabouts in the flow of pedestrians, and when it rains, the earth at the base of tree trunks turns into a lake of trampled mud.

Surprisingly, though, it is quite easy to get served, even in this chaos. You just have to be assertive *à la parisienne.** At fruit or vegetable stalls, you fill a plastic bag with cherries, bananas or tomatoes and then hold out the bag at the end of your arm, waving it under the seller's nose. Eventually, he will weigh it and ask for the money. Fish, cheese and chicken sellers have more organized queues, while smaller stalls may have no one waiting.

The fringe of the market is fascinating, too. There are always some semi-legal stalls selling books, socks, flowers and more herbs, and the street is lined with the traders' vans, all of them covered in graffiti. The clever traders get a tagger to paint every square centimetre of their van, so at least it looks tidier than the ones that are spider's-webbed with scrawly, illegible signatures and *arrondissement* numbers.

By 2 p.m., the market is winding down but the activity is still frenetic – now, green-suited cleaners are spraying the ground, shovelling cardboard boxes into a giant crusher and stacking wooden crates for collection. Poor people will be picking through the mounds of discarded food for fishtails, chicken feet, bruised pears, snapped and browned celery, or a tray of strawberries already turning into Roquefort.

For six or seven hours, twice a week, it is pure *Ventre de Paris*,

* For hints on surviving in Parisian queues, see Chapter 1.

just as Zola described it. And the best thing, surely, is that on market days, the streets of this poor neighbourhood are invaded by an army of people pulling home their shopping trolleys, crammed with fresh fish and seasonal fruit and veg. It's easy to imagine the scene in their households on market day – a bored teenager gets up from the couch, wanders into the kitchen and rummages through the food cupboards.

'Mum,' he or she moans, 'why haven't we got any Pringles?'

To which the mother replies, 'Shut up and eat an orange.'

No wonder they stay slim.

'Bacteria aren't dangerous'

It can be unnerving to watch all the food-fondling that goes on at a market, even more so to walk past a closed restaurant early in the morning and see boxes of lettuces, sacks of potatoes and trays of tomatoes sitting on the doorstep, left there by a delivery man who couldn't wait for the *restaurateur* to turn up. Surely, you think, the veg is going to need an extra scrub to make sure it is free of all the dirt that can come its way while it is lying in such a vulnerable place? And even then, would it really be a good idea to eat it?

To get an official view of the dangers of contamination from passing dogs, rats and inconsiderate humans, I went to visit Professor Gilles Brücker, just before he retired from his post as director of the Institut de Veille Sanitaire, France's health-monitoring institute. His role, he told me, was to tell the government how dangerous a particular flu virus might be, or outline the measures necessary to combat an outbreak of Legionnaire's disease, and keep tabs on the general state of the nation's health. A very healthy-looking doctor, he seemed totally at ease with the state of Parisian hygiene. As soon as I began to question Paris's hands-on relationship with food, he flew to its defence.

'You've got to get out of this phobia about touching food,' he said. 'People say that everything we touch is contaminated, and that everything that is contaminated is dangerous, but it's just not true.'

I had always thought that 'contaminated' was a slightly negative quality in food, but apparently not. Surely, I asked, he wasn't suggesting that bugs like e-coli and salmonella might be good for the human body?

'Of course not,' he said, 'but they are extreme cases. There are plenty of other types of bacteria that are not dangerous.'

'So it's OK to touch food and pass on bacteria that we might have on our fingers?'

'In some cases, yes. Cohabiting with bacteria is absolutely indispensable. The diversity of life is a fundamental part of our survival.'

I tried to explain my own reservations about the diversity of life that might end up on a baguette after it had been fondled by a *boulangère* who just touched a coin that someone had picked up out of the gutter. He conceded that this might not always be very hygienic, but was scornful of the idea that it was always dangerous.

'In many cases,' he said, 'touching a baguette like that would just be a perfectly acceptable exchange of everyday bacteria.'

So it's official. The body needs bacteria to survive, and Paris is a good place to come and stock up after living far too long in a sterile, plastic-bag and rubber-glove environment.

Little did I know that I was destined to put this theory to the test.

Give us this day our daily baguette

The baguette is far more than a vector for germ exchanges. It is also the most sensual, and most publicly fondled, Parisian food. An

'Just going to buy some nice pigs' feet for dinner.' This photo was taken outside a Parisian *charcuterie* back in 1970, but today only the headscarf would be different.

obvious phallic symbol, surely it can be no coincidence that the word is just one letter away from *braguette*, the flies on a pair of trousers.

The baguette is also a good indicator of a restaurant or café's quality of food.* If they serve up baskets of fresh baguette with the meals, it's an excellent sign – it means they probably use the nearest *boulangerie*, and go to fetch fresh bread whenever they run out. Personally, I snub restaurants that use mini-baguette rolls, which are almost certainly bought in bulk and always seem to be under-cooked. They're often stingily served, too, and you're lucky if you get a refill after your first ration of one roll per diner. No, the best eating places bring a basket of freshly sliced baguette to your table when your food is served, and will refill it on demand, or even spontaneously – for free, of course.

If I am sounding like something of a baguette nerd, it's because I am – officially. In March 2010, after more than a decade and a half of living in Paris, I was granted the honour of being a judge in the Grand Prix de la Baguette de Paris. (No, this is not a bread race – it means, literally, the grand prize for the Parisian baguette.) I had been selected to choose the city's best bread.

When I first received the letter from the Hôtel de Ville, I thought it must be a cruel joke. I assumed that only bakers and chefs were worthy of such an honour, or at the very least native-born Parisians. Aren't Oscars voted for by movie people, and isn't the manager of the French football team always a Frenchman?

I was convinced that a friend of mine had got hold of some headed notepaper and was having a laugh, especially because I knew that the result of the competition could have a profound impact on the nation's politics. As well as a cash prize and sackloads of publicity, the winner gets a year's contract to supply bread to the Élysée, the presidential palace. It seemed incredible that Paris would

---

* For more ways of spotting a good and bad restaurant, see later in this chapter.

entrust the task of deciding what the head of state ate for breakfast to a British writer whose website was at that very minute trumpeting the arrival of his new book called *1,000 Years of Annoying the French*.

But then an email came through from the office of Madame Cohen-Solal, the Deputy Mayor in charge of Commerce, Craftmanship, Self-Employed Professions and Art Trades, confirming the invitation. Apparently, someone in the department had read my books and had decided that I might know something about baguettes.

And, in fact, baguettes do loom large in at least two of my books that have been translated into French. In *A Year in the Merde*, there's a passage, often quoted to me by French journalists, about a visit to the *boulangerie*, which the hero Paul West describes as the only place in the world where the French will form an orderly queue (he's not quite right, but then he's only just arrived in the city). And in *Talk to the Snail*, I trace the pilgrimage of the baguette from boulangerie to restaurant table, noting every stage along the route where it is squeezed, sniffed and exposed to bacteria before entering the unsuspecting oesophagus of the Parisian diner.

In any case, I accepted the challenge *avec plaisir*, and I'm very glad I did, because it turned out to be one of the most Parisian experiences I have ever had.

Judging was to take place at the Chambre Professionnelle des Artisans Boulangers-Pâtissiers (an *artisan* being a 'craftsman') on the Île de la Cité, the part of Paris that has been inhabited since before Roman times, and presumably where the city's first loaves were ever cooked. The building houses grand but rather rundown offices, including, on the first floor, a banqueting hall the shape of a slice of *tarte aux pommes* – a long triangle, panelled in wood the colour of a well-cooked baguette crust. From the wall hangs a breadmaker's version of the tricolour, featuring an olive branch (make bread not war?), a pretzel and two baker's oars – the wooden paddles used to remove loaves from the oven.

The fifteen judges, most of them bakers or City Hall officials, sat at three long tables, one along each side of the triangle. I was between two bakers, both of them floury-fingered thirty-somethings, and one of them a previous winner of the prize.

'So have you delivered bread to the Élysée every morning for a year?' I asked him.

'*Oui,* twenty baguettes a day.'

His shop was in the 15th, the south of Paris – quite a hike across town to the 8th during rush hour, I sympathized.

'Oh, they wanted me to deliver it at eight every morning,' he said, 'but I said I couldn't get there before ten.' Even the President had no authority over a Parisian baker, it seemed.

'And did you ever see Sarko or Carla Bruni eating one of your baguettes?'

'Never even got invited in,' he grumped.

'Still, a great competition to win,' I said.

'Yes, my turnover went up 15 per cent because of it.'

Definitely a prize worth having, then, which might explain the incredibly strict entry requirements. Entrants had to be owners or employees of a Paris baker's shop listed in the city's business register, and their baguettes had to conform to the criteria laid out in decree number 93-1074 of 13 September 1993, which (in case you don't know it) specifies that a baguette must be between 55 and 65 centimetres long and weigh 250–350 grams.

Consequently, twenty-two of the entrants were immediately eliminated from the judging, thirteen of them for being oversized. I pleaded for the big ones to be retained – after all, who's going to complain about receiving too much bread for their money? This, though, was shouted down as a typically Anglo-Saxon obsession with quantity over quality. And rules were rules.

So far, so methodical, but anarchy quickly kicked in. Like most Parisian meetings I have attended, the theoretical agenda didn't turn out to be the actual one. First, a baker who had come along to be a judge wasn't on the list, and began complaining that he would have entered the competition if he'd known he wasn't going to be on the jury panel. He was given some judging forms and allowed to start tasting (rules are rules, unless someone French complains).

The main source of typically Parisian chaos, however, was the hygiene, or total lack of it. The waiting baguettes, all laid out as naked as a Saint-Tropez sunbather except for the ring of paper bearing their number, were heaped up on a table at one end of the room, in a tasty-looking logpile. When the judging began, the loaves were gathered up in batches of five (by bare-handed helpers) and taken to the tasting tables, where they were sliced, fondled, sniffed and chewed by the judges, all of whom had shaken hands before the competition began just to make sure that any bacteria picked up in the *métro* or on a door handle had been shared out evenly. During the whole judging process, no one wore gloves or used napkins. It was the food-hygiene equivalent of an unprotected orgy. At one point, a TV cameraman accidentally swept a batch of baguettes on to the floor. They were simply picked up and replaced on the table.

After my initial shock, however, I realized that this was the only way to get the authentic taste of a Parisian baguette. If the bread hasn't been through the bacterial obstacle course, it won't have that truly Parisian tang. The loaf must bear traces of deodorant, as if it had been hurriedly transported from *boulangerie* to café under a waiter's arm or clutched to his chest. It also has to have other people's fingermarks on it, because, realistically, before the bread is eaten it will probably have been squeezed by the baker, the shop assistant, at least one waiter or waitress and, if it has been served up and not eaten by one tableload of diners, it will have been re-served to a second table, possibly being tested for size and freshness by a few picky eaters along the way.

In short, we were road-testing these baguettes in real-life

conditions rather than giving them a sterile laboratory test. The winning loaf was going to be a worthy champion, fully capable of standing up to anything the city could throw at it.

And in the end, we all survived the bacterial onslaught and chose a winner – number 86, who turned out to be an immigrant from Senegal now working in Montmartre, in a *boulangerie* called the Grenier à Pain (the bread attic) in the rue des Abbesses. The food professionals approved – they knew him and his work, and were pleased with the choice. Even a foreign novice like myself hadn't distorted the vote.

Over the next couple of days, I waited anxiously to see whether I would come out in boils or collapse from a gluten overdose (try chewing on more than fifty hunks of baguette in an afternoon and see what it feels like), but nothing happened. And then I realized – the organizers had no doubt chosen me because I'd been in the city long enough for my immune system to have become acclimatized. Anything less than fifteen years and the competition would probably have been fatal.

Visitors to the city should not be worried, though. Exposure to small quantities of café-basket baguette over a short period of time is probably not dangerous, especially if they are consumed with a cleansing glass of wine.

Follow your nose

There are hundreds of guidebooks and websites recommending eating places, but often the best way to make sure of getting a great Parisian food experience is – and apologies for the pun – to trust your gut feeling. Aided, of course by your senses, and a little local knowledge.

It's also useful to have a few yardsticks by which to judge

Parisian eating places, which is what this section is going to be about.

I shall be confining myself to French restaurants – I'm presuming that visitors to the city rarely come here to eat Japanese or Indian food.* Of course, what we foreigners call a 'French restaurant' is just a plain restaurant to Parisians, although they do specify when a restaurant is regional. The most common regional cuisines available in Paris are Corsican, which is peasant food with an almost grudging touch of Mediterranean lightness; Auvergnat, which is a waistline-busting mix of meat, sauce and absurd quantity; and Alsatian, which has nothing to do with eating dogs. Alsatian food – *choucroute* (sauerkraut) and pork dishes – is common in brasseries, because a brasserie† is a large café that used to brew its own beer, and Alsace is a big brewing area.

Like most Parisians, when I go out to eat in the evenings, it's usually to a non-French place. If I eat out at lunchtime, on the other hand, I usually go to a French café. As anyone who has been to Paris will have seen, there is one of these approximately every 10 metres in every shopping street, so it can be difficult to choose. Living in Paris, however, I have the time to indulge in a lot of trial and error.

To test a café, I use my own personal yardstick, based on a dish that I first discovered when I came to work in Paris, and which has now become my lunchtime staple. It is *la salade de chèvre chaud*, or *le chèvre chaud* as the locals call it for short. Occasionally it's hidden behind a name like *salade bergère* (shepherdess' salad or, more correctly perhaps, goatherdess' salad), but a quick scan of any

* Though I might add here that most Japanese restaurants in Paris are run by Chinese, and that Parisians don't know enough about Indian cuisine to force the standard up. For authentic Japanese food go to the rue Saint-Anne, near the Palais-Royal, and for great Indian and Sri Lankan, between Gare du Nord and La Chapelle.
† On the subject of definitions, *bistro* is a general word usually used to mean a small café or cheap restaurant. And the difference between a café and a restaurant is the same as anywhere else – a restaurant is a place where you go for a meal rather than just a drink.

menu's *Salades* or *Entrées* section for the word *chèvre* will reveal it.

If there is no *chèvre chaud*, the café immediately goes down in my estimation, because it implies a certain laziness on the chef's part. There are, you see, several key elements to a successful *chèvre chaud* that take a lot of skill and judgement to get just right. It's a challenge, but a worthwhile one.

First, of course, the chef has to choose the goat's cheese, which comes in a baffling array of varieties. There is the log, with or without a Camembert-style white skin, and varying in diameter from about 3 centimetres to 5. There is the Rocamadour, a small yellowish disc, which is rare in Paris but very tasty. There's also the *chèvre* fritter, a pre-prepared breadcrumb-coated pat of cheese that, for me, is an abomination as scandalous as the screw-top wine bottle or the electronic drum machine – it's just not the real thing. And then there is the Renault Espace of *chèvres*, the Crottin de Chavignol. Literally, *crottin* means turd, but this should not put you off, because it neither looks nor tastes like one. It is a 3- or 4-centimetre-high round pat of cheese, shaped rather like a marshmallow, with, ideally, a slightly yellow skin and whiter flesh. It will vary in hardness according to its ripeness, but is usually pretty soft when cooked.

For the perfect *chèvre chaud*, one of these cheeses should be cut into slices about a centimetre thick and melted (though not entirely – the slices should keep their shape) on to toasted bread. Here again, there is a frighteningly large scope for cooking abuse. All too often, the bread will be industrial squares of under-baked white loaf – yes, even in France this exists. It's called *pain de mie* and sometimes it doesn't even have any crusts, so its sogginess beneath a thick slice of *chèvre* is easy to imagine. Occasionally you will be offered toasted baguette, which is OK when well grilled, but too often undercooked – the sign of a rushed kitchen. Ideally, I find, the cheese should be on a slice of *pain au levain* – an old-fashioned, dark-floured loaf – or *pain Poîlane*, a well-known brand of crusty, *levain*-type bread.

The key thing is that the bread and cheese should be grilled *together*. Sometimes, a piece of raw cheese may be put on pre-grilled bread and quickly heated – a clumsy clash of textures. Worst of all, a pre-prepared slice of bread and melted cheese will be put in the microwave, so that the whole thing will come out as floppy as – well, we all know what shouldn't be floppy.

There are various schools of thought on whether to add herbs on top, or honey. Personally, I'm a purist. Forget the kinky stuff, and give it to me naked – let the bread and cheese breathe.

Even once a careful chef has got the ingredients and the cooking right, there's the quantity to consider. How many slices of goat's cheese should be on each various-sized piece of bread? And how many pieces of bread will be riding on top of the salad? Anything under three slices of goat's cheese and you're being down-chèvred, I feel, unless it's advertised as *tartine de chèvre*, which is, in fairness, just a piece of bread and cheese.

Then there is the salad itself to be considered. This doesn't apply only to *chèvre chaud*, of course. Has the chef settled for a straightforward heap of lettuce? Or do you get a variety of leaves, and maybe even cherry tomatoes, walnuts, pine nuts, and pieces of fresh apple? It's a real test of the café's generosity and imagination.

And finally there's the dressing. One look at a chef's salad dressing says volumes about him or her. A few well-defined squirts of sweetish, yellowish liquid means it's probably out of a bottle. Some chefs do mix their own dressings and put them in a plastic container for ease of use, but nothing looks quite like one of those homogenized, starched, monosodium-glutamated supermarket vinaigrettes, and if you get the slightest whiff of an industrial dressing, it's probably safest to rip the café out of your guide book (perhaps after checking that there's nothing useful on the other side of the page).

If, on the other hand, you're given a homemade dressing,

personally I'm happy with anything tangy, especially if I can taste real olive oil. Though I'm not convinced that balsamic goes very well with *chèvre chaud*. It tends to dominate too much.

All of which is a very detailed, highly personal way of saying that one dish that you enjoy can tell you everything you need to know about the chef and his or her menu. A café that gets your favourite dish right will probably make a good job of everything else, too. So if you have time for trial and error, it's the most reliable way of picking your regular eating-place while you're in Paris.

It's also a good idea to try and take a look at the chef. In many cafés, the kitchen opens out into the bar, so you can watch the cook at work. This can be very revealing. Take a look at the menu written on the blackboard and then compare it to what's going on in the kitchen. Is the chef cutting up cheese for the *quiche au bleu*? Slicing potatoes for the *gratin dauphinois*? In this way, even in a simple-looking corner café, you will often see proof that the food is going to be fresh and cooked by a pro.

In one café where I sometimes arrange morning meetings, the chef is on permanent show, constantly chopping, grating and mixing in his tiny kitchen. And even though this is a modest lunch place for people working in nearby supermarkets and a pensions office, the chef is always dressed in a white jacket and pale-blue checked trousers, and makes almost everything by hand. He is also a highly choosy buyer.

One morning, I was standing at the bar having a coffee when the butcher's rep came in with the monthly bill. The two men said their *bonjours* and then embarked on a detailed conversation about meat-carving. The chef was complaining,

'*Le rosbif, le rosbif*, why can they never cut it right? Look.' They went into the kitchen and the chef took a tray of red meat out of one of his fridges and showed it to the rep. They stared and commented, and I overheard the chef ending the conversation with 'that's not how my *grand-mère* used to cut it'. No pre-packed, pre-cooked, reheated food in this place, that's for sure.

On another day, I watched the same chef grabbing a handful of red jelly from a pot, melting it in a *bain marie*, and then slowly painting it over a couple of dozen freshly prepared strawberry tarts. Anywhere else, he might have been adding the final touch to some pre-prepared desserts. But here, his assistant was ladling *crème pâtissière* into pastry bases to make the next batch, while a bowlful of glistening fresh strawberries was waiting to be set on top.

And this, remember, is a simple neighbourhood café on a not-very-rich street corner in unfashionable northern Paris. You don't have to go to famous addresses or obey your guidebook to find good food. Often, it's just as easy to follow your nose.

Menu for success

Leaving out the more obvious considerations such as 'Do I like the feel of the place?' and 'How does the food look on the plates of people eating there?' here are a few more ways of spotting a good and bad Parisian eating-place:

- Is there a waiter or waitress standing outside, hustling for custom? Bad sign. In any decent café or restaurant, all the waiting staff are busy serving customers.
- How many people are impatiently waiting for their food? A full restaurant can be a good sign, of course, but if there are more people waiting than eating, the place may only be full because it's trendy, and not because of the quality of the food and service.
- At lunchtimes, does the restaurant look as though it is catering for groups of Parisian colleagues? If so, this is a huge plus point. The general standard of lunchtime cafés and restaurants is

An empty café terrace, a tempting sight. But ask yourself – why is it empty? Similarly, if it's full, take a look at the customers: are they munching merrily, or gazing around in desperation, hoping to spot a waiter? Choosing the right place to eat is a tricky business, which, happily, is explained in this chapter.

far higher in office districts because the chefs have to keep workers happy five or six days a week. (In the evening, though, when the demanding workers have gone home, the same café might bring in a less experienced chef, so beware.)

- Take a careful look at the menu, which by law must be on display outside the restaurant. Is it translated into several languages? Almost certainly a bad sign. Parisians are inherently snobbish and don't respect the taste – gastronomic or otherwise – of foreigners, so an establishment that caters mainly for tourists won't make as much of an effort. As in other countries, a restaurant that offers no linguistic help to foreigners can actually be the best place for foreigners to eat.

- Does the menu have a handwritten *plat du jour*, either on a Post-It or a blackboard? It should. A short menu with a *plat du jour* is far better than a long, varied menu without, because the ingredients will have been bought in specially.

- In the *Poissons* section of the menu, is there a fish other than salmon? If not, the chef is mechanically ordering in salmon rather than dipping into the veritable shoals of fresh fish that flow into Paris. Despite its distance from the sea, it has one of the best fish markets in Europe. Sometimes, chefs will propose a *duo de poissons* – two fish in the same dish. Again, if one of these is salmon it's not a great sign.

All of the above may sound very picky, but if you're in Paris for a weekend, you may only have time for three or four meals at a restaurant. And in a city so obsessed with good food, and so full of it, there's really no reason to eat badly.

And so *bon appétit*, which, by the way, is pronounced without the final 't' – it's 'bonapay-TEE'. A snooty Parisian once told me that it is considered slightly vulgar to say this before eating, as though there were some absurd risk that you might *not* eat well in France. But most Parisians seem happy to say it, and it would be churlish not to do likewise, a bit like not saying *bonjour* because you're bound to have a wonderful day in Paris.

Though the above-mentioned snooty Parisian was partially right – if you avoid the obvious tourist traps and *über*-trendy places where people go to be seen rather than eat, it is fairly difficult to eat badly here, and easy to eat wonderfully well without risking bankruptcy.

Worth his weight in chintz. Englishman Charles Worth (1825–95) came to Paris and invented *haute couture*. And amazingly, Parisians acknowledge their debt to him.

9

FASHION

La mode domine les Provinciales, mais les Parisiennes dominent la mode.
(Fashion dominates Provincial women, but *Parisiennes* dominate fashion.)

JEAN-JACQUES ROUSSEAU, EIGHTEENTH-CENTURY
WRITER AND PHILOSOPHER

EVERYONE COMES to Paris hoping to witness first-hand the elegance for which Parisians (and especially *Parisiennes*) are famous. This, though, can lead to disappointment. I often see tourists wandering along the boulevard Saint-Germain thinking, Why are so many men dressed in jeans and sports-brand T-shirts, just like they are at home? And those women in cargo pants and plain blouses – can they really be *Parisiennes*?

Well, yes, they are. The sobering fact is that Paris is a fully paid-up member of the global brand conspiracy. Most Parisians wear clothes that could be bought in any shopping mall in the Western world. Even the trendy cultural elite is singularly lacking in creativity. I recently went to a gallery opening in the Marais and thought someone had turned the lights out. Literally everyone in the fifty-strong crowd was wearing black. Fashion itself seemed to have become the victim.

You do, of course, see some very classy, elegant people

walking about the place, but their elegance will probably have a lot to do with the way they wear their clothes, whatever the brand. You might also spot girls who look like models. That's because they *are* models – seven-foot-tall female stick insects, their portfolios under one arm and their ears bunged up with headphones to block out comments from passing men. These are the wannabes, pounding the streets from audition to audition, drawn to Paris in the same way as actors flock to LA or zebras to a crocodile-infested waterhole.

Because despite all the globalization in its shopping streets, Paris is still a *capitale de la mode*, and home to most of the top surviving *haute couture* houses. And it's not only the models who come here wanting a slice of this fashion cake. A large proportion of visitors to the city are willing to spend a small fortune to take home something with a genuine Parisian brand stamped, sewn, engraved or welded on to it. They could just as easily buy it online, but only in Paris can they experience the thrill of going to *the* shop, founded perhaps by *the* creator of the brand, and staffed by people so beautiful that it is almost sexually exciting to be mistreated by them.

The most intense clothes-related sado-masochism goes on in a part of Paris called the *triangle d'or* (golden triangle), a section of the 8th *arrondissement* just to the southwest of the Champs-Élysées. Here, along the tree-lined avenue Montaigne, French fashion houses like Dior (at no. 30), Nina Ricci (no. 39), Chanel (no. 42 – presumably numbers 5 and 19 were already taken), and Chloé (no. 44) have their showcase Paris stores, housed in some *très chic* apartment buildings. Casually littering the street, double or triple-parked, there are often Ferraris or top-range 4WDs, apparently abandoned or strategically positioned as decor to heighten the ambiance of luxury (though in fact these have usually been left this way by provocative valet parkers).

The fashion stores themselves are often set back slightly from the pavement, as if to give shoppers a chance to stop and take in some oxygen after the shock of reading the numbers on the credit-card machine – and, of course, to recover from the breathless thrill of taking part in Paris's permanent fashion show.

The experience is similar over on the other side of the Champs-Élysées, near Concorde. The same brands and more sit nose-to-tail along the much narrower rue du Faubourg Saint-Honoré, which offers Paris's best chance of being bundled off the pavement by a sublimely dressed and coiffed *Parisienne* rushing to find a taxi after buying the perfect shoes for her lunch date. Here, the atmosphere of luxury is heightened not by valet parking but by limos ferrying diplomats and politicians to and from embassies and the Élysée Palace down the street.

Yes, Paris's fashion industry is at the heart of the city's establishment, as it has always been . . .

Kings and queens of the fashion world

It is often said these days that most of us live under a kind of fashion tyranny, dressing as the magazines order us to, or the department stores allow us to. But it wasn't much different in centuries past, when anyone who could afford it had to emulate their rulers or be excluded from high society.

This was especially true during the reign of Louis XIV (1643–1715), who believed almost literally that the sun shone out of his royal posterior, and wanted everything that clothed it to be suitably divine. He therefore summoned the best tailors from all over Europe to his court to make baroque outfits for him and his nobles. Lace and ribbon-covered culottes, shoes decorated with roses, bouffant blouses, pheasant-feather hats – and that was just the men. Women wore tight corsets, low-cut dresses, and trains that got longer as the lady rose up the social ladder (which she often did by taking all her clothes off).

The magnificence of this non-stop preening influenced not only the rest of France, but most of Europe, except those countries under the yolk of Puritanism, of course, where the merest buckle was regarded as a temptation sent by Satan.

Although Louis and his successors managed to bankrupt France with their unsuccessful wars and botched colonialism, Paris hung on to its luxury tailoring industry, and the city became a popular shopping spot for European aristocrats. Anyone with some money to spend could find a tailor capable of making an outfit that would be the talk of the town back home.

All this could have been called Parisian *haute couture*, but it took an Englishman to pin the concept down and turn the tailor from a craftsman indulging the whims of the noble customer into the tyrant of taste that is today's *styliste*.

Worth his weight in chintz

Charles Worth was born in Lincolnshire in 1825 and went to London as a teenager to become an apprentice draper (a merchant selling cloth and sewing materials). He apparently spent most of his time bookkeeping, but developed a passion for dress design. So when his apprenticeship finished, he immediately left for Paris to work for a textile merchant who also sold ready-made clothing. Here, Worth began to make dresses that won prizes at London's Great Exhibition of 1851 and the 1855 Paris Exposition Universelle. Soon, he had enough private customers to set up a company of his own in the rue de la Paix, a new, chic street built on the site of a monastery that had been demolished after the Revolution.

It was at this point, in 1858, that Worth created the business model that made Paris the fashion capital it is today, and he did this by introducing three revolutionary concepts.

First, by his sheer self-confidence and by sewing in labels saying 'Worth, 7 rue de la Paix', he convinced everyone that his dresses were not just clothing but works of art. Secondly, he showed potential customers how magnificent they could look by modelling the dresses on real women rather than simply draping his creations over a tailor's dummy. And thirdly, he held fashion shows, dictating to women what they would be wearing the following season.

This was not yet a democratization of fashion – the dresses were handmade and richly decorated, and would be individually tailored to fit the rich *clientes*. But Worth got the royals to come to him rather than vice-versa. First Princess Metternich, wife of the Austrian Ambassador, began patronizing his shop, closely followed by her friend the Empress Eugénie, wife of Napoleon III. Soon, the rue de la Paix shop was turning clients away, and its reputation was sealed.

In 1868, Worth was instrumental in the creation of the Chambre Syndicale de la Haute Couture Parisienne, and as we all know, once a French *syndicat* (union) gets involved, nothing will ever change again. Which is why all the Parisian *haute couture* houses, from Chanel to Dior to Yves Saint Laurent and beyond, have followed the same basic model – create a look, imbue it with Parisian exclusivity, and make people worship you.

In short, Charles Worth invented not only *haute couture* but the whole concept of luxury branding, which has been as much a part of Paris's appeal for the last century as the legs of its Eiffel Tower and those of its can-can dancers.

France has a habit of denying foreigners credit for things they wish they had invented themselves, like the guillotine and the baguette.* Charles Worth, though, is an exception. Today, Paris's *haute couture* industry is completely open about its debt to this Englishman. The highly prestigious École de la Chambre Syndicale

---

* For more details see my book *1,000 Years of Annoying the French*.

de la Couture Parisienne, where big names like André Courrèges, Jean-Louis Scherrer and Yves Saint Laurent studied, runs a history course entitled *La Mode depuis Worth* (fashion since Worth). Not 'since Louis XIV' or even 'since Chanel' – since Worth. Quite an accolade.

The only stain on this shimmering cloak of honour is one that Parisians have made by accident. They find it very difficult to say 'th', and can't believe that a word with 'or' in the middle should rhyme with *fleur*. They therefore have a nasty habit of mis-pronouncing the name of their English benefactor as 'wart'.

Ich bin un Parisien

These days, Parisian fashion is schizophrenic. On the one hand, brands like Chanel, Dior, Chloé, Louis Vuitton and Givenchy are seen as the ultimate in Parisian chic. On the other, they all hire, or have hired, foreigners to create or nurture this Parisianitude – big names like Karl Lagerfeld, John Galliano, Stella McCartney, Marc Jacobs and the late Alexander McQueen.

Granted, England brings in foreign managers to train its football team, but that is precisely to get them playing like stylish foreigners rather than clodhopping Englishmen. Surely handing the image of a Parisian fashion house over to a foreign designer is like a top sushi restaurant recruiting a Belgian chef?

Well, yes and no. Take Karl Lagerfeld, for example, *directeur artistique* for Chanel, the Parisian fashion brand *par excellence*. He was born Karl Otto Lagerfeldt in Hamburg, and speaks French with an almost comedy German accent, popping up in the media like some modern incarnation of a Prussian envoy to the court of Louis XIV. How, you might justifiably ask, could he possibly represent – embody, even – Chanel, which he has done almost continuously since 1982? Well, for a start, behind that accent lurks a grammatically impeccable and very witty French. Secondly, in his black-and-white formal outfits, with their touches of silver, he seems to have adopted classical elegance as his everyday lifestyle. And thirdly, for all his eccentricities, Lagerfeld is a consummate professional. Since his arrival on the Paris scene in 1959, he has been artistic director of several fashion houses, and is credited with salvaging two of them – Chloé and Chanel – from an imminent slide into obscurity. Under his directorship, Chloé became *the* chic brand of the mid-'60s, and was seen hugging the figures of Jackie Onassis, Brigitte Bardot and Grace Kelly, aka Princess of Monaco.

To achieve this, Karl did much more than bring a German touch to French *couture* – which was, in fact, the last thing the French brands were looking for. They wanted a designer who would make their clothes look even more Parisian, and his or her nationality was a secondary consideration.

Grafting foreign talent on to Paris fashion is a complex process that was explained to me by Susan Oubari, a Paris-based Californian who works as a go-between for American buyers and Parisian fashion houses, especially during the twice-yearly rush of Fashion Week. 'It doesn't matter what nationality they are,' Susan told me. 'If a foreign designer, or any designer, is to be a success, they have to be able to work within the structure of the company. They need to get on with the boss, who will be a pure businessman, work with the creative people, and keep the financial department happy. They might be forced to compromise on some of their designs, or make way-out designs fit a very down-to-earth budget.'

And these Anglo-German designers don't get hired just because the French think they will be more realistic about the business side of things, either. 'The important thing,' Susan emphasized to me, 'is for the designer to be able to go into the archives, and mix the old with the new. They have to study old collections, understand what the brand is about, and look at the reasons for its past success.'

German designer Karl Lagerfeld may look like an action doll and talk like a
Prussian Duke, but he is the essence of Paris fashion, known by the French as
'le Kaiser de la mode'.

It's rather like taking a classic car and designing a model that today's drivers will want. The new model can't turn its back on the past – it has to capitalize on it. Lagerfeld's Chanel designs are therefore not pure Lagerfeld, they're carefully crafted *über*-Chanel.

And the traffic isn't all one-way. The fashion house, and Paris itself, leave their mark on the designer. Karl Lagerfeld, the longest-serving of the big-name foreign designers in Paris, has been turned into a French institution. He was invited to design a coin to celebrate the centenary of Coco Chanel's birth, he has appeared on a special-edition French Diet Coke bottle, and he has even been awarded the Légion d'Honneur, which as the award's statutes put it, is usually given to those who have shown twenty-five years of 'eminent merit in the service of the Nation'. In short, the fashion industry has made sure that the German designer has become woven into the fabric of Parisian life.

Creating *le buzz*

The head *styliste* at a top Parisian fashion house has to do more than create saleable clothing – he or she has to generate a buzz, and, again, the fashion house doesn't care if this is a German, American or British buzz. The only important thing is for the brand name to be in the magazines and on the celebs' backs and backsides. This is why people with their own strong image, like Lagerfeld and the eccentric Galliano, or a famous name, like Stella McCartney, are perfect. In any case, the world of Parisian fashion may all look very refined and elegant, but it is governed by hard-nosed commercial thinking of a type few would associate with France, supposedly the capital of bad service and work-shy workers.

The hardest work of all goes on behind the scenes during Fashion Week. The shows themselves don't really have that much of an impact on ordinary Parisians – a few trendy restaurants are suddenly fuller than usual of thin people with designer sunglasses and ever-active iPhones, TV newsreaders will raise an amused eyebrow while introducing a few seconds of models gangling along catwalks, and occasionally a public space like the Gare de l'Est forecourt will be partly cordoned off so that models can prance up and down without bumping into commuters.

However, the important thing is that even someone like me, who can't conceive how a handbag can possibly cost more than 50 euros, is aware of Paris Fashion Week. And this is thanks to some very un-Parisian backroom work by the industry. Susan Oubari explained the mechanics:

'Before the week begins, a Parisian brand will bring in experienced sales people to cater for each different set of buyers. Americans will be hired to sell the collection to Americans, Italians for Italians, and so on. They will see a presentation given by the marketing people about the concept behind the collection, the techniques and materials used, and how to sell it into different markets. These sales people will then go away and prepare their pitches to the buyers who will – hopefully, if the catwalk show itself goes well – come to the showrooms.'

The danger is, of course, that the sellers might live up, or down, to everyone's preconception about French service – this being the total failure to notice that someone wants serving, and/or the shrug of indifference if the customer complains. But Susan assured me that the welcome given to potential fashion buyers bears no resemblance to the reception she got the first – and last – time she dared to order a coffee while sitting at a Parisian café table laid for lunch: 'People from the fashion house will be on hand to welcome the buyers, in English or whatever language it takes. They'll ask about their hotel, recommend restaurants and parties, all the while gauging reactions to the clothes. The French want to make sure that all the international buyers get a magical Paris experience, so that they'll come back again. It's not what we imagine about France at all.'

Furthermore, like movie directors, the fashion shows will use the Opéra, the Grand Palais, the Tuileries, the Louvre, all the big monuments, getting the city to sell their clothes for them. All of which points to the conclusion that Paris's fashion houses are discreetly undermining some key myths about the city. They're proving that the Parisian artistic establishment does not have to be elitist and set in its ways. When necessary, Paris can treat its culture simultaneously as art – to be swooned over – and as a business – to be ruthlessly sold.

And they're also showing that French customer service can be as good as any in the world.* But only when it really wants to be, of course.

Paris libéré

Being a Parisian fashion designer has to be a bit like singing opera at La Scala or surfing in Hawaii. You are where it's at. You have, as the French would say, arrived. To find out how this feels, I talked to Marie-Christine Frison, a *Strasbourgeoise* who started her career designing handbags and accessories for Nina Ricci, and who now co-runs her own fashion company, AD&MCF.

As well as designing for other clients, Marie-Christine and her partner have their own brand, Bandits Manchots ('one-armed bandits'), for which they are currently developing a line of postcards made of leather. Marie-Christine got the idea from seeing rolls of unused cowskin after the launch of a collection of chic handbags. It

---

* This is something I have long said. See my book *Talk to the Snail* for an explanation of how it's often the customers who are to blame for bad service.

was top-quality material, dyed in beautiful colours, that was destined for the dustbin or the incinerator because the fashion house wasn't going to use it once the season was over. Bandits Manchots bought the leather and had it cut into postcard-sized rectangles, on to which they have printed messages and tattoo-like motifs. To me, it seemed a very Parisian idea – taking a seemingly down-market concept like a postcard and raising the tone a notch. The kind of thing Jean-Paul Gaultier introduced into French fashion in the '80s, and that Karl Lagerfeld is continuing with schemes like his limited-edition Diet Coke bottle.

I put the point to Marie-Christine as we sit in a café in the 9th *arrondissement* that, perhaps like her postcards, is trying its best not to look too chic, and looking all the more chic for doing so.

'I never thought of it as a Parisian idea,' she says. 'I never try to be Parisian.'

'But when you started at Nina Ricci, didn't they tell you that they wanted your designs to be Parisian?'

'No. They expected the designs to reflect the spirit of the brand, with a soft, romantic feel. And my job was simply to take the art director's wishes and make them reality. No one talked about being Parisian. Sorry, this isn't helping you at all, is it?'

'Yes, of course it is,' I lie, being as courteously Parisian as I can. 'But what about when you arrived in Paris, didn't you notice something typically Parisian about the way people looked?'

'Oh yes. But it wasn't because their clothes looked Parisian.'

'No?'

'It was more an impression that they were free. The girls all had a relaxed way of walking, as though they were free to dress the way they wanted. They had the freedom to match very incongruous things, which we couldn't do *en province*. Outside Paris, you continuously have to ask yourself, "Does my shirt go with my trousers?" In Paris, you never ask that. You take a whole bunch of things that shouldn't go together and you wear them together, and that creates a look.'

'A Parisian look?'

'Yes, I suppose it is.'

Pausing only to offer a short prayer of thanks to the gods of fashion in their 8th *arrondissement* temples, I try to push home my advantage.

'So Parisian fashion is based on being unconventional?'

'No.' Marie-Christine shakes her head. 'Parisians are not unconventional at all, because they all go with the group.'

Damn, back to square one.

'A while ago,' she continues, 'some photographers put on an exhibition of pictures of teenage Parisian girls who they had just stopped in the street. And the girls all looked almost exactly the same. They were all holding their bags the same way—' Marie-Christine holds out her arm, crooked at the elbow, the wrist bent, and sags slightly under the weight of a large handbag full of school-books, and I instantly picture the crowds outside *lycées* at going-home time.

'But *en province*, don't girls look like that?' I ask.

'No. They'd love to, but they're too *coincées*.' (Meaning uptight or stuck in their ways.) 'Provincials go to the same shops as the Parisians, the big international brands, but they don't dare pick out very different things and wear them together. Parisians look a lot more relaxed about what they're wearing.'

'So it's got a lot to do with self-confidence, then?'

'Yes, and sophistication. Not in the sense of being elegant, but in the sense of knowing how to buy things that look almost exactly like what everyone else is wearing, but are slightly different, and probably made by the latest hip brand. It's part of their education. They observe, imitate and adapt.'

'So maybe this is the definition of a Parisian look,' I suggest. 'You select what you want from everything that's on offer in Paris –

and there's a hell of a lot on offer – and you make it your own.'

'Yes, but within limits. You can't be a total eccentric like some Londoners. In Paris, there's a kind of general dress code you have to respect. And at least teenagers are a bit creative, unlike the *bobos*.' These are the forty-plus bourgeois Bohemians who don't want to wear business suits. 'The *bobos* all buy exactly the same things from the same shop. They go to L'Éclaireur [a chain of arty lifestyle shops, with a name meaning scout or pioneer] and they buy clothes, candles, furniture, everything. *Bobos* will even have the same air freshener in their toilet. So they'll look laid-back, as if they don't care, but it's all very sophisticated because everything is expensive and it's the latest, trendiest stuff.'

'And is it all French stuff?'

'No, but that doesn't matter in Paris. For example, I pay 300 euros to get my hair cut and dyed—'

I interrupt her with a gasp – not because she has admitted that she's not a natural blonde, but because Parisians never usually reveal the price of anything expensive. It's a sign that we're getting into serious territory.

'I go to a private apartment,' she continues, 'not some place on the street – you have to know where it is. And absolutely *everyone* goes there. It's the hippest place in Paris. And the hairdresser is Australian.'

'*Australian?*' The man whom the hippest *Parisiennes* allow to cut their hair comes from the capital of canned beer, kangaroo poaching and burping?

'Yes, but it doesn't matter. Paris recognizes quality. It takes what is best from everywhere and makes it its own.'

Like Chanel taking Karl Lagerfeld, and Dior taking Galliano. It's what Susan was telling me. It all fits. This, then, seems to be the definition of Parisian style. It's quite simply your choice of the best of everything. The choice will be slightly limited and conventional, but it's the mix of ingredients that counts. It's like a giant French salad bar – you can have what you want, but only if it's in season. There's no danger that anyone will expect Parisians to wear an airline pilot's hat with a tutu and football boots. So they'll always look and feel relaxed. It's a great recipe for success – and anyone can do it.

There's only one more thing I need to know. As a middle-aged Parisian who doesn't want to wear business suits, exactly what fragrance of air freshener should I be using in my toilet?

'Just go to L'Éclaireur,' she tells me, 'and sniff. You can't go wrong.'

Shopping in a country where men wear *slips*

The posh fashion stores in the 8th *arrondissement* will all have sales assistants who speak English, as well as the language of any country that is famous for sending wealthy visitors to Paris. Many cheaper stores in the city centre will also have English-speaking sales staff, especially if they're fresh from school. But even if you're forced to go native, buying clothes doesn't have to be an intimidating linguistic experience. While the French naturally have plenty of their own words for fashion items (*chemise, jupe, pantalon, haut, chaussures, sac à main*, etc.), they also use a fair number of familiar English words.

There are, however, a few grammatical and pronunciation guidelines that must be obeyed:

1. Some clothing words look like English but aren't. These 'false friends' include:
    robe, which is a dress, not a bathrobe
    veste – a jacket

slip – a pair of underpants (male or female) rather than a ladies' underskirt

culotte – a general word for knickers, and not trousers that look like a skirt

blouse – an overall rather a women's shirt (that's *un chemisier*)

cravate – a normal tie, not something worn by Noël Coward

costume – a men's suit rather than fancy dress

tissu, which is fabric and not something you sneeze into (while *matériel* means equipment rather than material)

habit – an item of clothing rather than a routine

baskets – training shoes rather than something to collect strawberries in or throw basketballs at, and

talon – a heel, and nothing to do with an eagle's claws.

2. Other words have been slightly adjusted for French use, and should be treated with caution: *un jean* is a pair of jeans, just as *un short* is a pair of shorts and *un bermuda* is a pair of long shorts. Basically, anything with two leg holes is singular in French. This also explains why *une culotte* is a pair of knickers, and *un caleçon* a pair of boxer shorts. Similarly, *un collant* is a pair of tights, while a pair of stockings, which are not joined at the gusset, is plural – *des bas*.

3. Generally, to be understood, it is necessary to pronounce all relevant English words with as stereotypical a French accent as you can muster, putting the stress on the second syllable as though you were angry with the item of clothing you are talking about. So . . .

Un T-shirt is 'un tee-SHARRRT'.

Des baskets are 'day basss-KETT'.

Où est le sportswear? is 'Oo-ay le sporrtss-WHERE?'

Having just one syllable, a small size is simply 'un SMOLL'. But if you want something in a medium you must ask for 'un may-d'YUM' and a large is 'un larr-djj'.

Appropriately, shopping itself follows the 'angry second syllable' rule – it's 'le sho-PING'.

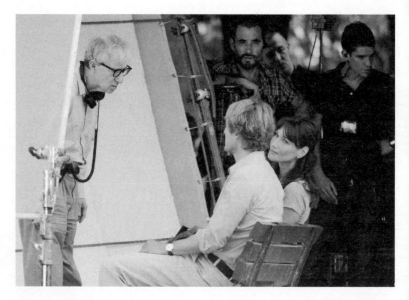

To encourage film shoots, Paris will lend or hire out almost any part of the city – including, apparently, First Lady Carla Bruni-Sarkozy, here filming with Woody Allen in 2010.

10

CINEMA

Quand les Américains tournent un film, ils visent le monde entier.
Quand les Français le font, ils visent Paris.
(When the Americans shoot films, they aim at the whole planet.
When the French do it, they aim at Paris.)

JEAN-JACQUES ANNAUD, FILM DIRECTOR

Ciné qua non

PARISIANS LOVE film. The city is overflowing with cinemas. Almost every major *métro* junction has them – Bastille, Les Halles, Opéra, Odéon, Stalingrad, Montparnasse, place de Clichy. According to the events guide *Pariscope*, the city has seventy-seven cinemas – more, in fact, because some, at Opéra and on the Champs-Élysées for example, have not just several screens but also several annexes in different buildings. This means that on average (and admittedly averages are dangerous things) there is about one cinema per square kilometre in the city. In the Latin Quarter it feels more like one per square metre. And they all seem to be flourishing. When a big new film comes out – French or foreign – there are long queues and full houses everywhere. Major foreign releases will be shown in most cinemas in *VO* (*version originale*), not just for ex-pats but because Parisians don't mind at all if they have to read subtitles. And in the studenty Latin Quarter there are still several tiny independent cinemas where, for slightly more than the price of the DVD, you can sit and watch a low-definition copy of a classic movie while causing yourself chronic back pain on the ancient seats.

Paris is so *cinéphile* that I have even seen sexy young women wearing Woody Allen T-shirts. Of course, they might have been friends of his wife, but even so, Woody probably doesn't get that kind of treatment in any other city.

And the relationship between Paris and cinema is very much a mutual love affair. The city is one of the movie industry's most bankable stars – it's an actor (or actress, perhaps) with eternal appeal. And make no mistake, Paris knows this very well. The city may look effortlessly elegant when it appears on screen, but behind the scenes it is constantly promoting the movie career of its streets and monuments, making sure it gets its name up in lights and its face in front of the camera at every occasion.

Mission possible

Any film shot in Paris has an instant added ingredient. Having the city as the backdrop to your screenplay is like serving Champagne at dinner – it becomes an event.

At its best, Paris looks sensational (parts of it have, after all, been rather well designed), and a few landscape shots of the City of Light in your movie are sure to bring a touch of class and glamour where there was none before. *The Devil Wears Prada*, for example, used the Petit Palais, the Pont des Arts and the fountains of Concorde to make its characters look chic. If the producers had wanted realism, they could have filmed the Paris Fashion Week section of the story in traffic jams on faceless boulevards, where visiting fashion journalists spend a fair amount of their time. But that's not why producers send their actors to Paris.

Similarly, *The Da Vinci Code* was a real gift to both Paris and the producers. The movie used fairly accurate studio mock-ups of the interior of the Louvre, as well as classy shots of the real museum, the Palais-Royal and Saint-Sulpice church. And ever since the Dan Brown phenomenon began, visitors to the city have been able to take guided tours of the book/movie locations.

This has created problems for real Parisians. A friend of mine who was living near Saint-Sulpice quite reasonably wanted to get married there. However, her bridegroom-to-be had the misfortune of being English, so the parish priest sat them down for a long interrogation scene, grilling them not only about their opinion of the sanctity of marriage and whether their future children would be Catholics, but also to make sure that they didn't want to get married at Saint-Sulpice just so that the guests could start digging up the aisle in search of cryptic messages.

And Parisians suffer smaller inconveniences every time a big movie shoot comes to the city – a whole neighbourhood can be blocked off by catering vans, make-up trailers and trucks that seem to contain enough lengths of cable to run an extension lead to the tip of the Eiffel Tower. Even a small shoot will involve an army of young people with walkie-talkies whose first job in the movies (at least one hopes it's their first job) involves standing in the rain asking drivers to wait while a scene is shot.

Amazingly, most Parisians accept this intrusion into their lifestyle almost meekly. Under normal circumstances, anyone not wearing a police uniform who was trying to get cars to stop would be ignored, insulted or hooted at, but a film shoot seems to expose a rare seam of patience in the city's drivers. Waiting for a movie director to get his shot seems to be an acceptable reason for being stuck in traffic, on a par with a serious accident or bomb scare, and certainly much more tolerable than, say, a convoy of limousines taking world leaders to a conference.

This tolerance is reflected in the city's seat of power itself, the Hôtel de Ville. City Hall has a department called *Mission Cinéma*, created in 2002 by Mayor Bertrand Delanoë purely to protect Paris's role in the movie business. It sponsors film festivals, gives subsidies to twenty or so small independent cinemas, and makes films happen. And it obviously does a very good job – at any given time there are ten movies being shot in Paris, in some 4,400 approved locations – and that's only the official shoots.

I went along to meet Mission Cinéma's communications director, Sophie Boudon-Vanhille, to ask how she manages the city's screen career.

Her office was not at all what one might expect for the head of such a glamorous city's film bureau. No corner bay window overlooking the Eiffel Tower, no anteroom staffed by the *gardienne* of an appointments diary as impenetrable as *The Da Vinci Code*'s cryptex. It was a DVD-filled, film-poster-covered, paper-piled working room on the ground floor of a municipal building that looked out over a bus route, made glamorous only by the number of framed photos of stars thanking Sophie and Mission Cinéma for their help.

'Paris and cinema are *intimement liés*,' she told me, meaning the two are intimately connected, as if they were lovers.

'But isn't Paris just being used just for its looks?' I suggested. 'It has to put up with its already congested streets getting blocked, as well as the danger that it might become over-exposed.'

'On the contrary,' Sophie said. 'If a film producer wants the tax breaks given to French films, the shoot has to have a quota of French technicians, and this helps to keep the country's cinema industry alive. It creates jobs for Parisians, who are cheaper to hire because they don't need hotels.'

This is true – whole areas of the city like Jourdain in the 19th and the nearby suburb of Montreuil are home to masses of *intermittents du spectacle* ('occasional entertainment-industry workers') – directors, actors, cameramen, light and sound engineers, electricians and who knows what, all being paid generous un-employment money between shows and film shoots, on permanent standby, like fighter pilots waiting to be sent on a life-and-death mission to save French culture.

'We are also helping to raise the city's profile,' Sophie said. Well, what she actually talked about was *le rayonnement de la ville*, an expression that made Paris sound like a beacon. 'Movies attract visitors, so we do everything we can to make it easy for producers to set their films here.' As if to prove her point, a hubbub of activity erupts on the other side of the glass partition. It is, I am told, a production team asking for urgent permission to film.

'Will they get the go-ahead?' I ask, knowing how frustrating life can be in France if forms are not sent to offices well in advance.

'Of course.'

'Even if they want to film on the Champs-Élysées or outside the Louvre?'

'It depends. If someone else is filming there on the dates they want, they are too late. There is no favouritism. It is first come, first served, even if they want to film in Montmartre or on the Pont des Arts.'

And doesn't it annoy her, I ask, that everyone seems to want the same clichéd shots?

Far too diplomatic to answer directly, she tells me: 'To take pressure off over-used locations, we send screenwriters on guided tours of lesser-known areas and suggest that these might inspire plotlines. For example, to Rungis food market or on a trip with the Seine river police.'

This gives me a chance to quote some figures at her. On the excellent *parisfilm.fr* website, there is a long list of the fees charged to film at various types of location. It's all very scientific. The city's museums are divided into price categories – *Musée 1* includes the Musée d'Art Moderne, the Carnavalet and the Petit Palais (4,000 euros a day* plus a crew fee – for example, 400 euros if there's a crew of between eleven and twenty people); *Musée 2* includes smaller museums like Victor Hugo's and Balzac's former homes and the Musée de la Vie Romantique (2,500 euros plus the same crew fee as a *Musée 1*); while other less glamorous locations such as the catacombs and public libraries cost 480 euros plus the standard crew fee.

I ask Sophie about a couple of quirky charges. Apparently, it costs 400 euros to film by a canal, plus 40 to use a boat, and 62 for a bridge. Why 62?

Sophie looks up the list on her computer, shakes her head and confesses she has no idea who thought up that particular euro-earner for the city.

I have also noticed that some fees include royalties. So is Paris copyrighted? Can it charge a percentage of the box office for showing the Eiffel Tower?

'No, no,' Sophie says. 'It costs nothing to film Paris other than an administration fee to organize things. The only buildings that charge royalties are the ones whose architect is still living. The Louvre pyramid, for example. That is an image that still belongs to I. M. Pei. If it's in a film or a photo, he must get royalties.'

'But before he built his pyramid, the Louvre was free?'

'Yes.† And we don't charge anything for small shoots. For fewer than ten people, a production needs no authorization, except a police certificate, which is free. And we give subsidies to young

---

* These are fees per working day. In true French administrative style, Paris City Hall considers that films should be shot from nine to five, Monday to Saturday. Overtime costs 85 euros an hour, and Sundays, holidays and nights are 50 per cent extra. Some locations require the hire of a city worker, *un agent de la ville*, who will be paid 31 euros an hour overtime if a shoot overshoots.

† Note to self: get contract to add glass bubble to top of Eiffel Tower so it looks like a giant thermometer, and make fortune.

filmmakers to make *courts métrages* [short films]. We want young directors from the film schools to stay in Paris.'

'And can anyone make any kind of film they want?' I ask. 'For example, if someone wants to make a movie mocking Napoleon or Charles de Gaulle, will they get permission?'

As this has long been a personal ambition of mine, I hold my breath while she smiles at the idea.

'Yes, of course,' she finally says. 'We are not a censorship bureau. All we ask is that the filming won't shock the public or be dangerous.'

It's all very impressive, a perfect combination of Paris's love of cinema and its hard head for business. I'm sure every Hollywood actor and actress would love to have a manager as feisty as Mission Cinéma.

Paris on screen

So many films have been shot in Paris that everyone will have a different favourite. Most movie buffs will mention *A Bout de Souffle* (*Breathless*), which I love and disapprove of at the same time. It is fresh, daring and (yes) breathless, but I must confess I get annoyed at seeing Belmondo spend so much of his time smoking in bed. No wonder he's breathless.

They will also rave about *Hôtel du Nord*, the 1938 classic in which two suicidal lovers, who are staying at the aforementioned hostelry on the Canal Saint-Martin, meet a prostitute played by the inimitable (or rather, highly imitable) Arletty. She was a film version of Édith Piaf, an actress with an incredible Parisian accent. The film contains wonderful pieces of dialogue – one of the lovers laments, 'Ma vie n'est pas une existence,' to which the other replies, 'Tu crois que mon existence est une vie?' It's a piece of repartee so Parisian and philosophical that it's almost meaningless. The only trouble with *Hôtel du Nord*, though, is that it wasn't made in Paris – it was almost entirely shot on a studio set, an exact replica of the canalside.

So much for the obvious classics – the following are my own two favourite Paris films. Neither of them is very well known outside France, but each is quintessentially Parisian in its own way.

The first is the shortest and most graphic. And it certainly wouldn't get made today – even back in the liberal 1970s its director Claude Lelouch was arrested after the first public screening. It's *C'était un Rendez-vous* (which could be translated as *It Was a Date*), a nine-minute adrenalin rush that was filmed with a single camera in real time.

It is simply footage of Lelouch's Mercedes being driven by the director himself through the streets of Paris at five-thirty one August morning in 1976. He speeds through red lights, mounts the pavement, crosses on to the wrong side of the road to overtake, taking his camera on a manic tour of Paris from the Arc de Triomphe, down the Champs-Élysées, past the Opéra and Pigalle, and ending up at the Sacré Coeur in Montmartre to make the rendez-vous in the title – with a blonde babe.

Lelouch shot the film without permission, driving through real traffic with a camera strapped to his front bumper, adding nothing but a soundtrack of squealing tyres and a Ferrari engine that growls like a frustrated lion every time it has to slow down.

And it's not only the driving style that is typically Parisian. The film gives a perfect example of how drivers behave at the Étoile roundabout, even at legal speeds – that is, go exactly where you want to and don't give a damn what other people are doing. The movie also pays tribute to the city's cleanliness – almost the only vehicles about are refuse lorries.

And then there's the conclusion. A Parisian male can't just drive through Paris for the hell of it (or can't admit that's what he was doing) – it has to be to meet a *femme*.

Personally, I enjoy the film for its views of 1970s Paris and its sheer Parisian-ness. The streets are almost empty, especially out in the posh areas around the Arc de Triomphe, because Lelouch made his film in August. It's a testimony to how many Parisians desert the city during that month – and to how bored a Parisian can become if he's forced to stay at home.

Favourite number two is a film called *Le Grand Blond avec une Chaussure Noire – The Tall Blond with One Black Shoe*. It's a comedy made in 1972 starring Pierre Richard, a sort of French Charlie Chaplin of his day – an actor with a gift for slapstick and a poignant edge, who almost always plays the same character, a curly-haired, accident-prone seducer.

Le Grand Blond is a romping spoof of a spy movie with lots of street scenes and a highly Parisian plot. The two rivals for control of the French secret service are battling it out in a dirty *chien* eat *chien* war. To distract the pretender, the current head of the Sureté orders his men to go to Orly airport and choose a total innocent with whom they will 'make contact', thereby suggesting to their rivals that this is a master spy. The victim is a hapless classical violinist (Pierre Richard), the kind of social inadequate who wears odd shoes and doesn't realize that he's being followed by secret-service agents, even when they start shooting at each other.

What is so typically Parisian about that, one might ask? Well, he may be a misfit, but the violinist is having an affair with his best friend's wife (*bien sûr*), and when a *femme fatale* is sent to seduce him into revealing his (non-existent) secrets, he is so good in bed that she falls in love with him. Every Parisian male's ideal Parisian. Furthermore, the *femme fatale*'s dress is a Guy Laroche creation that is 1970s Paris personified – from the front it looks like a long, formal evening gown, but when she turns around, she reveals a *décolleté* that swoops down to expose a good inch of buttock cleavage. A million times sexier than Sharon Stone revealing all in *Basic Instinct*.

More importantly, perhaps, all the actors (including French screen greats Jean Rochefort, Bernard Blier and Jean Carmet) are superb, and there's a strong '70s Paris ambiance, with plenty of smoking, seduction and witty repartee. It's just a shame that the city doesn't inspire new films like it.

Liberté, Égalité, Ciné

Paris doesn't want films like *C'était un Rendez-vous* and *Le Grand Blond* to be forgotten. It wants to educate Parisians about cinema culture, which is why, as well as screening the latest releases, many cinemas also run frequent mini-festivals. They will show the current box-office hits at the same time as having, say, a Cary Grant week, an Almodóvar night, or a Suspense cycle. Just days after director Claude Chabrol's death in September 2010, five cinemas got together to organize a twenty-film retrospective.

The city has also created its own institution to make sure that film-lovers get a varied, balanced diet. Deep down in Les Halles, in a subterranean plaza a few dozen metres from one of Paris's biggest multiplexes, sits the Forum des Images, a film library and five-screen cinema financed by Mission Cinéma. The Forum shows classics, new independent films and obscure foreign productions from countries you didn't even know had a movie industry. It also has a direct educational role, inviting in school groups – a recent 'children's programme' included a movie by New Wave director François Truffaut. They start them young in Paris.

The Forum has a library of over 7,000 films, the oldest dating back to 1895, and *cinéphiles* can either go along to one of the showings advertised in the listings magazines or simply decide to nip underground and ask for a private screening of anything in the catalogue. The Salle des Collections has individual screens, sofas where two can snuggle up to watch a love story (though even in Paris there are limits on the degree of snuggling allowed) and small *salons* where up to seven people can gather for a collective movie experience. And in the evenings after 7.30 p.m., it's free. Yes, Paris provides legal video piracy – with comfy sofas.

The Italian painting section of the Louvre, back in the good old days when you could actually get quite close to the Mona Lisa. But it is possible to see great art in Paris without fighting the crowds.

11

ART

Le fou copie l'artiste. L'artiste ressemble au fou.
(The madman copies the artist. The artist looks like a madman.)

ANDRÉ MALRAUX, WRITER AND FORMER
FRENCH MINISTER OF CULTURE

What's Louvre got to do with it?

PARIS IS the spiritual home of Impressionism and Cubism and has played host to pretty well every other artistic –ism. It was the city where Picasso blossomed from a gifted teenager to a modernist giant and where Van Gogh turned himself from a gloomy Dutchman into a frenzied Frenchman. Before the First World War, it was practically impossible to sit in a Parisian café without being offered a cheap portrait by a future genius for the price of a glass of absinthe. In short, Paris is so arty that even Mona Lisa has set up residence here.

Well, that's the image that the city likes to project. And there are artists and galleries everywhere, doing their best to convince us all that the art scene is as vibrant as it was between the 1870s and the 1920s, when Monet, Manet, Morisot, Matisse, Modigliani and co. were painting so productively that Paris seemed in danger of being overrun with barely dry canvases. In fact, though, it's largely a myth – those good old days weren't really so good at all. In their early careers, almost all the city's most famous artists of the nineteenth and early-twentieth centuries were ignored or shouted down by Parisians.

When Gustave Courbet first began exhibiting his paintings in Paris in the early 1850s, for instance, his attempts at realism shocked the public and critics alike. They wanted art that depicted princes and heroes, re-enactments of legends or historical scenes, and Courbet was offering them just plain people – not graceful or godlike, but merely human. His 1853 painting *Les Baigneuses* (*The Bathers*) features one fat lady getting out of a river or lake, and another taking her stockings off ready for a dip. People were aghast at the tastelessness of the nude bather's fleshy buttocks and at the mud on the other woman's bare foot, which was interpreted as a symbol of immorality. The mud didn't symbolize anything, though – according to Courbet, it was plain old riverbank silt, and people weren't used to such literalism.

Others, including Édouard Manet, followed Courbet's realist lead, and had the doors of the artistic establishment firmly slammed in their faces. In 1863, so many artists were refused permission to exhibit their paintings at Paris's annual art fair, Le Salon, that they set up an alternative show, Le Salon des Refusés, with the blessing of Emperor Napoleon III, who agreed that the public should be allowed to decide what they liked. They did just that – the show was a total flop, and the critics had a field day. One called the paintings 'sad and grotesque', but added that 'with one or two exceptions, you laugh as heartily as at a farce at the Palais-Royal' (home of the Comédie Française).

Fifteen years later, the critics were even more horrified. A young man called Claude Monet, who had been invalided out of the army after catching typhoid, began expressing his relief at being alive by painting what he saw in front of him, preferably outdoors instead of staying cooped up in a studio. And given that life was short, he felt the need to paint quickly, capturing the moment, and preferred to finish his paintings there and then rather than touching them up later. This inevitably made his work look hurried and blurred. Take his *Impression: Soleil Levant* (*Impression: Sunrise*) for example. In a swirl of blue-green mist, we can just make out the masts, cranes and smoke stacks of Le Havre harbour. A black silhouette hovers in the mid-distance. It seems to be a boat carrying two men, although it might also be a walrus doing backstroke. And in the centre of the painting sits a bright orange splodge – the sun. No subtle gradations of colour here, no tapestry of dawn light woven into the clouds – it's just a splodge.

Today, this is considered a masterpiece, but in 1874, when it was first exhibited, the art critic (and unsuccessful painter) Louis Leroy slammed it in the satirical magazine *Le Charivari,* inadvertently creating history when he lambasted Monet and his friends for being incapable of painting things in detail, and damned them all as mere *Impressionistes.*

And in 1876, at the second public showing of the new artists' work, a critic went even further:

The rue le Peletier is a street of disasters. At the Durand-Ruel gallery, an exhibition has just opened that is alleged to contain paintings. I entered, and my horrified eyes beheld a terrifying sight – five or six lunatics, including one woman, have got together to exhibit their work. I have seen people shake with laughter on seeing these pictures, but my heart bled when I saw them. These would-be artists call themselves revolutionaries. They take a piece of canvas, splash on a few random daubs of colour, and then sign it. It is a huge fraud, as if the inmates of a madhouse had picked up stones by the roadside and imagined they had found diamonds.

The gallery-owner, Paul Durand-Ruel, was so frustrated at Paris's inability to understand the Impressionists that he took his trade elsewhere, opening premises in London, Brussels, Vienna and

New York, all the while paying artists like Monet, Auguste Renoir and Camille Pissarro a monthly salary so that they wouldn't starve.

It wasn't until the early-twentieth century that these Parisian painters started to get recognition at home, and even then, it was largely thanks to private collectors, many of them foreign, who were coming to Paris to snap up Impressionist canvases for a song.

By then, a new generation of artists, including Henri Matisse and the recent immigrant Pablo Picasso, were suffering the same fate, being jeered at for their 'childish' style and desperately courting rich ex-pats like the writer/heiress Gertrude Stein. They would troop along to her dinners and cocktail parties, hoping to sell a painting that would not only pay the rent but would also hang on Gertrude's wall and be spotted by other rich ex-pats. Again, the mainstream Paris art establishment turned its back on the local talent, and even alleged that people like Matisse were creating rubbish for gullible American tourists.

All this sounds horrific, but one could argue that at least the Impressionists, Post-Impressionists, Cubists, Dadaists, Surrealists and all the other innovative '–ists' had something to react against. Opposition gave them energy and a sense of purpose; it goaded them into perfecting their ideas so that everyone would become convinced of their validity.

These days, on the other hand, more or less anything goes, and – in my humble opinion – Parisian art as a movement has stagnated. The focus is more on the artist than the art. This was true of Picasso, too, but he was so incredibly productive and innovative that he never seemed to let the cult of personality get past his studio door. For some new Parisian artists, though, personality is everything. Their art is all about *moi* . . .

Look at my navel

Parisian-born Sophie Calle, for example, has made her life her art. She is highly intelligent and therefore comes up with clever ideas. For example, in the early '90s she had an exhibition of photos of the spaces left on museum walls by stolen paintings. Yes, it's a funny concept, but it's a bit of a one-liner. Once you've seen one empty space, haven't you seen them all?

The most recent example of this style of 'clever' art in Paris was an installation called *Monumenta 2010* at the Grand Palais. For this, the artist Christian Boltanski filled the 13,500 square metres of the Grand Palais's immense, glass-roofed central hall with clothes. Visitors walked around piles of rumpled old coats, shirts, pullovers and trousers, heaped in one central stack and a grid of small squares that looked like plots in a cemetery. Meanwhile, booming out of loudspeakers was the slow thump of human hearts beating, a chilling sound because subconsciously everyone is afraid it will stop at any moment. And although this was taking place during one of the coldest winters in recent years, the heating was turned off so that spectators could experience the full desolation of what they were seeing – a monument to the victims of genocide. An honourable intention, no doubt, but its effect as art was slightly diminished given that reviews of the exhibition were sharing newspaper space with reports of homeless people freezing to death in the streets of Paris – *due to lack of warm clothing*. It was bit like organizing a sound installation of ocean waves on the day after a tsunami.

Surely, though, new Parisian art can't have disappeared completely into a black hole of its own pretension?

The answer, fortunately, is *non*. There are still Parisian artists out there creating work that tries to titillate the eye as well as the intellect, and one of the best ways of seeing them is to go to their studios.

To do this, it is not necessary to hang around in Montmartre cafés chatting up anyone with paint brushes stuck behind their ears. At various times of the year, usually in spring and autumn, all the artists in a certain area of the city hold a weekend of open days.

The biggest concentrations of artists' studios are up in the north of Paris, around Montmartre and Belleville, and there are also open days in the south, in the 14th *arrondissement*. You can consult listings on the internet at www.parisgratuit.com/ateliers.html, but unless you're looking for a specific artist, the best thing often is to go to the hub of the neighbourhood and follow your nose, or rather your ears – Parisian artists rarely seem to create without musical accompaniment, preferably either old French chansons, Bob Marley or bleeping techno.

Open the *porte*

The steeply rising rue de Belleville has long been a neat little Chinatown, with end-to-end restaurants, but the streets immediately to the east and north have suffered from the kind of urban regeneration that involved demolishing old buildings and then saying, 'Hmm, what shall we do now?' In most cases, the answer was, 'Stick up a cheap, ugly apartment building that will start to crumble in ten years.' Elsewhere, it was more a case of, 'Let's brick it up and leave it to decay, and then maybe someone will give us a grant to build a cheap, ugly . . .' etc.

The destruction was caused by a city plan at the end of the 1980s to turn the area into a *zone d'aménagement concerté*, literally a concentrated redevelopment zone, but after several years of demolition, the plan was shelved, leaving the area scarred but at least half intact.

More recently, many empty buildings have been squatted by

artists, and lots of the old shops have also been taken over by *créateurs* of various kinds – jewellers, clothes designers, lampshade makers and the like. The artiness has even spread to some of the surviving traditional shops – a plumber's showroom and a grocer's both have façades that have been decorated by graffiti artists, with the consent of the owners, that is.

The rue Dénoyez, in which half the buildings are bricked up, is now a permanent outdoor gallery, with whole façades painted over. On the open day I attended, there was a large painting of a rhinoceros being pleasured by a gorilla and a crocodile, while itself doing erotic (but very painful-looking) things to a monkey with its horn. Its title was *Belleville Zoophilie*, or *Belleville Bestiality*, not something that most of us would want to commission for our living rooms, but very Parisian – there aren't many cities where such public displays of animal *amour* would be tolerated, even in the zoos.

It was also a reminder that, these days, many of Paris's most creative young artists work in a comic-book style. The French love *bandes dessinées*, or *BD*, and the cultural establishment is even beginning to acknowledge this form of art, so that the launch of a big French *BD* gets as much – and as respectful – media coverage as a new Monet exhibition.

Next to the rhino-led orgy, a young man was up a ladder, daubing blue paint over the walls and windows of a low-rise building. I watched as he made long, swooping strokes with his roller on a stick, and slowly a blue elephant came into soft focus, apparently charging at the owner of the café next door, who was watching anxiously, as though worried that the animals might stampede across his windows.

Wandering further along the street, I visited a ceramic artist called Guy Honore. Using an apartment-block motif, he had made sculptures of dream-like cities, one of which was painted white and lime green, and had large leaves overrunning the urban scene, like the ideal French *nouvelle ville*. And for art lovers with no space on their mantelpiece for a ceramic new town, he had used the same motif on a cute cubic teapot.

A few doors down was a kind of Parisian Andy Warhol who had taken the photos-to-paintings theme and given it a French twist, creating Pop Art portraits of the poet Arthur Rimbaud and singers Jacques Brel and Georges Brassens. Not exactly an original style, but Rimbaud's photo definitely deserves to be as iconic as anything that Warhol adapted.

Next I ventured into a dark studio hung with lengths of coloured fabric, some of them spliced down the middle with a splash of metal. The artist was sitting in a chair staring at me as I gazed around, and replied to my greeting with a questioning 'Bonjour?' Then I realized why she looked confused – it was a haberdasher's shop, and the metal-spliced pieces of material were zips. I apologized and left, though if I'd been a conceptual artist, I'd have bought the whole place, haberdasher and all, and sold it to the Musée d'Art Moderne as an installation symbolizing the way the modern French cultural establishment is zipped shut to truly iconoclastic ideas (except my own, of course).

Heading up the rue Ramponeau, I came to the demolition site that is La Forge. This is a group of studios in a former key factory that used to be hidden behind a large apartment block. The main building has been replaced by a large gap in the street line that is one day destined to be filled with social housing.

On the wall of the building next door, the artists who now occupy La Forge have created a six-storey-high mural, a scene of urban degeneration, with blood, skulls, decapitation and what looked like a massive pair of hairy human legs using the apocalyptic landscape as a footstool. There was also a gorilla head and yet another mention of Belleville Zoo, so I asked the first artist I could find why this was. A reference to the urban jungle, no doubt? No, the painter told me, it is a homage to the song 'Brooklyn Zoo' by Ol' Dirty Bastard. I looked this up on Google and found that it's a cute little ditty in which the rapper boasts that he has never been 'tooken out' by a 'nigga who couldn't figure how to pull a f*ckin gun trigga'. Not an influence that one might expect in the city of Monet, Manet and co., but then some Parisians aren't content to sit on their Impressionistic laurels. And it's more than mere imitation – the urban French have always idolized American rap culture, and, by mixing in their own *bande dessinée* styles, they have created something profoundly Parisian.

In the dozen or so studios in the old forge buildings, I saw spray-painters, photographers, a collage artist, a modeller, and even a conventional painter, a man called Pierre Chandelier whose studio walls were covered in highly Parisian canvases – slightly naïve apartment interiors featuring the kind of wacky furniture that an artist might own, plus cats, potted plants and views of rooftops out of the open window.

'The kids in the main studio call me the *sous-Matisse*,' he lamented – the 'sub-Matisse'. He was clearly a disciple of the great Henri M, and his vivid Pariscapes were exciting a couple of visiting Americans, who seemed especially pleased that the artist had been canny enough to create several small canvases that would fit in hand luggage, and not cost much more than the suitcase that was holding them.

Sadly, however, the bickering about who was the coolest artist on the block went deeper than disagreements about whether to apply paint with a spray or a brush. At the time of writing, a group of artists who had recently received permission to manage the site on behalf of the city were in conflict with the people who had originally squatted the place and set up studios. Locks had apparently been changed, and some of the older artists were forced to move out of their original studios into smaller spaces. The only consolation is that there seems to be room for everyone, so with any luck the situation will not get any worse.

And meanwhile, the buildings themselves are clearly enjoying being put to active use, as well as benefiting from some sunlight after all those years hidden behind an apartment building – the passageway between the two wings of the forge is now a leafy alley of grapevine, and when I was there, it looked to be preparing a bumper harvest of fruit.

Overall, then, the studio open day was a fascinating way to spend an afternoon, and an excellent chance to get a glimpse of what Parisian artists do before they are sidetracked by media attention and/or huge subsidies.

Artists, a protected species

Not all Parisian artists are forced to squat, however. If you walk around certain parts of Paris, you can see physical evidence of art's prestigious place in the city's architecture. In many buildings along the Left Bank of the Seine, the top floors have immense windows – these were purpose-built artists' studios. The same goes for apartment buildings along the boulevards around Pigalle, where gigantic walls of glass were included in the architects' plans, giving artists not only soft northern light but an inspiring view of Montmartre. These chic *ateliers* were designed for artists with a bit of personal capital or a generous sponsor, but in the late-nineteenth and early-twentieth centuries, the city also built less luxurious studios.

An old friend of mine, a sculptor called Lélio, used to live in the Villa Mallebay in the 14th *arrondissement*, a tiny paved alley lined with garages on one side and artists' studios on the other. Lélio's studio, one of several in a row of low, glass-fronted buildings, was made of panels salvaged by the city authorities from the pavilions at the great Paris Expo of 1889. The little house was basically three walls and a roof propped up against the building behind it, and it should probably have been condemned as unfit to live in. Lélio had built the toilet himself and plumbed it into a pipe that led he knew not where (in the 1980s, when developers bought some of the surrounding land, they discovered to their horror that there was an ancient, uncharted septic tank at the end of the lane).

The living quarters, where Lélio had, for a few years in the 1960s, housed a wife and two children, consisted of two perilous mezzanine levels, one of them too low to stand up on. The kitchen was barely big enough for a sink and a cooker, the bathroom was a shower cubicle and the floor was a layer of concrete on top of Parisian soil. The whole thing was heated by a stove with a clanky metal chimney twisting up through the roof.

When I knew him, Lélio was living and working alone in the studio, gradually filling the building with towering totems of wood and clay until there was barely room for a bed and a table.

Needless to say, art magazines regularly used to come and photograph the place – he was the embodiment of a Parisian artist. And, even more regularly, property developers used to try and buy the row of studios, whispering in municipal ears that these artists paying a few francs a month would be just as happy (and have far better plumbing) in a new building in some distant suburb. To the city's credit, it never listened, and Lélio worked in his studio literally until the day he died there.

The Villa Mallebay has now had modern houses imposed upon it, but elsewhere in Paris there are some unadulterated little villages of similar studios.

One of the best of these is the Cité Fleurie, on the boulevard Arago, a hamlet of thirty or so studios made out of building materials from the Food Hall at the Expo of 1878. Gauguin and Modigliani once lived here, but it was only protected from the developers thanks to a campaign by its artist residents in the 1970s. The Cité is now an historical monument, which explains the perfect upkeep – all the buildings are painted two shades of brown (mahogany for the door and window frames against a beige back-ground), and with their rustic beams and tiny, tree-shaded courtyards, the cottages are enough to make even the least-talented dauber take painting lessons just to qualify for such perfect accommodation. Because even today, tenants of the Cité have to be artists, although one suspects, peeping through the windows at neat bookshelves and tasteful living rooms, that not all of them are quite as active as my friend Lélio was.

In similar places that have been sold off for private ownership, such as the equally picture-postcard Cité des Fusains in Montmartre, where Renoir and Toulouse-Lautrec used to paint, any studio that becomes vacant is instantly snapped up by loft-hunters. The new non-artist residents then start complaining at the disturbance caused by a neighbour loudly sculpting wood or slapping paint on to canvas with too much expressionist abandon – while, of course, boasting to friends about how bohemian their new neighbourhood is. Parisian estate agents have a special label for the type of person who wants to buy an artist's studio – they are clients looking for *l'atypique* (the unusual). And I should know, because I was one of them. I once tried to buy a small place in the Cité des Fusains, and would have done so if it hadn't turned out to be a miniature rather than the large canvas I'd imagined it to be from the agent's description.

This competition with non-artists for studio space explains why Paris now tries to help artists find a studio. They can apply to the city for a special *HLM* (*habitation à loyer modéré* – low-cost housing) with a studio attached. On the application form, the artist can specify which floor their studio should be on, and stipulate a minimum surface area.

The offer is open to painters, engravers, sculptors, photographers, plastic artists, video artists and creators of installations. All they have to do is provide a CV, a portfolio, a letter of motivation ('I need a studio or I'll cut my ear off') and proof that they have signed up to the artists' social-security scheme (presumably, their medical cover includes testing for paint poisoning, marble-dust inhalation and feeling misunderstood). Every two months, a commission consisting of four city councillors and two artists meets to study applications.

No other professional body in Paris gets such preferential treatment for housing (except people like ministers, head teachers, firemen, and directors of institutions who might have to live at their workplace). There are, for instance, no special provisions for taxi drivers, bakers or waiters, all of whom contribute just as much to making sure that Paris stays Paris. There are none for writers, either, I should add, though we scribblers can apply for rooms in special residences, the only problem with them being that you have to live next to other writers, and there's only so much conversation about royalties, word counts and the use of the semi-colon that a balanced human being can stand.

Parisian artists in search of something more temporary can also apply for six months' free accommodation, plus a grant, to work in an artists' community near the Gare de l'Est. And if they get fed up with Paris, they can go and spend their grant in partner residences in Budapest, New York and Buenos Aires.

Paris's most prestigious *lycées* might do their best to force pupils to learn maths and physics and become engineers, but there are definite compensations for the kids who spend their time doodling.

Avoiding the museum queues

There are a dozen major art museums in Paris, the main problem being that there are slightly more than a dozen people trying to visit them. On a rainy day in spring or summer you can spend ten times longer queuing outside a museum than you will looking at the paintings. Even when you get inside, you have to join the crowds jostling to get a quick glimpse of a famous picture before the jabbing elbows and shoving shoulders eject you from your vantage point. An hour of waiting just to spend ten seconds in front of *The Painting Made Famous by the Da Vinci Code*.

Although it must be said that, thanks to Mona Lisa, some of the other picture galleries in the Louvre are relatively crowd-free. The French-painting rooms in the Sully Wing of the museum are often empty, and you can spend uninterrupted minutes exchanging doleful gazes with Watteau's *Pierrot* (the white clown), or admiring the shapely buttocks of one of Boucher's famous reclining nudes. There's even a largely ignored group of Impressionist pictures in the collection, donated to the Louvre by a certain Victor Lyon, a Parisian financier who had a sharp eye for art investments, to judge by his Monet snowscape, his gorgeous bathing nude by Degas, and several wallfuls of Sisleys, Renoirs and other household names. Though this doesn't, of course, save you the bother of queuing up to get in the Louvre.

There are, however, smaller museums dedicated to a single artist or genre where the crowds aren't so intimidating – the Musée Gustave Moreau for lovers of Romanticism, and the Musée Guimet for oriental art, for example. Even the Musée Rodin isn't always crowded, and has a large garden that is ideal for a picnic. But Paris can go one better than that – museums where there is almost no one, or where a short time queuing will yield unbelievable artistic rewards.

In the first category is one of my favourites, the museum dedicated to the abstract artist Jean Arp – or Hans Arp as he is sometimes known. He was born in 1886 in Alsace, which was then part of Germany, and came to Paris just before the First World War to work alongside rising stars like Picasso and Modigliani. When war broke out, Arp avoided conscription into the German army by having himself declared insane, and went to Switzerland to work

Abstract artist Jean Arp may not look like a bundle of laughs (he spent a lot of time in Switzerland), but if you go to his Parisian studio today, you will be invited to fondle his sculptures.

with the artist who later became his wife, Sophie Taeuber, and the Russian painter Wassily Kandinsky. The three of them founded a new movement, the most modernist of all, Dadaism – its philosophy: to reject all previous artistic conventions (except, of course, that of claiming to reject artistic conventions). Arp, Taeuber and Kandinsky began to produce abstract art and nonsense poetry, exploding the rules as a comment on the real explosions happening on the other side of the Alps.

After the war, Arp and Taeuber came back to Paris and accepted the offer of another modernist artist, Theo van Doesburg, to build a house on a piece of land he owned in the suburb of Clamart, not far from Rodin's second home in Meudon.

And it was there, interrupted only by yet another war, that Arp would live and work for most of the rest of his life. The house, designed by Sophie Taeuber, has now been turned into a museum that is one of the Paris region's best-kept artistic secrets.

It's not a deliberately kept secret – the museum would love to have more visitors. But it seems that hiding the house about 400 metres from the nearest suburban train station, even if that station is just outside Paris on the way to the slightly better-known Château de Versailles, discourages all but the hardiest art lovers.

I almost didn't find it myself, and wished I had a phone with Satnav, because the supposedly helpful road signs didn't help at all. When I got off the train at Meudon–Val Fleury station, the sign pointed to the 'Fondation A R P', as if the town didn't know that Arp was a man. They seemed to think he was an institution like the *Anarchistes pour la Révolution Perpétuelle* or the *Association des Restaurants de Poisson*.*

I climbed the hill, past the modernist house of Van Doesburg

---

* This bad signposting, I was later told, is due to the fact that the train station is in Meudon but the Arp museum is in neighbouring Clamart, and Meudon doesn't see why it should put up signposts to someone else's museums. *Vive la bureaucratie française.*

himself, a cube like a 3D Mondrian painting, and then turned right, seeing absolutely no one and hearing nothing except the chattering of birds. It was eerie. This was a neighbourhood of stone cottages, on the edge of Meudon forest, and I felt as if I should be identifying different species of tree rather than looking for an art museum. But after just a couple of minutes I found another sign, this time with 'Arp' spelt like a real name, and sure enough, a few metres further up the hill, there was a house marked *Fondation Arp*.

To someone more used to Rodin's palatial mansion near the Invalides or even Monet's villa out at Giverny, this place came as a surprise. It was tiny, a cuboid version of the other cottages in the neighbourhood, made of the local Paris stone, with a façade that looks like lumps of brown coral set in concrete.

I rang the bell on the gate and the lady in the office looked at me as if she was astonished to be asked to buzz anyone in. When I explained that I hadn't come to the wrong address or to read the gas meter, she called the guide, who clearly wasn't expecting to be needed that day, and I was given a personal tour of the house by someone who seemed genuinely pleased that a visitor was taking an interest in Arp.

And there was plenty of Arp to see. The three floors of the house were crowded with small sculptures, paintings and engravings, wooden Dadaist reliefs, a carpet and a tapestry, all of them in Arp's swirling abstract forms. It is highly unusual to see a studio so full of a famous artist's own works – Giverny, for example, has none.

There were also some pieces of Sophie Taeuber's furniture – homemade, primary-coloured units that were in effect Ikea fifty years before it was invented. And a small display of family photos included a picnic in the garden with James Joyce and Max Ernst, and some funny shots of Sophie and her sister in weird 'abstract' Dadaist costumes.

You don't have to be an art historian to enjoy the place, but you do have to like abstract art, and especially Arp's trademark blobby shapes. I do, and was not surprised to learn that the circular holes in his work are often supposed to be navels – he was a bit of a belly-button fetishist, apparently.* Similarly, his sculptures often manage to be exactly like – and yet not quite like – thrusting buttocks, smooth thighs, arched backs and bulbous phalluses. They feel erotic, but you don't know exactly why.

The eroticism came to a height when the guide got out a box of white gloves and invited me to caress the statues in the garden. This highly Parisian activity is, he told me, a regular part of any tour of the studio. So I went ahead, feeling inexplicably embarrassed at running my hands over the curves and into the holes of the statues. Doing the same thing at the Rodin museum would have been outright pornographic, but here the statues are abstract, and any resemblance to the human form is in the imagination. Even so, it felt like touching up the Venus de Milo.

When I left the museum, there was still no one disturbing the peace of this tranquil neighbourhood, no crowds of art pilgrims trekking up from Meudon. On the guide's advice, I walked up the hill to the end of the street, where there were some weird and wonderful modern houses – the weirdest of which had a façade of mirrors, with bright-yellow windows and doorframes, like a modernist Hansel and Gretel cottage. Close by, on a garden wall, there was a panel saying that the huge cedar tree nearby was a present from Napoleon's Josephine to her art teacher. This place really is part of Paris's art history.

* Plenty of Parisian artists are obsessed with gazing at their own navel, but at least Arp put it to creative use.

Monet, Monet, Monet

Visiting Paris without seeing some pictures by the Impressionists would be a bit like missing out on croissants. The problem being that croissants are made fresh every morning, whereas the Impressionists stopped painting over a century ago.

This is why there are almost always logjams at the permanent collections, and if there's a temporary exhibition – even something as sub-Impressionist as *Painters Who Once Met Manet While He Was Out Shopping* – the lines can stretch for a hundred metres. And that's just to use the toilets.

The Musée d'Orsay is the usual must-see for the Impressionist fan, and it does have some spectacular masterpieces, such as Renoir's *Moulin de la Galette*, Cézanne's card players and (to stray even further into Post-Impressionism) Van Gogh's bedroom in Arles. Strange, then, that in 2002 the Orsay's then director Serge Lemoine was quoted in a magazine interview saying that 'I am one of those who thinks that Impressionism is overrated.' It was a bit like a Pope expressing doubts about the Immaculate Conception, and Lemoine has now been replaced by a new director who says that Monet, Renoir *et al.* are 'ambassadors of our culture' and who markets the museum shamelessly as the 'temple of Impressionism'.* The only problem, of course, is that it has so many worshippers.

Giverny, Monet's house just outside Paris, is another Impressionist-lovers' pilgrimage spot. Personally, I was disappointed by my visit there. True, the house has a strong period feel, and Monet's collection of Japanese prints was gorgeous. And yes, walking around the lily pond, it was easy to imagine him daubing

---

* The 'temple' quote is from the museum's website. Funnily, on the page dedicated to the floor plan, the website also says that, 'The location of artworks is updated every morning, before the Museum opens, based on information from the previous evening.' It's as if the crush in the museum is so great that, like glaciers scraping down a mountain valley, the crowds shove paintings along the corridors.

paint on to his huge canvases in the tranquil dampness, but my overall impression (no pun intended) was, 'OK, cute house, but where are the Monets?' I'd always assumed that they'd all been sold off and re-hung on the walls of every major art gallery in the world. In fact, though, all the paintings that Monet kept for himself at Giverny were donated to a small museum on the western edge of Paris, which now houses the biggest collection of the artist's work in the world. This is the Musée Marmottan (or Marmottan–Monet as it calls itself in an attempt to draw attention to its star resident), in the 16th *arrondissement*. And the Musée doesn't stop at Monet – there are also wonderful paintings by Manet, Pissarro, Sisley, Degas, Renoir and my own favourite Impressionist, Berthe Morisot.

The pictures are housed in a small château that was once the hunting lodge of the Duc de Valmy, one of Napoleon's generals. When it was built in the early nineteenth century, it was way out in the forest, but the huge 16th *arrondissement* has caught up with it, and the lodge is now a few minutes' stroll from the *métro* station at Muette. After a period in the possession of the Marmottan family, who were politicians and art collectors, it was turned into a museum in 1934, apparently in an inheritance-tax deal. Since then, other collectors have followed the Marmottan family's example and donated their art to the museum, which is now eclectic and yet wonderfully focused.

A new exhibition area has been built to house the Monets, which include some of the old man's most famous works. I was astonished to stroll around the museum one weekday afternoon, almost untroubled by other visitors, and come face-to-face with the very painting that started the whole Impressionist movement – *Impression: Soleil Levant*. It's still a startling picture, with its bright-orange blob of sun that looks as if Marilyn Monroe had tried some lipstick, decided it was too bright and stubbed it out on the canvas. It's not surprising that the realism-addicted critics laughed. In its day, it was as daring as Lady Chatterley having sex with a servant. It just wasn't done.

And this is far from being the only masterpiece in the collection. There are some decidedly insulting views of London in the fog as well as plenty of lilies, a Japanese bridge and one of the painter's trademark haystacks. In the main house, there is also a small but wonderful Berthe Morisot room that feels like a family lounge decorated with priceless paintings, and a Napoleon room (Paul Marmottan was a collector of Napoleonic memorabilia) housing pictures from early in Boney's reign at the turn of the nineteenth century. These include a portrait of the legendary Josephine – a sultry, fiery-eyed beauty in a thrustingly low-cut dress, to whom no one in their right mind would say 'not tonight'.

All in all, even a northern Parisian like myself, for whom an excursion into the depths of the 16th *arrondissement* is something akin to crossing the Gobi Desert, can feel that a trip to the Musée Marmottan is worthwhile. It was totally crowd-free, except for one coachload of schoolkids who stuck together like a shoal of wide-eyed mackerel and were therefore easy to avoid. And I probably got there and back in no longer than it would have taken me to queue up at the Musée d'Orsay and get squashed into mackerel pâté.

Owning a piece of Parisian art history

Today, if you feel like buying a signed work of art by a famous Parisian like Arp, you can do so for around a thousand euros. It's not exactly cheap, but this seems a relatively small price to pay when you see the ludicrous sums spent on signed prints by people like Andy Warhol and Damien Hirst. And even if you don't have thousands to spend, there are still some excellent ways of taking home a piece of genuine Parisian art history.

The rue de Seine in the 6th *arrondissement* begins at the river that inspired its name and, after a meandering start, heads straight for the boulevard Saint-Germain. All along the street, there are small art galleries. Admittedly, some of what they sell is (to my taste, anyway) horrifically ugly. In one shop window, I recently saw a five-foot-tall bronze bull that looked as though it had been in a head-on collision with a train. Mostly, though, these galleries deal in tasteful and often very affordable pictures. The dealers inside can look a little snooty, but as Edina Monsoon pointed out in an episode of *Absolutely Fabulous*, they're only shopworkers, so there's no need to be scared off. And they're usually very courteous – after all, it's not as if they sell dozens of pictures a day, and they have central-Paris rents to cover.

I went to the rue de Seine to hunt for affordable Parisian art, and began in a gallery that was running an exhibition by one of the best-known French contemporary artists, Ben. He's not a Parisian (he's from Nice) but he has a very Parisian wit. He's known for writing cryptic messages on canvases in his characteristically curly, rather old-fashioned, handwriting, usually in white paint on a black background.

It turns out, though, that as far as prices are concerned, he takes himself more seriously than I thought. A canvas inscribed *chef d'oeuvre inconnu* (unknown masterpiece) was listed at over 8,000 euros. It was the same price for another, in red writing on white canvas this time, saying ironically *beau et pas cher* (beautiful and not expensive). And it would have cost only slightly less to acquire *c'est quoi l'idée?* (what's the idea?). Like I said, it's very Parisian – cheekily denying the importance of art while trying to sell it at whacking great prices. All good fun, though, and a signed print at 100 euros might actually have been good value. If not, a black Ben pencil case at 5 or so definitely was.

Next, I went into one of the small galleries specializing in prints, and said I was looking for something Parisian. The woman showed me a view of the Eiffel Tower.

'Not quite *that* Parisian,' I told her, adding that I was interested in anything by artists who lived in Paris.

She laughed. 'Well, they all lived here at one time or another.'

She showed me a postcard-sized photo of the Pont Neuf when it was wrapped in fabric in 1985 by Christo (a pseudonym for two people, Christo Javacheff and Jeanne-Claude Denat). The card was framed, signed by Christo (presumably the man) and came with an authenticity stamp on the back. It was as Parisian as you get but, at 350 euros, it seemed to me to be a bit expensive for a postcard.

The dealer left me to browse through her folders of prints and I quickly found some pictures that were much more to my taste. A series of black-and-white engravings of ballet dancers – slightly more realistic than Degas' drawings of the same subject – by Auguste Brouet, a late-nineteenth century Montmartre artist. They were all signed, and cost about 200 euros each, rather less than a Degas. There were also Arp-like abstracts by lesser-known artists, and various Parisian views drawn or painted between the early 1900s and the 1960s, all for a hundred or two. And in places like this, you can always haggle – subtly, of course, this is art, not a second-hand car.

I moved on to one of my favourite Parisian art galleries, Paul Prouté, in the section of the rue de Seine on the other side of the boulevard. It's an unfortunate name – in slang it means 'Paul farted', and the poor owner must go through hell whenever he reserves a hotel room by phone – but it's one of the best places to buy old art in the whole of Paris. The gallery was founded more than a century ago and feels as if the sales assistants have been stuck in a time warp ever since. Young or old, they're all quiet and pale, as though they never get out into the real world.

The walls are lined not with pictures but with wooden racks of folders, all stuffed with art. You can go in (you have to ring the bell and wait for a green light, so it's probably best not to go dressed as a punk or a samurai) and ask for whatever you want – they have everything. You're looking for sixteenth-century religious engravings? There's a file. Or nineteenth-century Italian water-colours, modern abstracts, English caricatures – it's all there.

As in the previous gallery, I asked for views of Paris – rather a touristy question, I thought, but it was welcomed with just as much courtesy as if I'd asked to see their signed Manets. And the three fat files I was given were a veritable goldmine, or inkmine. There were some fascinating seventeenth-century engravings showing Paris with sandy riverbanks and the Seine awash with boats of all sizes, at a time when the Tuileries ended in open countryside. There were also views of the Bastille when the prison was still standing proud at the gates of the city – a smallish medieval castle that would become world-famous only when it was knocked down. I also found nineteenth-century pictures of the shabby, shady Marais full of brothels and absinthe dens rather than gay furniture shops, and scenes of Montmartre as a real village, its windmills grinding out flour rather than can-can music. My favourites, though, were some large, hand-coloured eighteenth-century prints of palaces and gardens, including a rustic-looking view of the Élysée, now the presidential palace, with some soldiers gazing rather threateningly at the artist. Revolution in the air, perhaps.

And all these slices of Parisian art history cost around a hundred euros, little more than a meal at a Michelin-starred restaurant. Personally I'd opt to have a sandwich at the corner café and buy the art.

Oh, and I did find an Arp on my travels – a beautiful little signed engraving, showing (I now know) a couple of bulbous navels. And from what I saw, Arp's prices are going up. Art collectors have been warned . . .

A bid for glory

Another typically Parisian place to buy a picture or sculpture, and a relatively cheap one, is Drouot, the complex of auction rooms near the *grands boulevards*. It's a sort of Galeries Lafayette for everything secondhand – the difference being that you invent your own price. This is where most of the city's art and antique dealers buy, and where ordinary Parisians can acquire art at wholesale rates.

It's a bizarre place – a mixture of attempted modernity (the '70s glass building, the small escalators between floors) and old-school tradition (the red carpets, the armies of porters and the constant feeling that you're looking at the contents of Balzac's house), and gives off an air of impenetrability. Until recently, its workings were something of a mystery, but the walls of secrecy were torn down in late 2009, for a wonderfully Parisian reason . . .

At the time, Drouot's porters, responsible for moving all the objects for sale or pre-sale valuation into and around the building, were instantly recognizable by their black uniform with a sliver of red at the collar. They were nicknamed *Savoyards* because, for over a century, they were just that – in 1860, as a welcoming gift to the state of Savoie, which had just joined France, the Emperor Napoleon III made a rule stipulating that only people from that region could work as porters at Drouot. After 1980, non-Alpine natives were allowed to don the red collar, but their working practices still included some historical quirks – jobs were allocated amongst the Savoyards by a roll of the dice. Get a six and you were moving jewellery. Throw a one and it was wardrobes.

Their job was not confined to shifting things around – they were also responsible for making inventories of incoming lots, and this was what caused their downfall. In 2009, it was alleged that some of them had been unable to resist the temptation to make certain valuable objects go 'missing', including a Courbet painting. Such scams were especially easy, it was said, when houses were cleared and their contents put up for sale to pay death duties. Grieving relatives had usually helped themselves to the best items, so they weren't going to notice the disappearance of *grand-mère*'s antique clock, her silver candlesticks or (apparently) her pre-Impressionist painting.

According to an article in the *Figaro* newspaper, a group of Savoyards were also accused of a much more subtle scam – when a load of furniture arrived, they would take the doors off a wardrobe or the cushions off a chair and then buy the incomplete object at auction at cut price. The wardrobe or chair would then be re-assembled and sold, in perfect condition, for a hefty profit.

Their whole operation was foolproof, the *Figaro* said, because if a complaint was made, the missing item or parts would instantly be 'found' and all suspicions quashed.

At the end of 2009, eight of the 110 porters were tried for theft, at which point the French media pounced upon the story with unrestrained glee. Here was one of Paris's oldest art establishments being forced to wash its dirty *lingerie* in public. It was reported that, by holding on to fraudulently acquired objects for six months and then selling them at Drouot via a 'friendly' auctioneer, some of the Savoyards were doubling their already ample salary of 4,000 euros a month.

In August 2010, a judge ruled that the Savoyards were collec-tively answerable to a series of highly imagistic charges – *association de malfaiteurs en vue d'un ou plusieurs crimes* (frequenting wrong-doers with a view to committing one or more crimes), *complicité de vols en bande organisée* (conspiracy to commit organized-gang theft) and *recel de vols en bande organisée* (receiving stolen property as an organized gang) – the kinds of accusations usually aimed at Corsican gangsters. The Savoyards' reign had come to an end, and they have since been officially disbarred from working at Drouot, and replaced by polo-shirted newcomers.

The auction house has also appointed, for the first time ever, a director general who is not an auctioneer – he's a manager and, effectively, security man in chief.

Despite the scandal, the auction house's Zola-esque frenzy of activity hasn't slowed down. Look at the calendar of upcoming sales on their website, drouot.com, and on almost any given day (including Sundays) you can find sales of anything from nineteenth-century drawings and vintage *haute couture* to clocks, coins, books, militaria, and (in the week I am looking at now) buttons, oriental art, carpets, wine, perfume bottles, picture frames ('ancient and modern') and Armenian paintings.

Drouot has more than a dozen sales rooms, and it is fascinating to wander in, browse the objects laid out for pre-auction viewing, and then drop into a sale that is in full swing. There is nothing to stop anyone going in to watch, and there's little danger of buying anything by accident, even if you have the most violent nervous twitch, because if you're not a regular, you really do have to wave energetically and catch the auctioneer's eye to bid.

Even so, ordinary members of the public have as much chance as the professionals of picking up a real bargain. Dealers will usually stop bidding for an object once the price reaches half of what they think they can sell it for, and they won't buy anything they're not sure of getting rid of, so if you see a faded painting in a battered frame and can be bothered to wait for its number to come up (lots go at a rate of about one per minute), then you have an excellent chance of winning the auction.

And it really does feel like winning a Parisian game. The object you covet is solemnly carried forward by a porter, the auctioneer reads out its description, and then you quickly find out if anyone else has taken a fancy to it. If they have, and put in a low bid, you can have the satisfaction of seeing their surprise when you pitch in with a higher offer. After that, it's like poker – a matter of nerves. You have to decide your maximum limit and play to it. Hold out, and your opponent might give up. If not, and you go beyond your limit, you can end up with a serious case of post-adrenalin depression. You 'won', but at what cost? Did you really pay 100 euros for that dust-encrusted mishmash of paint and its cracked square of peeling wood? Weren't you planning to spend no more than 20? And was that a glimmer of disdain in the auctioneer's eye as his hammer came down?

Well no, it probably wasn't, because Drouot, rather like one of Paris's old *bordels*, is a place where all tastes are equally valid. One man's coffee stain is another man's abstract masterpiece, and as you carry your prize away, you are on an equal footing with the person who has just bought a Louis XVI commode or a Louis Vuitton suitcase. What's more, these days there's no danger that you'll see a sly grin on a Savoyard's face as he recognizes something that had 'gone missing'.

Painting by numbers

If you do decide to try your luck – and your nerve – at an art auction, it is essential to practise oral recognition of French numbers, because there are some very different numbers that sound alarmingly similar. Make a simple mistake, and you could end up bidding rather more than you bargained for.

For example:

vingt-quatre = 24
quatre-vingts = 80

cent deux = 102
deux cents = 200

cent trois = 103
trois cents = 300 (etc., up to 109/900)

mille cent = 1,100
cent mille = 100,000

mille deux cents = 1,200
deux cent mille = 200,000 (etc., up to 1,900/900,000).

Though one would hope that if you suddenly caused the bidding to jump from, say, *mille deux cents* (1,200) euros to *trois cent mille* (300,000), the auctioneer would stop and ask for confirmation.

And if you win the bidding, you'll hear the auctioneer call out, 'Adjugé!' – sold. At which time you just have to hope that you got your numbers right . . .

The ad said 'furnished', but it didn't specify *how* furnished. Apartment-hunting in Paris requires the attention to detail of a micro-biologist.

12

APARTMENTS

On croit souvent qu'un appartement est bas de plafond, alors qu'il est tout simplement haut de plancher.
(You often think that an apartment has low ceilings, when in fact it just has high floors.)

Pierre Dac, French comedian

One foot on the ground

WHAT SHOULD you do if you like Paris so much that you want to become a more frequent Parisian? Or even a permanent one? Lots of people decide to do so, and go native by buying a place here. These include French people, too. Many of them live in the deepest, darkest provinces but have a Parisian *pied-à-terre*, or 'foot on the ground' – a rather painful image, as if they are stuck halfway while trying to disembark from a rowing boat. And for the unprepared, buying an apartment in Paris can feel a lot like that.

Even native Parisians often find buying property in their city a stressful, confusing process, because it is a relatively new experience for them as a sociological group. Until only ten or fifteen years ago, renting was so easy and cheap that buying wasn't something that Parisians usually bothered about. Most middle-class couples were happy to pay the monthly rent, and spend what savings they had on a *résidence secondaire* – the weekend/holiday house on the coast, just outside Paris, or *au pays* in the region of France where one of their families came from. Then, once they'd dragged the kids through the education system, they simply stopped paying their Parisian rent (usually by passing the lease on to a family member) and retired to the *résidence secondaire*, which had long been paid for. It was a gloriously cosy system that, ever since the building craze under Haussmann in the mid-nineteenth century, had divided Paris in two – the rich who owned the apartment buildings, and the less affluent, but often comfortably off, who rented.

Even twenty-five years ago, a typical Parisian estate agency was a narrow, dingy shopfront with a few handwritten cards in the window. The atmosphere inside was dusty and paper-swamped, like the office of a solicitor on the verge of retirement. Often they were just that – lots of properties were sold by *notaires* acting for families who'd inherited them and couldn't decide which brother or sister was going to live there. Commissions on sales were huge – up to 10 per cent – so there was no need to achieve a high turnover. Four or five family-sized apartments a year could provide a very healthy second income for a solicitor. Apartments could moulder for weeks or months in a file on a *notaire*'s desk, waiting for one of his clients to mention that they might want to invest in property.

Buying to rent wasn't attractive, either, because tenants' rights had been set in stone by a post-war law aimed at repairing the trauma of the Occupation. From now on, it was announced on 1 September 1948, the French were going to occupy their rented homes at the same rent practically *ad infinitum*. The *loi de 1948* fixed maximum rents, stipulated that rental agreements were completely open-ended, and that tenants could be evicted only if the landlord or landlady intended to live in the apartment or give it to his or her children – although it was impossible to budge any tenant over sixty-five or on a low income. And even when eviction was possible, the owner had to give six months' notice and offer the tenants 'equivalent' housing elsewhere, the notion of equivalence being so vague that a tenant could hang on for years claiming that the new place wasn't as conveniently located, didn't have a bidet etc., etc. And the worst thing for landlords was that these '1948' tenancies could be passed on from parent to child or sibling to sibling. Renting out was little more than charity work.

Given these conditions, many owners gave up and sold the apartments, either 'occupés' (and therefore much cheaper), or directly to the occupants, who had first refusal anyway. Meanwhile, almost no new apartments were coming on to the rental market – why build and rent out a place if you knew that it was going to be squatted at a government-capped rate?

It was therefore to try and reboot the rental market that, in 1986, the French government overturned the *loi de '48* – without pulling the carpet out from under existing tenants' feet. Now, if a tenant moved out, the owners could charge what they liked for a new lease rather than adhering to a capped rent. But instead of freeing up the rental market, this only created a new stagnation. Rents rose so sharply that prospective new tenants had to provide almost impossible guarantees – this was when it first became common for young people to turn up at rental agencies carrying a dossier stuffed with their own and their parents' pay slips, the deeds to their grandparents' country house, a letter from their boss guaranteeing the company's survival for the next twenty years, and a promise to sell their kidneys if they were late with the rent.

Meanwhile the new rent-hiking policy sent speculators knocking at the doors of Paris's richer *arrondissements*. Did the family by any chance have an apartment building that it wanted to get rid of? If the answer was yes, a couple of months later, men in suits would be tramping up and down staircases, bribing tenants to leave or forcing them out by doing renovation work – one of the few escape clauses in the 1948 law was that tenants could be removed during *travaux* and their rent increased because the apartment had gained significantly in *confort*.

As planned, the number of 1948-type rentals began to fall, but even this legal eviction policy didn't always prove efficient because of the high number of old (and therefore unmovable) tenants, and the sheer doggedness of Parisians whose whole lifestyle was based on a rent that had barely increased since their mum and dad moved into the apartment forty years earlier.

Abandoning the plan to rent out whole buildings at extortionate rates, many of the speculators began to cut their losses and sell individual apartments. At last, private ownership entered the Parisian consciousness and, with renting less secure and banks offering fixed-rate mortgages, it suddenly became very fashionable to buy. In short, Paris went from no market at all to a boom in only a few years. And unlike an internet bubble or mobile-phone bonanza, it was a small, finite market – Paris is only so big, and there are only so many apartments that can be bought. Until France decides to move its capital elsewhere, or foreigners lose interest in the city's sex appeal, property is going to be highly sought-after.

There is good news, however, and it is twofold. First, there is a fairly high turnover in apartment sales. And secondly, not all of Paris has so far revealed its potential *charme* and been gentrified out of reach.

The question is, how to cash in on these good tidings?

Location, location, location*

The first consideration is, of course, can I afford to buy a *pied-à-terre*? And if you look in the estate agents' windows in the parts of

---

* This title is a shameless French property pun – *la location* means rental (location would be *la situation*). The joke is in totally the wrong place, because this chapter is about buying not renting, but it's just more proof that in France puns crop up at the most inappropriate times.

town that attract the most visitors, the answer would probably be no. But that, quite frankly, is not a problem, because those areas have a major disadvantage – do you really want to come to Paris only to sit in the local café with your morning croissant and listen to people at the other tables saying things like, 'Avez-vous du *normal tea*?' and 'Vous n'avez pas de cappuccinos?' Even if your lack of linguistic skills means that you might want to say something similar yourself, it'd be nice to be the only one doing so. Some cafés in the central *arrondissements* – especially the 6th – have more customers reading the *International Herald Tribune* than *Le Monde*, and waiters who will immediately address you in English. You might as well be in your local fake French café.

In any case, unless you're very rich, the only affordable apartments in these *arrondissements* will be the top-floor *chambres de bonne*, the old servants' quarters, most of which have now been converted into studios. These can seem remarkably cheap, until you realize that they're up six flights of stairs and that your neighbours are all students, who are so relieved to have escaped from *chez Maman et Papa* that they live as wildly, noisily and nocturnally as possible. Combine these factors with the statistic about top-floor apartments being the easiest to burgle (the thieves creep across the rooftops) and the fact that many *chambres de bonne* share a toilet on the landing (even if you don't have to share, your landing is still going to smell like a public convenience) and you might decide that a posh *arrondissement* is not for you after all. Besides, there are some fairly central neighbourhoods (and let's face it, Paris is so small that most of it could be described as 'fairly central') that are safe, attractive, affordable and very Parisian . . .

Double agents

When looking to buy a Parisian apartment, the easiest solution is probably to go into one of the estate agencies, sit down and tell your life story. Well, that's what it will feel like, because what the agents usually do is spend ten minutes or so taking your name (which, if you're foreign, you will have to spell several times before they get it right), your mobile number, home number, work number, email address and the shoe size of your uncle's donkey. Once this ritual is over, the agent might well inform you that the apartment you saw in their shop window is now sold (it was probably sold months ago, but looks good so they leave it in there as bait), but they have several 'similar' properties, which all turn out to be totally dissimilar.

The agent will then promise to to call you on all your phone numbers, email you and send a singing telegram as soon as something comes in.

Which, to be fair, they probably will, about a year later, when you have already moved into your new Parisian apartment. This happened to me once, and I told the agent he was too late. But he kept ringing for about another two years, at one point even saying, 'Oh well, maybe you'll be thinking of moving again soon.'

There are, of course, agents in Paris who specialize in dealing with non-Parisian buyers, and whose training includes lessons in how to be less Parisian. The trouble with these is that they usually sell apartments in the most tourist-heavy parts of Paris, and assume that foreign clients will want to visit the Louvre, the Panthéon or the Pont Neuf every morning on their way to the *boulangerie*.

Perhaps the worst thing about Parisian estate agents, though, especially for a buyer who is not *au fait* with the complexities of the Parisian market, is that if an apartment has any kind of major flaw – and they often do – the agent is there to hide the fact. Of course, we all know that that is an estate agent's basic function in any city in the world, but in Paris they can actually get away with it. If a British estate agent tells you that a house is leaning at a 45-degree angle 'to let more light into the ground-floor windows' or that 'Yes, the back garden has got 10 yards shorter since that storm but the council is going to stop the cliff erosion next week,' the lies will be revealed as soon as you get the surveyor's report. In France, though, there is no surveyor's report. As long as the subsidence isn't caused by termites, asbestos or lead paint, the buyer will remain in the dark about any inherent problems with the building.

I once visited a building that had a green-black stain running down half the façade, from about the third floor to street level, on either side of the gutter downpipe. When I expressed concern about this, the agent said that the *syndic* (the building's management company) was going to repair it – it was just a leaky gutter. Inside the building, there were deep cracks in the walls of the stairwell, but again I was assured that the *syndic* was on the case.

I visited the apartment, which was fine in itself, and asked to see the latest *compte rendu de réunion des copropriétaires* (the report written by the *syndic* after every annual owners' meeting, which has to be made available to potential buyers). The agent said he would send it, but 'quite honestly there was nothing interesting in it', and in any case, I really ought to make an offer straight away – he had several other clients interested, including one who was coming up specially from Marseille to re-visit the apartment that very afternoon, and was probably going to buy it.

This was, of course, a tactic straight out of Chapter One of *Selling to Gullible Idiots*, so I trusted my instincts and said *merci* but *non merci*. But, just out of interest, I hunted around and found the building's *syndic*. I called them, saying I was a potential buyer, and the person on the other end of the phone actually laughed. The *syndic* was, she said, in the process of tearing up that building's management contract. The owners could never agree amongst themselves to do any repairs, the façade was about to collapse on to passers-by, City Hall had already threatened legal action, and anyone buying an apartment there right now might as well throw their money in the Seine, which was where half the building would end up if things didn't get better very quickly.

Which was not exactly what the agent had told me.

Neighbourhoods can have their own surprise drawbacks, too, of course. A street lined with cafés can seem picturesque in the daytime, but be transformed into a yelling, music-thudding, bottle-smashing battlefield at night. It is no longer true that the French know how to hold their alcohol. They've discovered binge drinking and are suffering all the consequences, as are the people who live where they have their binges.

On the other hand, the office building next door to the apartment you're visiting can be as silent as newly fallen snow in the evening but shudder and hum like a battleship's engines on a summer's day when you want to sit on your balcony reading Proust. The agent will know this and make sure you visit when the apartment, and the neighbourhood, is *très calme*.

Now I am not saying that all Parisian agents are dishonest, of course. No doubt, there are as many helpful, truthful agents as there are in any other city. It's just that, like all people paid on commission, they can be tempted to bend the truth slightly to make a sale. All the more so because even with green sludge covering half a building's façade, there will be someone willing to buy an apartment there.

Doing it direct

The way to avoid the clutches of an agent is to buy direct from the owner. The most common way of doing this is to answer one of the ads in the property magazine *De Particulier à Particulier* (from non-professional to non-professional). The ads also appear on their website, www.pap.fr. If you're looking to buy, you want the *annonces de vente*, and if you just want to rent, the *locations* (as I said earlier, *location* means rental rather than geographical position).

In theory, buying direct from the owner is cheaper because of the lack of commission, but some owners are greedy and clearly base their asking prices on ads they have seen in agencies. And there is no reason why an owner should be more honest than an estate agent – after all, the owners are on 100 per cent commission.

I have heard various sellers' tales about the scams they pulled to get a buyer. One man lived across the landing from a terribly noisy family. The daughter would stay at home all weekend listening to her radio at full volume, and bad French pop at the decibel level of a 747 taking off can scare away even Parisians. The owner therefore offered the girl a month's supply of M&Ms if she would agree to turn the music off whenever he was arranging viewings. Sure enough, the following silent Saturday, the place was sold.

In short, since it is illegal in France to view apartments armed with a lie detector or truth serum, buying a Parisian *pied-à-terre* is all about instinct. In a way, it's a lot like falling in love. Either there's a spark or there's nothing, and it's all a matter of taste. If you can fall in love with someone who has green sludge running down their face or who stands at a 45-degree angle, then *c'est la vie*.

C'est un toilette, ça?

I recently went on to www.pap.fr and found that, like all things fundamentally Parisian, nothing had changed in the years since I first went hunting for a small apartment.*

* For an only slightly exaggerated account of that debacle, readers might like to look at the 'Octobre' chapter in *A Year in the Merde*.

This time, things began smoothly, with a search page. I agreed that I wanted to *rechercher un bien* (a property), ticked the *appartement* box, typed in the postcodes that interested me (75003, 75011, 75019 – the 3rd, 11th and 19th *arrondissements*, my own favourite band of central and northeast Paris), chose a maximum *surface* (area) of 30 square metres, and my idea of a maximum price for a *pied-à-terre*, remembering not to put commas between zeros because French websites think they're decimal points, then hit *rechercher* and got eleven ads – not many, admittedly.

I immediately realized why there were so few ads – only one of my chosen *arrondissements* had come up. This wasn't a serious bug, however, because at the bottom of the list the site tells you how many similar ads are in all the other *arrondissements*, so you can click there whenever you want.

The first thing I did was *trier les annonces* – sort the ads, asking for the most recent first. These are marked *annonce nouvelle du . . .* plus the date. I knew from past experience that the ones listed as *annonce mise à jour* (updated) were probably sold, especially as I was looking for the size of apartment with the quickest turnover – there are investors galore looking to put their savings in stone rather than let the stock market evaporate them away, as well as a whole generation of Parisians trying desperately to evict their stay-at-home student kids into an apartment so they don't have to keep yelling at them for smoking in the toilet.

These days, the jargon* used in the ads actually means something to me, both the literal meaning of each term and its (often very different) implications.

The first ad needed no translation, however. It was a *chambre de bonne* with, if I was interpreting the photo correctly, a toilet beneath its only window, right next to the kitchen units – ideal for

---

* For a full, translated list of the French vocabulary used in property ads, see the Scrapbook section of my website, www.stephenclarkewriter.com.

anyone with digestive troubles or who had recently escaped from prison, but not much else.

The next place was the complete opposite – three times the size of the live-in toilet but only twice the price, near but not too near République (a great *métro* junction for getting anywhere in Paris in minutes), very pretty, very well laid out. And, when I phoned, very sold, only two days after the ad had appeared.

Browsing further, I found five or six decent-looking apartments of various sizes, and rang up. Each time it was a mobile phone, and each time I had to tell the voicemail, 'J'ai vu votre annonce dans le *Particulier*, et je voudrais visiter l'appartement.'

And although I had pronounced my phone number very clearly and didn't sound at all like an estate agent trying to hassle the owner, only two people called back. The others, I guessed, must have sold already. Speed is of the essence.

Anyway, I finally got a bite, and one Saturday at ten in the morning, I stood outside a grey, middle-class nineteenth-century building near the Père Lachaise cemetery, and keyed in the door code I'd been given. I then keyed it in again. And again. I took a deep breath, tried one more time and phoned the owner to ask for the correct code. Voicemail, of course, but it didn't matter because as I was about to leave a frantic message, a man came out and held the door open for me. Another deep breath, this time to smell the staircase. Pretty neutral – a good sign. No bizarre food smells, no medieval dampness, no stale cigarette smoke.

The ad had said *sixième ascenseur*, sixth floor with lift, but I didn't fancy the look of the minuscule cabin that had been slotted down the middle of the staircase. I once read an article in a French paper about how often lifts break down and how difficult it is to call out the repair people at weekends. Two days standing in a matchbox? *Non merci.* I opted to go up on foot.

Six floors isn't bad as long as you don't expect to speak for ten minutes after your arrival at the top of the stairs, and I soon found

A 'romantic garret' in the 1940s. Today, in the Latin Quarter, this cupboard-sized apartment would cost about as much as a château in Auvergne – and be snapped up instantly.

myself hyperventilating comfortably in a low-ceilinged, but quite attractive, corridor. It had a varnished tiled floor, making it look as though it was made from large toffees, and a definite artist's-garret feel, with the water pipes picked out in dark velvet red against the creamy white of the walls.

The owner had told me *sixième droite*, sixth floor on the right, and although I could see three doors to my right, it was easy to spot which was the apartment for sale. The door was ajar and I could hear a loud voice dictating the address over the phone.

I knocked, noting that the lock was flimsy and would have to be replaced, and, getting no reply, pushed open the door to see a typically Parisian tableau – an open window with a body leaning half out into the street, a cigarette in one hand and a phone in the other. The owner, a fifty-something man with longish grey hair and a leather jacket, beckoned me in as he carried on making a date for another viewing. Holding his cigarette even further outside, as if to offer a puff to the pigeons, he gestured at me to look around.

The place was listed as 18 square metres, so there wasn't a whole lot to see. A room painted dirty white, with a cheap laminated table and fold-up chair against one wall (the apartment was being *vendu meublé* – sold furnished), a sofa smothered in a sort of chocolate-brown blanket cum tent in the other. Also a fake-pine chest of drawers with an Olympic-rings effect of mug stains and a few stubbed-out cigarette craters.

As I admired the furniture, the owner, still talking on the phone, made a dismissive gesture as if to say, All yours if you want them, you don't even have to buy the apartment.

Wondering if I would ever get a personal interview, I went into the next room. Half its width was taken up with a pair of kitchen units, one of which had a much-used electric ring on top, the other a stainless-steel sink. Next to these, on the same wall, was a shower cubicle, with a plastic curtain that looked brand new, and a beige plastic concertina door behind which there was a sort of toilet. I say sort of toilet because it had a bowl and a cistern, but was squat and slightly square, as if it would have preferred to be a sink. It was sitting on a white box that was plugged into the wall. I wondered whether it wasn't some kind of built-in sex toy – the vibrating toilet seat. It all looked vaguely familiar, and I wondered if I hadn't seen one in an old French film.

'Bonjour!' The owner came in behind me, apologizing for having been on the phone. He took my name, crossed me off a list and began to tell me, rather amicably, everything I already knew from the ad.

I interrupted him.

'C'est un toilette, ça?' I asked.

'C'est un sani-broyeur,' he said, and it all came flooding back – almost literally. When I first arrived in Paris, I spent a couple of weeks using one of these. Or rather, one week using it and another week waiting for a plumber to come and fix it. The *sani-broyeur* is a devilishly clever invention, and has allowed countless French apartment owners to stop using the shared loo on the staircase and install their own facilities, even when (and this is the key point) there is no regular-sized toilet downpipe within range. These machines can be plumbed in to a normal water outflow pipe, hence the *broyeur* (grinder) part of their name.

Instinctively I reached out and flushed, always a good thing to do when visiting an apartment. A toilet that doesn't work is a good indicator that things might not be so well maintained elsewhere.

The *sani-broyeur* sucked away the water in the bowl, and then did its grinding.

'You can get really silent ones now,' the owner said, waving his telephone perilously close to the bowl.

I honestly didn't want to know.

'Why are you selling?' I asked. Again, a key question. If the owner looks cagey, there could be trouble afoot. A messy divorce or inheritance dispute between rowing siblings can sink a sale.

'We're retiring to the *campagne*,' he said. 'I'm selling everything.' He looked too young to be opting out of work, but this was France and he was of the generation that had it good. If he'd worked since leaving school, he could get a full pension. Selling off his Paris property and moving to the *résidence secondaire* would allow him to grow old very comfortably.

Meanwhile, something else had just occurred to me. I went back and stood in the doorway to the other room. The apartment had seemed big for 18 square metres, and now it hit me.

'Where's the bed?' I asked.

'C'est un clic-clac,' he said, meaning a fold-out bed.

Of course. And there was no wardrobe, either, or nook to hang a clothes rail. To be liveable, the room would need filling with furniture. The place wasn't furnished as much as half-furnished.

The owner's phone started ringing, and with a quick *excusez-moi*, he took the call and began to confirm that the place hadn't been sold yet and *oui*, the caller could come and visit straight away.

I gestured as if to say I had to go. The owner smiled and nodded goodbye – he could tell I wasn't interested, but he knew that someone else would be.

'Non, non – un sani-broyeur,' he was saying, 'like all the studios on this floor. There's never been a problem.'

I was already halfway to the stairs.

An apartment 'under the roof'

My next visit was very different, mainly because the apartment was extremely tempting, and if I'd had the money (and the need for a *pied-à-terre*, of course) I'd have snapped it up.

It was in the 19th, above Belleville. Not exactly in the centre of town, but an area that is becoming trendier by the day, while keeping most of its traditional shops. The ad was for a *grand studio* in a courtyard, 'under the roof' (that's where all apartments are, you hope, but top-floor places are often advertised using this evocative image of living amongst the roof beams), with a mezzanine, which can allow you to split a studio into two rooms.

I inquired when the owner would be holding viewings and she said, 'All Saturday starting from nine.'

At nine on the dot I was there, but I wasn't the first. In the courtyard – more of a lane than a mere courtyard – there was a middle-aged man taking photos with an iPhone. I went into the *bâtiment de droite*, nodding appreciatively at the note by the door apologizing to neighbours for wedging it open – a good atmosphere in the building, it seemed.

The stairs were bare wood but not in a neglected way, and the stairwell was graffiti-free (there is zero tolerance in any decent Parisian building). Just like my favourite restaurants, it wasn't chic but it didn't need to be.

Pushing open the door (which had a nicely solid lock), the first thing I saw was a woman of about sixty being interviewed by a small thirty-something man who was taking careful notes on his copy of the *Particulier*.

'Et les charges, c'est par mois ou par trimestre?' he asked. (Were the building charges per month or quarter?)

'Par trimestre,' she answered and he tried not to look relieved.

I said *bonjour*, wiped my feet and stepped forward, and the lady waved her arms as if to shoo me further in. She had a bemused but happy look on her face like an artist whose work has un-expectedly become fashionable, and now everyone wants to visit her studio. On the table by her side, there was a blank *compromis de vente* – a sale agreement. She was obviously willing to sign that very morning.

The apartment was everything the ad had promised – simple, blemish-free white walls and a ceiling with no signs that someone had been filling in cracks overnight. An open kitchen-dining area, a living room complete with a sofa, an armchair, an old dresser and TV corner, a double bed up on the mezzanine, and – holy of holies for a studio – a real toilet. The bathroom seemed to have a young couple living in it, but they turned out to be viewers who were squatting on the edge of the bath (yes, it even had a bathtub) discussing whether to put in a bid, and looked nervously up at me as though they were afraid I'd heard their maximum price.

There was a radio playing classical music, so I gestured to the owner (who was still being interviewed) whether it was OK to turn it off. A radio can cover up annoying sounds like a humming air-conditioning unit or a nearby clothes workshop – Paris still has lots of sweatshops with buzzing sewing machines. I listened, opened the window and stuck my head out, listened again, and heard only the distant traffic noise. Excellent sign for a Saturday morning.

Satisfied, I went to hover by the owner and the man taking notes for her biography.

'C'est la première semaine?' he was asking – was it the first week it had been in the paper?

'Oui,' the owner said. I didn't think she'd need a second.

The interviewer nodded, and told me to go ahead with my question – for him, it was thinking time.

I started my own interrogation, hitting the seller with all the essential questions – *charges*, approximate electricity and gas bills, the date of the last *réunion de copropriété* (owners' meeting), when the next *ravalement* (expensive façade clean-up) was due, whether the *toit* (roof) was *en bon état* (good condition – obviously she was going to say yes, but it's worth asking to see the reaction), whether the building was planning any other communally paid work such as a renovation of the courtyard, and, apologizing for being indiscreet, why she was selling. Again, no one is ever going to say, 'Because the neighbours hold all-night bongo and firework parties and breed cockroaches which they feed to their pet baboons,' but it's always interesting to ask.

'I retire in three months, so I won't be coming to Paris any more,' she said.

'So this is your *pied-à-terre*?'

'Yes, I come here for one or two weeks a month. And my husband joins me now and again, of course. I'll be sad to sell after fifteen years, but the children have places of their own, and we can't justify the expense.'

All in all, it was the equivalent of the car with one careful owner.

'Er, Madame . . .' The couple from the bathroom were looking even more nervous. Time to put in a bid, it seemed. I didn't blame them. The apartment was sensibly priced, excellently located, and had a great feel to it. Lived-in, but by someone who loved the place.

'Go ahead,' I told them, and they closed in.

Out on the landing, the guy who'd been conducting his interview was on the phone, and seemed to be telling his girlfriend that she ought to have come with him because he was sure the apartment was going to sell.

Going downstairs, I met the man I'd seen in the courtyard. An investor, I decided, looking to buy to rent. The polite thing to do would have been to wait on the landing and allow him to pass, but I pretended not to have seen him and clattered halfway down the flight of stairs between the second and first floors.

'Oh, désolé,' I apologized, and turned as if to go back up.

'Non, non, je vous en prie.' He beckoned me to come past, not managing very well to hide the fact that he thought I was being impolite.

'Non, j'insiste.' I turned, walked back up the stairs and gestured him through. As he passed, thanking me, I told him, 'The apartment doesn't interest me, anyway.'

'Non?' He looked intrigued.

'Non,' I said, not wishing to elaborate, but with the slightly pained look on my face that is achieved by picturing a *sani-broyeur*. 'Bonne visite,' I wished him, and went on my way.

With any luck, I'd wasted enough of his time, and instilled enough doubt in his mind, to let the young couple seal the deal.

Taking the plunge

This chapter doesn't pretend to be an exhaustive housebuyers' guide, so I won't even try to go into all the legal niceties of property deals. But the most reassuring thing about buying in France is that a deal is a deal. Buyer and seller sign the *compromis de vente* (pre-sale agreement), with no lawyers present, and the seller then has seven days in which to panic and retract, without incurring any penalties. Once those seven days are up, the buyer has to pay 10 per cent of the sale price to the seller's solicitor (*notaire*) as a deposit, then usually has three months or so to put together the finances and find their own solicitor to oversee the transaction.

Buyers can pull out and get their deposit back if the bank refuses a loan or if the obligatory checks (for asbestos, termites, lead paint, etc.) aren't satisfactory, but they are in no danger of being gazumped.

This protection explains why apartments sell so fast. If you visit an apartment that has been advertised in the *Particulier*, you have to go along with ink in your pen and the courage to sign there and then. And you have to phone up the instant you see the ad. Even an hour's hesitation can lose you the deal. Owners selling direct usually want a quick, clean sale at the asking price, so that they don't have to repeat the trauma of having their apartment invaded by hordes of people demanding to know how well their toilet works. And if they haven't overpriced their property, they will find a buyer, and fast. If you aren't willing to act quickly, it's probably better to go to a slower-moving agent.

For people who are trying to get a feel for what's on the market, just doing a few prospecting visits can therefore be useful, and highly revealing. I was once shown around an apartment by a man who looked like a strait-laced French physics teacher, but who was arm in arm with a young Asian ladyboy. He seemed to be selling his lifestyle more than his apartment.

I fled another place because the people trying to sell it were an estranged couple who couldn't even stand to look at each other, let alone negotiate a deal. I could almost hear their lawyers arguing about prices and dates above the echoing silence of their dead relationship.

On the other hand, I bought an apartment from an old shop-keeper who was complaining that the Marais was turning too trendy, and that traditional shops like his vacuum-cleaner store would soon be going out of business. He couldn't wait to leave, and the price came tumbling down.

The moral of the story is that even if the apartments you visit are awful, at least you will have learnt something about Paris and how its citizens live. Not that I'd recommend viewing property as a tourist activity, of course. That would be too cruel to my fellow Parisians . . .

APPENDIX 1
ADDRESSES

VOILÀ THE addresses, phone numbers, websites, emails, etc. – *les coordonnées* as the Parisians would neatly say – of the cafés, restaurants, museums and other places of interest recommended in the book, chapter by chapter. If places occur in more than one chapter, they are listed at the first occurrence, unless they're so important that they need mentioning more than once. If I give the address or location in the main body of the text, I haven't listed it again here. And if I've missed any out, they're on the internet.

Opening times and prices may have changed since I did the research for the book, so please check before going, to avoid disappointment and/or bankruptcy.

And please remember that, as I said in the chapters concerned, some of these places have been recommended not because they are centres of excellence but because they're interesting from a sociological viewpoint. If you get ripped off, insulted or just plain disappointed there, please just put it down as a valid Parisian experience.

NB: Listings are in alphabetical order, and to make things simpler, I have ignored the *le, la, l'* and *les* before names. I've also given the postcodes because they tell you which *arrondissement* the place is in, e.g. 75009 is the 9th *arrondissement*, 75020 is the 20th, etc.

1 Parisians

L'Antenne, 27 rue François Premier, 75008. Tel: 01 47 20 77 39. *Métro*: Franklin D. Roosevelt.

L'Avenue, 41 avenue Montaigne, 75008. Tel: 01 40 70 14 91. *Métro*: Franklin D. Roosevelt.

Bar Ourcq, 68 quai de la Loire, 75019. Tel: 01 42 40 12 26. *Métros*: Stalingrad, Laumière.

Le Bonaparte, 42 rue Bonaparte, 75006. Tel: 01 43 26 42 81. *Métro*: Saint-Germain des Prés.

Café Charlot, 38 rue de Bretagne, 75003. Tel: 01 44 54 03 30. *Métros*: République, Filles du Calvaire.

Le Concorde, 239 boulevard Saint-Germain, 75007. Tel: 01 45 51 43 71. *Métro*: Assemblée Nationale.

La Coupole, 102 boulevard du Montparnasse, 75014. Tel: 01 43 20 14 20. *Métro*: Vavin.

Les Éditeurs, 4 carrefour de l'Odéon, 75006. Tel: 01 43 26 67 76. *Métro*: Odéon.

Enfants Rouges market, rue de Bretagne, 75003, entrances just opposite the Café Charlot (see above, in this chapter).

La Flèche d'Or, 102*bis* rue de Bagnolet, 75020. Tel: 01 44 64 01 02. *Métro*: Gambetta.

Les Gladines, 30 rue des Cinq Diamants, 75013. Tel: 01 45 80 70 10. *Métros*: Corvisart, Place d'Italie.

La Grande Épicerie, 24 rue de Sèvres, 75007. Tel: 01 44 39 81 00. *Métro*: Sèvres–Babylone.

Mama Shelter Hotel, 109 rue de Bagnolet, 75020. Tel: 01 43 48 48 48. *Métro*: Gambetta.

Musée Marmottan, 2 rue Louis Boilly, 75016. Tel: 01 44 96 50 33. *Métro*: Muette. Website: www.marmottan.com. Open every day except Monday, 11 a.m.–6 p.m., and Tuesdays till 9 p.m.

Le Nemours, 2 place Colette, 75001. Tel: 01 42 61 42 16. *Métro*: Palais-Royal.

Le Pause Café, 41 rue de Charonne, 75011. Tel: 01 48 06 80 33. *Métro*: Ledru-Rollin.

2 Pavements

Hôtel Meurice, 228 rue de Rivoli, 75001. Tel: 01 44 58 10 10. *Métro*: Concorde.

Lycée Janson de Sailly, 106 rue de la Pompe, 75016. *Métro*: Rue de la Pompe.

Vespasienne, outside Prison de la Santé, boulevard Arago, 75014 Paris. *Métros*: Saint-Jacques, Denfert-Rochereau. Tel: As far as I know, *pissoirs* don't have phones.

3 Water

Canal de l'Ourcq: boats from the Bassin de la Villette and the Parc de la Villette go up the canal to northern suburbs like Pantin, Bondy and Aulnay-sous-Bois. Every weekend from the end of May to the end of August. Saturdays 1 euro, Sundays 2 euros. A chance to see old industrial sites (renovated and very much not) and, sadly, homeless people's camps. A piece of advice – don't decide to get off at the terminus and find a cosy restaurant. There's almost nowhere to eat and only poor neighbourhoods to see. Come back with the boat.

Chez Clément, 9 place Saint-André des Arts, 75006. Tel: 08 99 23 48 14. *Métro*: Saint-Michel.

Pont de l'Alma, bridge at the exit of *métro* station Alma–Marceau.

The *Zouave* is on the up-river (eastern) side.

Quai Saint-Bernard, near the Institut du Monde Arabe: dancing happens here every night in July and August, unless it's raining. It's all semi-improvised, and all free. Being a French event, it's strictly categorized into rock'n'roll, tango, salsa, hip-hop, etc. *Métro*: Jussieu.

Sewers (Égouts de Paris), opposite 93 quai d'Orsay, 75007. Tel: 01 53 68 27 81. *Métro*: Alma–Marceau. Open Saturday–Wednesday, 11 a.m.–4 p.m. from October to April; and 11 a.m.–5 p.m. May–September.

Water-themed guided tours, Eau de Paris, see the website: www.eaudeparis.fr/page/pavillon/parcours-conferences?page_id=93

4 The *Métro*

Basilique de Saint-Denis, the ancient royal cathedral north of Paris. Saint-Denis is better known for the Stade de France and occasional rioting, but this cathedral was the first-ever gothic building, and the burial place of all French kings up to the Revolution. April–September 10 a.m.–6.15 p.m., Sundays 12 noon–6.15 p.m.; October–March 10 a.m.–5 p.m., Sundays 12 noon–5.15 p.m. *Métro*: Basilique de Saint-Denis.

La Flèche d'Or, see Chapter 1 listings.

Parc André Citroën, a large modern park in the 15th *arrondissement*, worth a visit to take a fixed-balloon ride 150 metres up to see the Paris skyline, including the nearby Eiffel Tower. Adults 12 euros at weekends, 10 euros weekdays, reductions for young people. Open every day from 9 a.m. until 30 minutes before the park closes (usually at dusk). To check that day's opening times, tel: 01 44 26 20 00. *Métros*: Javel, Balard.

5 History

Arènes de Lutèce, hidden behind the walls at 51 rue Monge, 75005, or accessible via the garden in rue des Arènes. *Métros*: Place Monge, Cardinal Lemoine, Jussieu.

Café de Flore, 172 boulevard Saint-Germain, 75006. Tel: 01 45 48 55 26. *Métro*: Saint-Germain des Prés.

Chapelle Expiatoire, square Louis XVI, 29, rue Pasquier, 75008. Tel: 01 44 32 18 00. *Métros*: Saint-Lazare, Saint-Augustin, Havre–Caumartin. Open 1 p.m.–5 p.m., Thursday, Friday, Saturday, as well as on most bank holidays, and Bastille Day (14 July).

Musée Carnavalet, 23 rue de Sévigné, 75004. Tel: 01 44 59 58 58. *Métro*: Saint-Paul. Open 10 a.m.–6 p.m., every day except Mondays and (to quote the museum) 'Sundays from Easter to Pentecost'.

Thermes de Cluny, part of the Musée du Moyen Âge, 6 place Paul Painlevé, 75005. Tel: 01 53 73 78 16. *Métros*: Cluny–La Sorbonne, Saint-Michel. Open every day except Tuesday, 9.15 a.m.–5.45 p.m. Closed Christmas Day and New Year's Day.

6 Romance

Amour, hotel and restaurant, 8 rue de Navarin, 75009. Tel: 01 48 78 31 80. *Métros*: Pigalle, Saint-Georges.

Bassin de la Villette, large canal basin just northeast of Stalingrad *métro* station. Big, wet and greenish-brown. You can't miss it.

Café Restaurant Le Temple, 87 rue Turbigo, 75003. Tel: 01 42 72 30. *Métros*: Temple, République.

The Champ-de-Mars gardens stretch between the École Militaire and the Eiffel Tower, and are open all the time. *Métros*: École Militaire, Bir-Hakeim.

La Coupole, see listings for Chapter 1.

Hôtel des Grandes Écoles, 75 rue Cardinal Lemoine, 75005. Tel: 01 43 26 79 23. *Métro*: Cardinal Lemoine.

MK2 Quai de Loire, MK2 Quai de Seine, cinemas on either side of the Bassin de la Villette (see above, in this chapter).

Palais-Royal gardens, 75001 Paris, main access points at 6 rue de Montpensier, or behind Le Nemours café (see Chapter 1 listings). *Métro*: Palais-Royal. Open at 7 a.m., and close at 8.30 p.m. between 31 March and 1 October; 9.30 p.m. in June and September; and 10.30 p.m. between 1 April and 31 May.

Pont des Arts crosses the Seine just west of the Île de la Cité. *Métro*: Louvre-Rivoli. (It will probably need a phone number soon, so you can book a place at sunset.)

Le Ritz, 15 place Vendôme, 75001. 01 43 16 30 30 (and ask to book a table in *le bar* or *le jardin*). *Métro*: you really want to go to the Ritz by *métro*? Why not – I always do. Opéra and Concorde are both handy.

La Villa Royale, 2 rue Duperré, 75009. Tel: 01 55 31 78 78. *Métro*: Pigalle.

7 Sex

Le Chabanais brothel. It was closed in 1946, you naughty person.

Le Crazy Horse, 12 avenue George V, 75008. Tel: 01 55 26 10 10. *Métro*: George V, Alma–Marceau.

Musée de l'Érotisme, 72 boulevard de Clichy, 75018. *Métro*: Blanche. Open seven days a week, 10 a.m. to 2 a.m.

8 Food

Aligre market, place d'Aligre, 75012. *Métro*: Ledru-Rollin. Market hall open every day except Monday. Big food market and flea market on Sundays.

Café Voisin, rue Saint-Honoré – closed in 1930, and stopped serving camel and elephant long before that.

Le Grenier à Pain boulangerie, 38 rue des Abbesses, 75018. Tel: 01 42 23 85 36. *Métro*: Abbesses.

Joinville outdoor food market, rue de Joinville, 75019. *Métro*: Crimée. Thursday and Sunday mornings.

Musée Carnavalet, see Chapter 5 listings.

9 Fashion

Bandits Manchots, website: www.banditsmanchots.net.

L'Éclaireur, *bobo* shop: for various branches, see www.leclaireur.com (the website is a Parisian experience in itself).

10 Cinema

Forum des Images, Porte Saint-Eustache, Les Halles, 75001. Tel: 01 44 76 62 00. *Métro*: Les Halles. For full opening times and prices, see: www.forumdesimages.fr.

The paris.fr website offers downloads of bilingual *Parcours Cinéma* or Paris film trails, little guides listing the main locations of (at the time of writing) a dozen or so films. And they don't stick to intellectual French productions – *Rush Hour 3* has a *Parcours* (presumably because the producers spent a fortune filming at the Eiffel Tower, the Invalides and the Opéra). Even the cartoon

Ratatouille has one, though the animators probably didn't do any of their graphic wizardry down in the real sewers. According to Mission Cinéma, there will be more of these *Parcours* on line soon.

11 Art

Pierre Chandelier, painter, see www.chandelier.free.fr.

Cité Fleurie, 65 boulevard Arago, 75013. *Métro*: Les Gobelins.

Cité des Fusains, 22 rue Tourlaque, 75018. *Métros*: Place de Clichy, Blanche.

Drouot auction house, 9 rue Drouot, 75009. Tel: 01 48 00 20 20. *Métro*: Richelieu–Drouot. Check www.drouot.com for sales dates. It is a French company, so there isn't generally much activity in July, and none at all in August.

Fondation Arp, 21 rue des Châtaigniers, 92140 Clamart. Tel: 01 45 34 22 63. Train station: Meudon-Val Fleury on Line C of the RER. Open Friday, Saturday, Sunday, Monday, 2–6 p.m.

La Forge de Belleville, 23–5 rue Ramponeau, 75020. *Métro*: Belleville. For events and art classes, check www. tracesabelleville.org. However, due to the dispute between the different groups of artists in the studios, the information might not be exhaustive.

Guy Honore, ceramic artist, 14, rue Dénoyez, 75020. *Métro*: Belleville.

Journées Portes Ouvertes (artists' open days), see listings at:
    www.parisgratuit.com/ateliers.html
    www.ateliers-artistes-belleville.org
    www.ateliersdemenilmontant.org
    www.montmartre-aux-artistes.org
and others.

Musée Marmottan, 2 rue Louis Boilly, 75016. Tel: 01 44 96 50 33. *Métro*: Muette. Website: www.marmottan.com. Open every day except Monday, 11 a.m.–6 p.m., and Tuesdays till 9 p.m.

Paul Prouté, 74 rue de Seine, 75006. Tel: 01 43 26 89 80. *Métros*: Mabillon, Odéon.

Villa Mallebay, starts at 88 rue Didot, 75014. *Métros*: Pernety, Alésia.

12 Apartments

De Particulier à Particulier property sales magazine, commonly called *Le Particulier* for short, comes out every Thursday. All ads also appear on their website, www.pap.fr.

APPENDIX 2
FURTHER READING

THERE ARE a dizzying number of books about Paris, including my own. Here are some classics written by French authors. They're mainly fictional works, but no less accurate for that.

Guy de Maupassant was a fun-loving civil servant who finally succumbed to syphilis. In short, an archetypal nineteenth-century Parisian gentleman. His *Mademoiselle Fifi* is a collection of short, easy-to-read stories published in 1882. One of these is 'Une Aventure parisienne', the tale of a provincial wife who comes to Paris to 'try vice'. She samples absinthe, artists, theatres and casual sex. Another of the stories, 'Nuit de Noël', is about a young man who decides to go out and find a prostitute to share his Christmas dinner. And to act as dessert, of course. He finds a pretty, plump girl, takes her home and gets a surprise when they go to bed.

Émile Zola's *Le Ventre de Paris* (1873) and *Au Bonheur des Dames* (1883) are two portraits of Paris by a man who would have been making social documentaries if TV had been invented. *Le Ventre de Paris* is all about the food markets at Les Halles and the way that the well-fed Parisians allow both their tummies and their political convictions to go flabby. *Au Bonheur des Dames* is a kind of antidote to the *Shopaholic* novels – Zola describes the working conditions in Paris's first department store.

J.-K. Huysmans (who clearly inspired Harry Potter's creator when she was looking for a *nom de plume*) was a Parisian writer who dabbled in Satanism and general decadence before settling down to become an author. His *Croquis parisiens* (1880) are, as their name suggests, short sketches of the racy Paris he knew, including the Folies-Bergère.

Raymond Queneau's novel *Zazie dans le Métro* is a book that really should be read in French, and read aloud. Queneau plays constant games with phonetic transcriptions of the way working-class Parisians spoke at the end of the 1950s. It's the story of a brattish provincial twelve-year-old, Zazie, who comes to Paris to see the *métro*, and gets swept away by the surreal nocturnal activities of her uncle Gabriel, a heterosexual man who is forced to make a living as a cross-dressing cabaret artist. The novel is so much fun that it is almost impossible to believe Queneau was a mathematician and an associate of the elitist, humourless Jean-Paul Sartre.

Photo Acknowledgements

xiv: © Bettmann/Corbis; 23: SaverioTruglia/Getty Images; 28: Roger-Viollet/Getty Images; 44: Frank Huster/Getty Images; 47: David Allan Brandt/Getty Images; 52 © John Kellerman/Alamy; 60: Getty Images; 63: Getty Images; 68: Roger-Viollet/Getty Images; 80: author's photo; 98: Roger-Viollet/Getty Images; 120: Roger-Viollet/Getty Images; 124: Owen Franken/Corbis; 129: AFP/Getty Images; 133: Keenpress/Getty Images; 154: Benaroch/Rex Features; 167:Roger-Viollet/Rex Features; 174: Getty Images; 184: Jacques Pavlovsky/Sygma/Corbis; 195: Bob Peterson/Getty Images; 198: Getty Images; 206: © Photos 12/Alamy; 216: AFP/Getty Images; 228: © Iain Masterton/Alamy; 243: Getty Images; 258: Clément Guillaume/Getty Images; 270: Time & Life Pictures/Getty Images.

INDEX